And I Remember Spain

Edited by Murray A. Sperber

And I Remember Spain

A SPANISH CIVIL WAR ANTHOLOGY

Macmillan Publishing Co., Inc.

NEW YORK

Copyright © 1974 by Murray A. Sperber

All rights reserved. No part of this book may be reproduced
or transmitted in any form or by any means, electronic or
mechanical, including photocopying, recording or by any
information storage and retrieval system, without permission
in writing from the Publisher.

Macmillan Publishing Co., Inc.
866 Third Avenue, New York, N.Y. 10022

Library of Congress Catalog Card Number: 74-2644
First American Edition 1974

Printed in the United States of America

Dedicated To

Mavis King Bamberger
who Served in Spain
with Spanish Medical Aid
from December, 1937
to February, 1939

Acknowledgements

I wish to thank the many people who have helped and encouraged me in my *idée fixe*, the Spanish Civil War, throughout the years. I must thank a number of institutions who have provided financial and professional assistance.

I owe specific thanks to my friend and mentor, Tom Flanagan, and to Ralph Rader, John Henry Raleigh, and Alex Zwerdling (all of the University of California, Berkeley); to Scott Sanders and Lee Sterrenburg (of Indiana University); to my editors at Rupert Hart-Davis, Grant MacIntyre and Alan Brooke; to Evelyn Cramer and Joanne Eustis who helped assemble the manuscript; and to my wife, Aneta.

The Canada Council, Ottawa, Canada, awarded me two years of generous grants to research the subject of writers and the Spanish Civil War in Europe. Tony Shipps of the Indiana University Library was tireless and invaluable during the final year of research. And the Research and Advanced Studies Department of Indiana University aided me in assembling the final manuscript of this book.

I owe a special debt to those persons and corporations who were kind enough to grant me free copyright permissions. Since my personal profits will go to the Spanish Refugees Aid Society, these gifts will greatly increase the amount of money that I will be able to contribute to that worthy cause. Thus, I must especially thank: Sam Atyeo for the excerpt from his unpublished memoir, *Up and Down Under: Being the Author's Adventures in Art and Diplomacy*; Arthur Koestler for 'Koestler's Own Story', *News Chronicle*, May 23–8, 1937; Jacques Maritain for 'The Idea of a Holy War'; T. C. Worsley for the selection, 'Malaga Has Fallen', from *Penguin New Writing*, ed. John Lehmann, Spring, 1939; Elizabeth Dos Passos for the North American copyright permission for the selection from John Dos Passos' *Journeys Between Wars*; T. Stanhope Sprigg for the selection from the letters of his late brother, Christopher Caudwell [St John Sprigg]; Browne and Nolan Ltd for the selection from Eoin O'Duffy, *Crusade in Spain*; *The Chicago Tribune* for the Jay Allen dispatch, August 30, 1936; Diana Crawfurd Ltd for the selection from Martha Gellhorn, *The Face of War*; *The Guardian* for the selection from Alexander Werth's dispatches from Spain, December 1937–January 1938; Lawrence and Wishart Ltd for the selection from John Sommerfield's *Volunteer in Spain*; A. D. Peters and Co. for permission to reprint the selection from Evelyn Waugh's *Scoop*; Hart-Davis, MacGibbon for the selections from Gustav Regler's *The Owl of Minerva* and Ilya Ehrenburg's *Eve of War 1933–1941*; Mary Hemingway for the excerpt from Ernest Hemingway, *The Spanish Earth*; and *Time and Tide* for the article by J. Leslie Brewer, 'Too Late?'; and *The Spectator* for the Louis MacNeice article, 'Today in Barcelona', and the Stephen Spender article, 'Pictures in Spain'.

In addition, I must make the following legal copyright acknowledgements: the Louis MacNeice poem, from *The Collected Poems*, is reprinted in America by permission of Oxford University Press, New York, and in the rest of the world by permission of Faber and Faber Ltd; the Estate of John Cornford, Jonathan Cape Ltd, and Pat Sloan, the editor of *John Cornford: A Memoir*, for the selection from that work; David Higham Associates Ltd for the selection from Douglas Jerrold, *Georgian Adventure*; the Hutchinson Publishing Group Ltd for the selection from Cecil Gerahty, *The Road to Madrid*; The Hogarth Press Ltd for the Stephen Spender poems from *Poems for Spain*; *The New Statesman* for the W. H. Auden article, 'Impressions of Valencia', and for the Stephen Spender articles, 'Heroes in Spain', and 'Guernica'; Curtis Brown Ltd for the selection from Roy Campbell, *Flowering Rifle*; Oxford University Press, New York, for the North American permission to reprint the Herbert Read poems, which in England are reprinted by permission of Faber and Faber Ltd from *Collected Poems*; A. M. Heath and Co. Ltd and the Estate of the late John Dos Passos for the British copyright permission for the selection from John Dos Passos, *Journeys Between Wars*; Chatto and Windus with The Hogarth Press and Wesleyan University for permission to reprint 'A Moment of War' and 'Words Asleep' from *The Sun My Monument* by Laurie Lee; The Society of

Authors and the Estate of George Bernard Shaw for the excerpt from *Geneva*; Constable and Co. Ltd for the letter of George Santayana in *The Letters of George Santayana*, ed. Daniel Cory; Editions Gallimard for the selections from Simone Weil, *Ecrits Historiques et Politiques* (1960), and Pierre Drieu La Rochelle, *Gilles* (1939); the Yeats poem, 'Politics', in the United States is reprinted with permission of The Macmillan Company from *Collected Poems* by W. B. Yeats, and in the rest of the world, by permission of M. B. Yeats and the Macmillan Companies of London and Canada; Wm Heinemann Ltd and Harcourt Brace Jovanovich Inc. for permission to reprint the excerpt from Antoine de Saint-Exupéry, *Wind, Sand, and Stars*; Secker and Warburg Ltd and Harcourt Brace Jovanovich Inc. for permission to reprint the selection from Hugh (Humphrey) Slater, *The Heretics*; Curtis Brown Ltd and Hodder and Stoughton Ltd for the selection from G. L. Steer, *The Tree of Gernika*; Libraire Plon and The Bodley Head for the selection from Georges Bernanos, *Les grands cimetières sous la lune* [*A Diary of My Times*, translated by Pamela Morris]; Mrs Sonia Brownell Orwell, Secker and Warburg Ltd, and Harcourt Brace Jovanovich Inc. for permission to reprint the selection from George Orwell, *Homage to Catalonia*; *The New York Times* for permission to reprint the news articles on Hemingway; Mrs Wyndham Lewis for the selection from *Revenge for Love*.

Table of Contents

Preface

The purpose of this anthology is to collect in one volume the best, or excerpts from the best, international writing on the Spanish Civil War. This literature falls into several categories: original, previously unpublished works; selections by well-known authors returned to print after a lost generation; pieces by less famous writers deserving discovery; the works of foreign authors often unfamiliar to English language readers (some translated here for the first time); and, finally, a few justifiably famous selections.

The one limitation of the anthology is that for cultural and language reasons none of the works or authors are Spanish in origin. It was agreed by the editor and publisher that because of the richness and accessibility of the non-Spanish writing on the war, a full and more coherent single volume would result from this limitation. Possibly the title should be *International Writers and the Spanish Civil War*.

The general aim of the anthology is to reproduce for the reader, by means of the best literature on the subject, the milieu of the late 1930s, and the Spanish Civil War, and the special feelings that war provoked in both international participants and spectators.

Introduction

The Spanish Civil War was not 'The Last Great Cause', as a recent book called it (every last cause, especially lost ones, qualifies for that title, including the next great cause), nor was it, as some critics suggest, the last time in human history when men believed that they could triumph over war machines (World War I ended that myth – if men still believed it after the invention of gunpowder). The Spanish Civil War was an apocalyptic moment – and not the final one either.

At the time, many writers considered the war apocalyptic. Arthur Koestler called it 'the Apocalyptic flood', and John Dos Passos saw the war mirrored in some paintings of 'enormous Apocalypses'. André Malraux tried to define it more explicitly. He called a section of his *L'Espoir* 'Prelude to Apocalypse', and in the section's concluding passage he has one of his characters exclaim: 'The apocalyptic mood clamours for everything right away . . . That apocalyptic fervour is ingrained in every one of us; and there's the danger. For that fervour spells certain defeat, after a relatively short period, and for a very simple reason: it's in the nature of an apocalypse to have no future.' (*Man's Hope*, p. 118.)

Although Malraux's novel only showed the Republican side of the conflict, he realized, and all the writings and oratory from the Nationalists proves, the war was apocalyptic for all participants. The Anarchists, traditionally strong and active in Spain, awaited the lifting of the veil, the New Jerusalem. The Communists and Socialists wished to usher in Marx's utopia. Even the Liberals of the Republic believed that the new age had come.

On the other side, the Nationalists had begun the war with the cry '*Arriba España*' (Spain arise). They viewed their struggle as much more than a military *coup d'état*. Almost all were Catholics, supported by the rigorous Spanish Catholic Church and they saw their fight as a holy war – a crusade to purge the *Rojos* from Spain and to resurrect the pure Spanish state. Like many religious zealots, they harkened to a vision of a previous golden age: they placed it in Spanish history but they might as well have longed for Eden. Fighting for Franco and his Burgos Government were such militants as the Monarchists (restore Alfonso XIII), the Carlists (restore Don Alfonso Carlos: a purer, more fanatical version of monarchism), the Spanish Foreign Legion with its battle cry '*Viva la Muerte!*' and the Moorish troops from Africa. In addition, the Falangists, the emerging political party on the Right, patterned themselves on the Nazis and Fascists and called for a new totalitarian state and social order.

Initially, in late July 1936, the *junta* (principally, Franco and Mola) failed to seize more than a third of the country. This enabled the Republic to call out a militia and the Leftist political parties to arm themselves. Thus began a war of a people against an entrenched power (most of the professional army remained loyal to their religious and class interests – the Right). With such antagonists, and with hatreds descending through centuries of Spanish history, what might have been a military coup against the Republic on July 17 1936 quickly became an apocalyptic drama.

Traditionally men have participated in rather than studied apocalyptic dramas. Although the Judeo-Christian Apocalypse originates in *The Book of Daniel* and the Maccabean revolt, and it occurs in most centuries since (for example, Cromwellian England), only recently has there been serious scholarship on the subject. This scholarship attempts to explain apocalyptic moments as recurring historical phenomena and it seeks the political and psychological causes behind the phenomena. The most eminent scholar in this field is Professor Norman Cohn. In his work, *The Pursuit of the Millennium*, he describes – from *The Book of Daniel* to the twentieth century – 'the paradigm of what was to become and to remain the central fantasy of revolutionary eschatology':

The world is dominated by an evil, tyrannous power of boundless destructiveness – a power moreover which is imagined not as simply human but as demonic. The tyranny of that power will become more and more outrageous, the suffering of its victims more and more intolerable – until suddenly the hour will strike when the Saints of God are able to rise up and overthrow it. Then the Saints themselves, the chosen, holy people who hitherto have groaned under the oppressor's heel, shall in their turn inherit dominion over the whole earth. This will be the culmination of history; the Kingdom of the Saints will not only surpass in glory all previous kingdoms, it will have no successors. (Cohn, p. 4.)

The turning of one's enemies into demons – therefore, non-humans – is always a crucial act in war psychology, but when the war is apocalyptic, like the Spanish Civil War, the demonology becomes boundless and the 'Reds' or 'Fascists' appear as fantastic creatures of terror and revenge. A people's militia becomes for one side an avenging angel, and for the other the devil's crew; in the same way, African soldiers are sanctified by the Church so that they can participate in the holy war, or cursed and feared as a black demonic horde. The peasants and workers of Spain justifiably believed that their almost ageless suffering was intolerable, but when the 'hour' struck and they were 'able to rise up', they acted out their revolt in terms of their apocalyptic fantasies and they burned churches, killed clergy, and murdered many of the bourgeoisie.

Nationalist Spain responded in a similar way. The property classes and the Church also felt oppressed (but are fears of property loss as oppressive as poverty?) and they acted in a blood-thirsty manner. July 24, the declaration of the Nationalist Government, was their 'hour ... to rise up' and they considered themselves 'the Saints of God'. General Mola announced:

'Spaniards! Citizens of Burgos! The Government which was the wretched bastard of liberal and Socialist concubinage is dead, killed by our valiant army. Spain, the true Spain, has laid the dragon low, and now it lies, writhing on its belly and biting the dust. I am now going to take up my position at the head of the troops and it will not be long before two banners – the sacred emblem of the Cross, and our own glorious flag – are waving together in Madrid.' (Quoted in Hugh Thomas, *The Spanish Civil War*, pp. 180–1.)

And as the elect, although the Nationalists had hardly 'groaned under the oppressor's heel', they felt justified in purging Spain of its devil's crew – the majority of the population.

The Saints were on the Left as well. As Hugh Thomas points out:

> For the conversion of the working class of Spain to revolutionary ideas, the Church, which was to suffer so much in consequence, had paradoxically prepared the way. The Church's communalism, its puritan hostility ... made the ideas of [the Anarchist] Fanelli seem merely an honest continuation of the old faith. The religious character of Spain also made converts to the new collectivism, as it had made the liberals more passionate, less ready to compromise, more obstinate than any other similar group in Europe. (Thomas, p. 41 fn.)

Because they believed themselves secular Saints, when the political parties of the Left felt that 'their turn [to] inherit dominion over the whole earth' had arrived, they saw nothing wrong in killing all those who did not belong in the new world (including, at times, former allies on the Left). Because this was 'the culmination of history' and 'it will have no successors', why hesitate to kill those persons who do not belong in utopia?

Sucked into the Spanish whirlwind were foreigners of many nations and political beliefs. First the Nazis and the Fascists, with their consciously apocalyptic slogans and ideology, sent aid to Franco. The Germans dispatched the fearsome Condor Legion to perfect its aerial warfare, including the systematic bombing of civilians; the Italians sent the Black Shirts and although they marched with the appropriate steps and songs, they proved less effective in battle than the Germans. There were also foreign volunteers for Franco – mainly Catholic, almost always on a religious crusade – but they proved more military trouble than their propaganda value was worth. The Nationalists, through the world-wide offices of the Catholic Church, also elicited much aid and sympathy for the fight against the Spanish church-burners and nun-rapists.

The most famous volunteers, however, were the men and women who came from Western countries to fight for the Republic. The majority were organized by the World Communist Party, the Comintern, into the International Brigades, but many fought with Anarchist or militia groups. Most of these volunteers were veterans of Leftist political campaigns within their own countries and the experience of frustrating and unresolved struggles propelled them to the climactic Spanish Civil War.

For the English 'Spain' offered a release from the smug lies and boredom of the Baldwin, then the Chamberlain National Government. For Americans it allowed a break from 'fortress America' and the isolationism of the 1930s. The French Leftists, frustrated over the failure of Leon Blum's *Front Populaire* government to achieve social change, saw Spain as the true struggle (and one they hoped to take back across the Pyrenees). And all of these nationalities regarded the Spanish war as the first opportunity to fight the Anti-Christ himself, Hitler and/or Mussolini (in the same way that the other side saw the war as the first battle in the crusade against demonic world Communism). For the political émigrés from Germany, Italy, and eastern Europe, Spain also offered a chance for personal revenge against Hitler, Mussolini, Horvathy, and other dictators. Even the Russians, who were sent by Stalin to prop up, then manipulate the Republic, developed so much political idealism that they were purged upon their return to the Soviet Union. Finally, many persons who remained at home shared the apocalyptic feeling – perhaps more so because of the added guilt of not going to the war.

Few statements summarize the nature of the Spanish Civil War more accurately than Norman Cohn's conclusion that for each individual and for each age believing itself to be apocalyptic, the 'social struggle is imagined as uniquely important, different in kind from all other struggles known to history, a cataclysm from which the world is to emerge totally transformed and redeemed'. (Cohn, p. 308.) Only by applying such insights can we begin to explain the fantastic events of the Spanish Civil War and the flood of words written about it.

*   *

The great intellectual is a man of subtleties, of fine shades, of evaluations; he's interested in absolute truth and in the complexity of things. He is – how shall I put it? – 'anti-Manichean' by definition, by nature. But all forms of action are Manichean, because all action pays a tribute to the devil; the Manichean element is most intense when the masses are involved. Every true revolutionary is a born Manichean. The same is true of politics, all politics. (*Man's Hope*, p. 392-3.)

Once again, Malraux points to a central paradox of the Spanish Civil War. How could intellectuals – with their task of making discriminations, seeing nuances and subtleties – join an event that all participants saw clearly as good or evil, black or white. The apocalyptic mentality sees the world in Manichean terms (the Manicheans themselves, an early Christian sect, awaited the Apocalypse) and, as Malraux implies, to act is to choose. To decide to kill is to make even narrower choices, in fact, to limit choices to a final either/or.

The intellectual is 'interested in absolute truth': he begins with and seeks an ideal against which reality always falls short. Thus, even if he could go to the Spanish Civil War because he thought he saw ideal truth there, he would soon find – because his talent and training force him to such discoveries – a discrepancy between his ideal and reality. For this reason, few intellectuals could participate easily in the war or in the politics of the war: their desire for intellectual purity was immediately offended by the inevitable political compromises.

'But all the forms of action are Manichean'; the nature of choosing to act is both to assign right to a particular action and to foreclose other possibilities. Usually this situation has kept intellectuals from joining political causes – and those who have signed up have been attacked by fellow intellectuals for their choice and the very act of choosing (Julien Benda's *Trahison des clercs* is a classic of this genre).

The 'Manichean element is most intense when the masses are involved'; this connection, probably more than any other single element, allowed Western intellectuals to 'suspend' their traditional 'disbelief' in action in order to participate in the Spanish Civil War. Because they could convince themselves – and were supported by Marxist ideology – that proletarian revolution was inevitable, the generation of the 1930s could either temporarily suppress their anti-Manichean instincts or, like Malraux, paradoxically transcend them (articulate and still fight). Although Malraux is an intellectual when he steps into his aeroplane, he soon transforms himself into a killer: 'Yet at the same time the old savage instinct of the bird of prey has taken hold of us. With the centuries old wheeling flight of hawks, we circle . . .' (p. 69 below.)

Most intellectuals, particularly the British, were less mentally and physically agile than Malraux. They held their anti-Manichean nature in abeyance for the Spanish war but when the Apocalypse did not arrive and did not justify their choice, they felt doubly disillusioned. Often they turned in great bitterness from politics or at least from the politics of the parties of mass revolution. Some even ended in the camp of anti-Communism – thus, never really breaking out of the Manichean mentality.

It is this apocalyptic-Manichean mentality that characterizes most of the writing on the Spanish Civil War. Whether the author was a professional writer before the war or not, usually 'Spain' compelled him or her to literary expression – but in good or evil, black or white terms. Indeed, the apocalyptic mood was so startling that it prompted many people to write for the only time in their lives. The volume of writing on the war is stupendous: there are at least 1,500 titles in the English language although there were only about 5,000 English-speaking volunteers. No other single event in our history produced such a proportion of literature to participants. Unfortunately, much of the Spanish Civil War writing, particularly the apocalyptic kind, is almost un-readable today. It is often worse than propaganda, it is doom-saying and blasphemy, and although fantastically illuminated, its madness makes it impenetrable.

Of the 1,500 titles, which ones are still worth reading? Many writers, ordinary professionals and journalists, turned out yards of material; only a few transcended their perishable prose to write remarkable pieces about the war. Other authors, some literary cubs and lions, barely controlled their Spanish war efforts and, no doubt, they were embarrassed subsequently by them. (Not only did many writers who were Manichean for the duration later regret it but often, in spite of original merit, they attempted to rewrite or they failed to preserve their pieces on Spain. W. H. Auden, with his great poem 'Spain', did both: first he rewrote it and now he will not reissue it – or allow it to be reprinted.) From these established writers, a handful of pieces are worth exhumation.

The very best literature on the war does not come from any definable group of writers. All the ordinary cliques and schools, such as Bloomsbury, do not apply. Because the apocalyptic mood informs almost all the writing on the war, works should be seen against the background of events and not as aspects of individual or group literary careers. And no particular author, not even those who were familiar with Spain before the war, was especially prepared to write about it (for example, the English novelist Ralph Bates had lived in Spain from the early 1920s, and although he wrote endless propaganda about the war, in fact, his pre-war novel *The Olive Field* is far superior to his war writing). Therefore, any literary collection on the Spanish Civil War will produce a mixed and odd list of contributors.

Regardless of the author, the very best literature on the war shares a certain quality. It comes from those authors who caught – in two meanings of the word: were infected by and re-created – the apocalyptic mood. Although they participated in it, they did not part from their senses and as a result they produced some extraordinary work. Their accomplishment keeps their writing alive: we want to read about the Spanish Civil War as a shattering moment but we have to see it from our distance – we know that the millennium did not descend. Those men and women who wrote from inside but were aware of the Apocalypse quickly gain our attention and sympathy. They capture the time and mood of 'Spain' and they look ahead, especially to the inevitable tragedy.

This anthology begins with a poem by Louis MacNeice (Canto VI, *Autumn Journal*) because his lines especially catch the apocalyptic mood:

> *And I Remember Spain*
> *At Easter ripe as an egg for revolt and ruin,*
> *Though for a tripper the rain*
> *Was worse than the surly or the worried or the haunted faces.*

MacNeice describes the eve of war. The Easter symbolism, with its images of decay and resurrection, conveys the war's special meaning. Like most pre-war 'trippers', MacNeice hardly realized that 'the peoples' mind / Was tunnelling like a mole to day and danger'. And it is only in retrospect that he sees how the commonplace of Spain was transformed into the great moment for his generation:

> *And next day took the boat*
> > *For home, forgetting Spain, not realizing*
> *That Spain would soon denote*
> > *Our grief, our aspirations:*
> *Not knowing that our blunt*
> > *Ideals would find their whetstone, that our spirit*
> *Would find its frontier on the Spanish front,*
> > *Its body in a rag-tag army.*

Editorial Note

Like the editor of most anthologies, I found that I had both too many and too few pieces from which to choose. Too much unprintable writing and too few selections of unquestionable merit, too many works on the principal and dramatic events of the war, especially the Battle for Madrid, and too few to convey the war's totality and corrosive tragedy. Therefore, like any editor, I had to choose.

But before selecting, it was necessary to order the anthology into a coherent shape. The too natural order would be to follow the history of the war. But since many events occurred in different parts of Spain and Europe and America simultaneously and the importance of others was only realized years later, I decided to order less according to chronological event – although there is a general movement forward from 1936 to 1939 – than to shape by the writers' points of view. The purpose of this form and the division of authors into sections according to it – The Volunteers, The Reporters, The Tourists, The Literary Homefront, and The Witnesses – is to avoid the shape of formal political and military history and instead, to attempt to re-create through the literary works the sense of the Spanish war for foreigners in Spain and also, the war's special meaning abroad. (And partly because of this general theme of international writers looking at Spain through outsider's eyes, no Spanish writing is included.)

When historians consider writers and their works they often

examine them as if through the reverse end of a pair of binoculars: a perfectly shaped world but miniature and without distinctive marks or characteristics. By applying a literary category, point of view, as the organizing device I hope that the anthology transcends formal history and presents the writers and their works up close. In this way the reader (who can turn to the historians for the lists of battles and politicians) can experience the Spanish Civil War directly.

And I Remember Spain

Louis MacNeice

'Canto VI' from *Autumn Journal*

The poem is set in the spring of 1936, the eve of war.

And I Remember Spain
  At Easter ripe as an egg for revolt and ruin
Though for a tripper the rain
  Was worse than the surly or the worried or the haunted
    faces
With writings on the walls –
  Hammer and sickle, Boicot, Viva, Muerra;
With café au lait brimming the waterfalls,
  With sherry, shellfish, omelettes.
With fretted stone the Moor
  Had chiselled for effects of sun and shadow;
With shadows of the poor,
  The begging cripples and the children begging.
The churches full of saints
  Tortured on racks of marble –
The old complaints
  Covered with gilt and dimly lit with candles.
With powerful or banal
  Monuments of riches or repression
And the Escorial
  Cold for ever within like the heart of Philip.
With ranks of dominoes
  Deployed on café tables the whole of Sunday
With cabarets that call the tourist, shows
  Of thighs and eyes and nipples.
With slovenly soldiers, nuns,
  And peeling posters from the last elections
Promising bread or guns
  Or an amnesty or another

Order or else the old
  Glory veneered and varnished
As if veneer could hold
  The rotten guts and crumbled bones together.
And a vulture hung in air
  Below the cliffs of Ronda and below him
His hook-winged shadow wavered like despair
  Across the chequered vineyards.
And the boot-blacks in Madrid
  Kept us half an hour with polish and pincers
And all we did
  In that city was drink and think and loiter.
And in the Prado half-
  wit princes looked from the canvas they had paid for
(Goya had the laugh –
  But can what is corrupt be cured by laughter?)
And the day at Aranjuez
  When the sun came out for once on the yellow river
With Valdepenas burdening the breath
  We slept a royal sleep in the royal gardens;
And at Toledo walked
  Around the ramparts where they throw the garbage
And glibly talked
  Of how the Spaniards lack all sense of business.
And Avila was cold
  And Segovia was picturesque and smelly
And a goat on the road seemed old
  As the rocks or the Roman arches.
And Easter was wet and full
  In Seville and in the ring on Easter Sunday
A clumsy bull and then a clumsy bull
  Nodding his banderillas died of boredom.
And the standard of living was low
  But that, we thought to ourselves, was not our business;
All that the tripper wants is the *status quo*
  Cut and dried for trippers.
And we thought the papers a lark
  With their party politics and blank invective;

And we thought the dark
   Women who dyed their hair should have it dyed more often.
And we sat in trains all night
   With the windows shut among civil guards and peasants
And tried to play piquet by a tiny light
   And tried to sleep bolt upright;
And cursed the Spanish rain
   And cursed their cigarettes which came to pieces
And caught heavy colds in Cordova and in vain
   Waited for the right light for taking photos.
And we met a Cambridge don who said with an air
   'There's going to be trouble shortly in this country',
And ordered anis, pudgy and debonair,
   Glad to show off his mastery of the language.
But only an inch behind
   This map of olive and ilex, this painted hoarding,
Careless of visitors the people's mind
   Was tunnelling like a mole to day and danger.
And the day before we left
   We saw the mob in flower at Algeciras
Outside a toothless door, a church bereft
   Of its images and its aura.
And at La Linea while
   The night put miles between us and Gibraltar
We heard the blood-lust of a drunkard pile
   His heaven high with curses;
And next day took the boat
   For home, forgetting Spain, not realizing
That Spain would soon denote
   Our grief, our aspirations;
Not knowing that our blunt
   Ideals would find their whetstones, that our spirit
Would find its frontier on the Spanish front,
   Its body in a rag-tag army.

The Volunteers

The volunteers were a mixed crew. The writers in this collection represent the spectrum of international combatants: from workers and political functionaries, through middle-class intellectuals and literary stars, to right-wing hangers-on and crusaders for Christ (as well as a sprinkling of the naïve and foolish).

Of the English writers in this section, Douglas Jerrold was the only one on the Right. He relates how he helped begin the war by arranging for Franco's flight from the Canary Islands. John Sommerfield was more innocent. His enlistment and journey across France, as well as the waiting and the muddle, was less exotic than Jerrold's adventure but typical of the international volunteers for the Republic. John Cornford, a dedicated Communist, went to Spain on his own at the outbreak of war and fought with a militia unit at the Aragon front (he was killed a few months later; his life is recounted in an excellent biography, *Journey to the Frontier*).

General Eoin O'Duffy led the Irish Blue Shirt contingent to fight for Franco and Christendom (in the event, the group hardly fought and were more an annoyance than an aid). Between the lines of O'Duffy's pompous enthusiasm the reader glimpses an amazing, at times comic confusion. Frank Ryan led the Irish Battalion on the Republican side. His letters, although attempting an international viewpoint, reveal an Irish feud carried out in the midst of the Spanish Civil War.

Ray Harris, a naïve American, was in Spain with an American medical unit. Harris' innocence, too typical of the American volunteers, contrasts with the sharp awareness of Jef Last, a Dutch politico and writer. Christopher Caudwell [Christopher St John Sprigg], the brilliant British Marxist, died in the war as he had lived: unselfishly and with understatement. His letters and the letters about him say this remarkably well.

Of all the volunteers in Spain, André Malraux was the most

famous. Organizer and leader of the Republican air force, Espagne Escadrille, he also had the energy and genius to write the best single book about the war, *L'Espoir* (Man's Hope). After the Escadrille was disbanded into the Republican Air Force, Malraux toured Europe and America to raise money for the Republic. The article here, 'This is War', was sold to *Collier's Magazine* and it is one of the most unusual propaganda pieces of the time. Full of Malraux's paradoxes, it shifts between the war's reality and surrealism. Malraux also makes an important statement about the role of the writer in wartime:

> Madrid is being bombarded. I am following a man who lugs a manuscript as big as himself. People rarely write on paper of that size, and such a large manuscript naturally interests a writer. I stop the man:
> 'What is that manuscript of yours?'
> The sound of airplane bombs reaches our ears.
> 'It isn't a manuscript,' he answers gently. 'I'm changing the wallpaper in my apartment.'

Douglas Jerrold

From *Georgian Adventure*

Spain during the fateful months which followed the 1936 elections was saved by Primo de Rivera's Spanish Phalanx. There were, it is said, only 20,000 of them. But it was enough. I learned something of their courage and virtue at first hand.

I was sitting in my office one morning when I was rung up by Luis Bolin. Would I see a friend of his who was in London? I would and did.

I remember the day well. It was near midsummer of 1936, and I was trying to sell books and wondering greatly whether it was really worth while. When Luis Bolin's friend came in, I was pleasantly relieved. I anticipated a proposal to publish a pamphlet, the kind of heroic gesture appropriate to amateur politicians at midsummer in Mr Baldwin's England.

The Spanish are the most delightful because the most surprising of peoples. It would be supremely comic, if it were not for the encyclopedic ignorance which makes the lie sound plausible, to hear people say that they are even potential Fascists. They will never be Fascists because they are God's last, and therefore effective and sufficient, protest against the machine age. My new friend sat down as a man sits down when he has just dismounted after a long ride. He had, he told me, come on a bus, but that was clearly a terrestrial illusion. He had ridden across the sunburnt yellow plains of the Tagus straight into my room.

'Well,' he said, taking a good look at me and I at him (he was wondering, I could see, whether I was real), 'I won't waste your time. Bolin tells me that you're the only man in London who can help me. I want fifty machine guns and half a million rounds of SA ammunition.'

I said, as casually as I knew how, that I saw no difficulty about that. My new friend expressed neither surprise nor gratitude. It was, I gathered, the least he had expected. And, having disposed of this trifling business of question and answer, he went on to tell me all about it. It was, he put it to me, raising his voice ever so slightly to drown the hooting of paper merchants' and printers' vans outside, a question of saving a nation's soul. I said that I understood that such a necessity might easily arise. And then, for ten minutes, I listened to the realities of politics. The stories of murder, outrage and sacrilege are familar enough to me today; I have heard so many of them at first hand. The last three nights I dined in Spain, I found myself in each case sitting at table with women whose husbands had been murdered within the last six months. And these were all chance encounters. But that was not in Fleet Street, and the world in those days was younger. Yet I believed everything that I heard because of the manner of man who talked to me, and the way in which our conversation had begun. After a time I interrupted him. 'You want these arms to kill the murderers?'

'No!' His indignation rang through the room. 'We need them so that our people will have the courage to go on being murdered. As long as we are fighting for them, they will not give in, but if we stop – well, it will be Russia over again. And,' he added, 'Spain is not Russia. If Spain goes . . .'

'And how about payment?' I asked. Obviously we were in accord on every point, so the discussion reverted, as it always does in Spain (and of course we were in Spain; such a discussion could not be going on in Fetter Lane), to the severely practical without any apologies. Then we shook hands. 'I'll let Bolin know what I can do,' I said, and then I woke up and found myself on the steps of my office saying good-bye to a stranger.

Fifty machine guns, or was it five hundred? Or five hundred thousand? I went back to my desk and consulted my blotting paper. Yes! It had all been real! There it was in my execrable scrawl, as clear to me (but I hoped to no one else) as daylight – '50 MG – Hotchkiss preferred – and ½ million SAA'.

Then my door opened, and my ever-faithful colleague, P. V. Cave, put his head in. 'Well, did you sell him anything?' he asked cheerily. 'I think so,' I answered dubiously. 'Don't you *know*?' asked Cave, a trifle indignantly; he is always a bit suspicious of my commercial acumen. I confessed that I did not. It was a Spaniard, I added, by way of excuse. And Cave brightened. 'Oh, I thought it was an American publisher.'

Fortunately I was able to write to Bolin the next day and tell him that the matter we had discussed could probably be arranged, but as things turned out it was not until March, 1937, that I saw my unknown friend again. I was standing in the hall of the Grand Hotel in Salamanca when I heard a familiar voice behind me. 'After all, we didn't need those machine guns, but thank you all the same.' Then we shook hands and had a drink. Not till he had gone did I realize that he had not expressed the faintest surprise at seeing me . . . yet after all, why should he? He hadn't expressed any when I offered him the machine guns.

Odd though all this appeared at the time, it was commonplace by contrast to its sequel, which was not only a sequel but a consequence. It was just a fortnight later when Luis Bolin rang up and asked me to lunch. I looked at my engagements and suggested a day next week. 'No, no, I'm afraid it must be today. It's important.' I presumed that it was connected with my last Spanish excursion and suggested as much discreetly. Yes, it had a good deal to do with it. This was good enough for me and bad enough for my previously appointed guest, who luckily was on the telephone.

We lunched at Simpson's and de la Cierva completed the party. We began with appropriate gestures of conspiracy, *more Hispanico*. We must have a quiet table. By the time Bolin and de la Cierva, after much whispering, had rejected every vacant table in the room, hardly any one could have been unaware of our pressing need for privacy. Eventually, as if to secure the maximum of attention to our movements, Bolin persuaded the head waiter to ask a mild and unobtrusive citizen of London eating his saddle of mutton at a side-table to move elsewhere. We wanted to be quite alone. When we at last sat down, de la Cierva apologized for the delay; he found, he explained, the impenetrable envelope of secrecy in which for some weeks he had been obliged to shroud his movements very embarrassing at times. I was more than sympathetic, for it was clear to me that he had been for some weeks the most conspicuous man in London and Paris. I was not surprised to hear that, on his last visit to Paris, when he had decided on the Louvre as the best meeting place with his fellow-conspirators, he had gone there, 'quite secretly', he emphasized, only to find half the staff of the Spanish Embassy scattered round the galleries. But the inventor was a psychologist as well as a man of resource. He attached himself to a couple of ladies whose interest in art was obviously not rigorously exclusive, for, as he explained, no Spaniard, whatever his politics, would fail to retire in a situation of that kind.

By this time we had begun to eat, and as the atmosphere then was less electric, I thought it would be safe to broach what I imagined was the subject of our meeting. Had they, I asked, decided about the machinery we had been discussing? I gathered that they had not. And then it happened.

'I want a man and three platinum blondes to fly to Africa tomorrow.'

'Must there really be *three*?' I asked, and at that Bolin turned triumphantly to de la Cierva. 'I told you he would manage it.'

'Well, perhaps two would be enough,' Bolin said regretfully. 'But of course the man must have had some experience; there might be trouble.'

I said nothing for a moment and I saw anxiety spreading over their faces. It was real anxiety, so I explained that what was troubling me was the rival qualifications of three men, all of whom would be delighted to fly anywhere with two, though perhaps hardly with three platinum blondes. After all, there was the question of expense.

I was assured that need be no obstacle.

'Knowledge of Spanish?' I asked.

'But that's surely impossible,' said de la Cierva incredulously.

'Oh no,' I said, having made up my mind. 'May I telephone?'

I might telephone, and I did. I had been tossing up in my mind between George Fairfax, Francis Yeats-Brown, and Hugh Pollard, but after all the job was Pollard's by rights, for he had experience of Moroccan, Mexican, and Irish revolutions – and, of course, this meant war. And he knew Spanish.

'Can you fly to Africa tomorrow with two girls?' I asked, and heard the expected reply. 'Depends upon the girls.'

'You can choose,' said I in my best business accents. 'I'll bring two Spanish friends down to see you this afternoon.'

'Right,' said Pollard. 'I'll expect you to tea.'

'There's only one point I ought to mention,' I said as Hugh

was ringing off. 'The aeroplane may be stolen when you get there. In that case you come back by boat.'

'First-class?'

'Why not?'

'Right. Can do. Good-bye.'

That might have seemed the hardest part of my job, but there was still the business of getting to Pollard to be solved. Train was impossible and no one knew the way to Fernhurst. De la Cierva, the practical man, suggested buying a map, and so we finished our lunch and went to Philip's in the Strand. We bought our map of Sussex easily and as we were leaving Bolin said, 'Let's get a map of Spain and North Africa. It might be useful.' It was. The next time I saw that map was in General Headquarters at Salamanca.

Then to Fernhurst. I got them as far as the pub and then found myself lost, but I rang up Hugh again and got the final directions, and at last we arrived. All this time I had been told no more than I have put down here, but I am by profession a prophet and when I saw Pollard I took him on one side and explained to him, with an assurance that I could not possibly have justified, that his aeroplane, containing three self-styled English tourists, would be stolen, if the anticipated crisis arose, at the Canaries, to take General Franco to Morocco. But of course nothing was to be said about this that afternoon.

Round the table we got down to business. Passports, money, the route to Casablanca. Afterwards, anything might happen.

'Pack a gun?'

And again de la Cierva laughed, and said, 'This is incredible.'

Then began the most arduous search of all. Pollard's daughter was to be one of the party, but the other girl was out – no telephone inquiries could locate her. All that was known was that she was delivering chickens somewhere and that she hadn't got a passport.

And so the Last Crusade began on a hot July afternoon with four men searching frantically up and down Sussex lanes for a girl delivering chickens and who had not got a passport.

In despair we turned into the pub, and there, the heavens being kind and the bar being open, we found her.

'Dorothy, come here. You're going to Africa tomorrow,' Hugh shouted cheerfully.

'Africa, where's that? Who does it belong to?'

'Oh, you know, it used to belong to Cecil Rhodes, but now it belongs to Mussolini.'

'Oh, that place.' Dorothy, I never knew her surname, explained that the business of selling chickens could not very well be carried on from Africa. That was nothing, we could all put that right, we explained, with a highly liberal faith in the virtues of collective action. Money, passports, clothes, anything could be supplied, but go to Africa she must.

'Well, that's settled.' I suddenly realized that I was going to be late, very late, for dinner, and in any case there was nothing more to be said. Dorothy, I had noticed, kept her cigarettes in her knickers. She couldn't, she explained, afford a handbag. Obviously she was the type that went to Africa.

So we went home. Four days later, Calvo Sotelo was foully murdered by uniformed police in Madrid. Ten days later, General Franco, supposed to be safely relegated to the Canaries, raised his standard in Morocco. *Arriba España*! Luis Bolin was in Rome, and Hugh Pollard from the window of his bedroom in an hotel in Palmas heard the volley of musketry which began and ended the revolution there. And Dorothy was fast asleep. And on the balcony of the Town Hall at Seville a colonel of the Army Service Corps was making the shortest and best speech in the annals of revolution. He had been asked to occupy the Municipal Offices and to arrest the officials. He did what he was told, but only became uneasy when a large and curious crowd assembled and asked to be told what it was all about. He was a man of few words, and in any case he was by no means clear about it himself. However, he went out on to the balcony, and called for silence.

'Neither this,' he said, raising the clenched fist, 'nor this', giving the Fascist salute. '*Viva España.*'

And yet people say that soldiers are stupid.

John Sommerfield

'The Journey'

From *Volunteer in Spain*

Well, Paris is a nice place but we wanted to get to Spain. We hoped to be able to leave that night, but there were credentials and papers to be obtained. It had occurred to us, of course, that there would be other volunteers, but we had only thought of them as a few little groups like ours. We first began to realize that something important was happening when we got to the office.

In a not very large room full of smoke and voices men were sitting and standing about in the attitudes of those who have been waiting for days and have no hope beyond that of waiting for more days. They talked in low voices and various languages. At the end of the room was a table covered with strewn papers. Two men were sitting behind it in harassed attitudes. We waited.

'Looks like we'll be here for a week,' said John, and grinned.

The men behind the table communicated to one another in a curious tongue; it sounded like a Frenchman, mouth full, reading aloud from a Spanish newspaper and not getting on with it very well.

'Catalunyan,' said John. (He had been there, he knew.)

The strewn papers were forms. Men were filling them up, putting down things about their ages and military experience, their jobs and their politics, also next-of-kin.

More people arrived and the room grew stuffier and smokier. Mostly they were French and Poles, some of them pretty tough.

We advanced to the table, said our piece, were handed forms, and went through complications of mistranslation. What was my job? Author, perhaps. The French word was *écrevisse*? Something like that. But no, it turned out to be *écrivain*. *Écrevisse* was a lobster. 'Sommerfield, the celebrated English revolutionary lobster.' It was a crack to last for weeks.

When we had finished with the forms we felt that something

had been accomplished. We knew that we were going to get to Spain somehow, but all the same everyone felt that it was going to be very difficult and that all kinds of complicated and unexpected obstacles would interfere with our ambition. But the papers we had filled up were official-looking, Spanish, and it changed the whole situation in some way, so that it became more real, practical, instead of a slightly fantastic, hoped-for adventure.

So we went out and bought some revolvers and ammunition. We got small automatics; they went easily into the pocket and were useful things to have. I suppose that it would have been possible to have brought down a fair-sized dog at twenty yards with them if you were a pretty good shot. But still, it was very much a question of morale. They felt good in the hand, the short barrels were cold and shiny, and from out of the little round black hole in the end could come, we imagined, death, impelled by our own hands. It was decidedly good for the morale.

And, it turned out, the morale certainly needed a bit of reinforcing. We wanted to get to Spain, in a hurry. There was a war on, and we wanted to be in it, but soon. And it wasn't going to be soon. The next day came, and the next, and still we had not left. We hung about in cafés near the office, played endless billiards (and if there is a drearier game than French billiards I haven't heard of it), smoked hundreds of cigarettes, sat in sulky silence or talked dispiritedly of the dragging time, the conversation circling the same theme like the needle of a gramophone record caught in a single groove and repeating its phrase with maddening senselessness. We had to be ready to leave at a few hours' notice, and this stopped us from going far from the dingy arrondissement, and also it served to keep alive and irritated our impatience. Recollection of our automatics' cool comfortable fit in the hand was a comfort.

It was nearly a week before we left.

Quai D'Orsay station; people, intent upon departures and arrivals, scurried like ants under the echoing vault of the great roof. And we marched in, headed by Gustave, a cheerful, gnome-like little man who was in charge of us.

Everyone felt good, and talked at once, and you could hear them all down the corridor babbling excitedly in French and German and Polish and Italian. (Because there were quite a lot of Italians after all.)

Then the train began to move and the noise rose to a clamour like an upset beehive. And the Belge stood up and declaimed with great emotion, 'I am a Belgian, I am an aviator, I am going to Spain to fight for —' and everyone said shut up, and the train jerked and they all fell on top of him as they were shoving him back to his seat.

The lights of Paris were sliding by in the darkness and the train gathered speed to pound through the night.

The Belge slept, snoring a little. Antonio passed round a bottle of wine: sausages, with garlic in them, appeared; the atmosphere grew hot and rich. Boots and coats began to be removed. Antonio took off his scarf and windjacket, revealing a blue shirt, and then he took that off, and under it was a vivid blue pullover. And soon that came off too, disclosing yet another and more dazzlingly blue shirt with white stripes. (All this, of course, was accompanied with triumph and theatricals.) Michel sat quietly: his threadbare clothes and horribly worn shoes told a story of long unemployment that was borne out by his emaciated face and sunken eyes. There was something puzzlingly familiar to me in that face, which was so haggard and yet so youthful: his whole appearance and air reminded me of something that I knew very well indeed and yet could not remember.

Next to him was Marcel, deep in conversation with B, who was absolutely fascinated by his slang, the peculiar and sectarian argot of the toughs who frequent the Place de la République. Marcel was a small, dogged-looking person with a tremendous shock of reddish-brown hair, freckles, and a grin, a wide and friendly grin that every now and then suddenly became deprecating and rather unsure of itself. He was telling some great story of how he had been knifed by a Fascist. I couldn't follow the finer and more savoury details, and B was doing his best to translate in the manner of a ringside running commentary. Marcel reached his penultimate climax, paused dramatically, and began to take down his trousers.

'*Regarde*,' he exclaimed, and pointed to a long, red, newly healed scar that ran along the inside of his right thigh.

'So what happened?' we asked, after having been suitably impressed.

'Oh, I shot the swine,' he said, and roared with laughter. We looked at him with a certain amount of respect. Then it occurred to us that we too would be shooting the swine pretty soon.

'So you're well out of it,' we said. 'The cops must be after you.'

'But yes,' he said. 'Not for the shooting, though. They don't know it was me yet. But I dodged my military service.'

The train roared through the darkness, across the wide plain of central France. Once more everyone settled down, after having been wakened by Antonio's fall from the luggage rack where he had tried to compose himself for the night.

My eyes were closed, but I didn't feel like sleeping. I listened to the roaring engine-song, the sound of the striding pistons that bore us southwards and however fast they went they could not be fast enough for us now.

I opened my eyes and lit a cigarette. Then I found myself staring at Michel, trying to puzzle the meaning of the strange familiarity of his face that, now he was asleep, was more emaciated and mournful than ever. I felt that I had only to connect it with *something* for a whole forgotten complex of thoughts and feelings to be revealed.

Beside him Marcel dreamed with a child-like expression. And there was Antonio, his face in repose and without its vivacity and warm vulgarity, like a classic mask; under his thin shirt was sketched the outline of a Greek heroic torso.

I looked at all of them in turn, and somehow in each different sleeping countenance was a certain dignity, a beauty, something that they had in common that was hard to understand or explain, but that made me glad and proud that they were my comrades beside whom I would soon be fighting.

And then my eyes closed again of their own accord; everything was lost in the crushing roar of the train, that told of flying telegraph poles and departing landscapes, of the endless movement of shattered calm that spread outwards like a wake into sleeping countrysides, trembling upon the windows of farm-houses and across shivering grass, freezing small night animals into sudden stillness, briefly but continually touching the im-measurably remote and alien lives that dreamed or waked, suffered or rejoiced in the huge darkness through which we rushed.

The train ran right through the night and out into day again. The pale sunrise showed a different country, a rich and southern land-scape through which ran the turbulent travelled waters of the Rhône. One by one we woke, rubbed the grit from our eyes, stretched, lit cigarettes, yawned with an aching weariness, and became aware.

'I feel like hell,' said John.

'Yeh . . .' I grunted. 'I feel like hell.'

We headed for Spain; the endless rhythm of the jolting rail-joints had sung all night of the lessening miles to our dear objec-tive. But now we were deaf to that song; we peered with bleared and unappreciative eyes at the lovely river, and stretched, feeling saturated with the foul air and discomfort of the whole night.

'*Merde*,' said Michel, unheatedly, about nothing in particular. And he sighed deeply.

And as he sank back to sleep, letting his long arms fall trailingly at his side, I recognized him. The shape of his haggard, wistful melancholy was the very image of those unhappy circus boys that for a while Picasso had devoted himself to painting. I had always assumed that those sad and strangely moving figures were his own invention, that no possible models for them existed. But here before me in the living flesh was that lank resignation, so truly a copy of the painted figures that he hardly seemed to me to be an ordinary human being at all.

For a year a reproduction of one of those pictures had hung in my room and the time that I had spent in staring at it must have added up to many hours, hours in which I had shared so deeply of its melancholy that some of it had passed into the material of my own experience. To encounter its shape now, in this stuffy, hurtling compartment, on this journey, suddenly and for a moment brought into being again those old forgotten feelings, so that for a little while I was altogether removed from *this* atmosphere, and re-lived the incongruous sensations and thoughts of a period which I had for so long ceased to remember that it seemed to belong to the life of a stranger.

Then the train ran into Avignon, and it was time to count the remaining miles.

The Marseilles taximen mobilized themselves for us. From the back rooms of cafés, from the dozen obscure rooms and cellars in which we had been hidden during the day, we were collected by a fleet of taxis and whirled through busy streets, past lights and neon signs and crowded pavements, glimpsing for a few moments the secret and familiar life of an unknown city. Then there were long, dark, unpopulated roads, the lonely sound of trains and ships, the blank walls of warehouses, and then we came to the dock.

We got out. It was dimly lit, faintly sinister with the sound of lapping water and the peculiar dockside smell, the smell of ships and voyages and the outposts of land. Each of us felt an obscure compulsion to walk softly, listen, look round as if we expected to be challenged.

The huge white prow of the ship reared before us. I could see faintly the letters of her name and port of registration.

'Look,' I said softly. 'It's Spanish.'

In a moment now we would have left French soil, and surely before then someone would challenge us, some official (armed behind cold eyes with the whole machine of prisons and denials) would stop us and demand papers that we did not possess. It did not seem possible that we would be able to leave so simply.

And when we stepped on to the gang-plank I breathed a sigh of relief, as if we had come through some trial.

At the top of the gangway stood a sailor, an old man with a wrinkled, kindly peasant's face. He looked at us, raised his fist clenched in a salute.

'*Salud, camaradas,*' he said.

And I felt that now, at last, the final stage of our journey was about to begin.

The ship moved cautiously through the Mediterranean night.

That morning we had seen Barcelona, a smear of buildings and factory smoke low down on the horizon. But we had passed it by, heading still southwards to a port whose name we did not know.

Now we were in a danger zone. The ship's name had been painted out, she flew no flag, and not a single light shone aboard. The engines, working slowly, breathed out a muffled thudding. The ship was only a dim white shape moving in the darkness, out of which rose a faint murmur of voices; down pitch-black alley-ways cigarette-ends glowed like little stars. These were the clues to the eight hundred men that, between night sky and sea-bed, the ship bore within her iron bowels.

Somewhere one of the sailors was singing a *flamenco*, his voice low but pitched to the true *flamenco* note that sounds as if the singer was wailing of some great wrong at the top of his voice in an empty, echoing room.

Here was the ship and the night, the unknown danger and the urgent whisper of eight hundred lives packed close together, but the song was another thing, sounding of southern grief on lonely arid hills; it was something very old, and it had the richness of music that has been distilled from centuries of a people's experience. It seemed strangely irrelevant to this iron ship, this unknown danger, without meaning for the lives of these eight hundred. Here were factory workers, miners from Poland, men who had escaped from the concentration camps, exiles, and political refugees, the men of cities, of the electrically lit nights, of the loud street corners, of the labour exchange queues and the crowds at meetings and of the picket lines, the men whose song was the 'International'. They had carried the red banners through streets of great cities, the noises of machinery and traffic had attended their birth, their lives had been moulded by the struggles of classes: they were the vanguard of history. But the immemorial griefs and wrongs of this song were also theirs and it was in the age-long struggle against them that they had come together and so far.

John Cornford

Poems and Letters

From John Cornford: *A Memoir*

Full Moon at Tierz: Before the Storming of Huesca

The past, a glacier, gripped the mountain wall,
And time was inches, dark was all.
But here it scales the end of the range,
The dialectic's point of change,
Crashes in light and minutes to its fall.

Time present is a cataract whose force
Breaks down the banks even at its source
And history forming in our hands
Not plasticine but roaring sands,
Yet we must swing it to its final course.

The intersecting lines that cross both ways,
Time future, has no image in space,
Crooked as the road that we must tread,
Straight as our bullets fly ahead.
We are the future. The last fight let us face.

Where, in the fields by Huesca, the full moon
Throws shadows clear as daylight's, soon
The innocence of this quiet plain
Will fade in sweat and blood, in pain,
As our decisive hold is lost or won.

All round the barren hills of Aragon
Announce our testing has begun.
Here what the Seventh Congress said,

If true, if false, if live or dead,
Speaks in the Oviedo mauser's tone.

Three years ago Dimitrov fought alone
And we stood taller when he won.
But now the Leipzig dragon's teeth
Sprout strong and handsome against death
And here an army fights where there was one.

We studied well how to begin this fight,
Our Maurice Thorez held the light.
But now by Monte Aragon
We plunge into the dark alone,
Earth's newest planet wheeling through the night.

Though Communism was my walking time,
Always before the lights of home
Shone clear and steady and full in view –
Here, if you fall, there's help for you –
Now, with my Party, I stand quite alone.

Then let my private battle with my nerves,
The fear of pain whose pain survives,
The love that tears me by the roots,
The loneliness that claws my guts,
Fuse in the welded front our fight preserves.

O be invincible as the strong sun,
Hard as the metal of my gun,
O let the mounting tempo of the train
Sweep where my footsteps slipped in vain,
October in the rhythm of its run.

Now the same night falls over Germany
And the impartial beauty of the stars
Lights from the unfeeling sky
Oranienburg and freedom's crooked scars.
We can do nothing to ease that pain
But prove the agony was not in vain.

England is silent under the same moon,
From the Clydeside to the gutted pits of Wales.
The innocent mask conceals that soon
Here, too, our freedom's swaying in the scales.
O understand before too late
Freedom was never held without a fight.

Freedom is an easily spoken word
But facts are stubborn things. Here, too, in Spain
Our fight's not won till the workers of all the world
Stand by our guard on Huesca's plain.
Swear that our dead fought not in vain,
Raise the red flag triumphantly
For Communism and for liberty.

W. 1936

A Letter from Aragon

This is a quiet sector of a quiet front.

We buried Ruiz in a new pine coffin,
But the shroud was too small and his washed feet stuck out.
The stink of his corpse came through the clean pine boards
And some of the bearers wrapped handkerchiefs round their faces.
Death was not dignified.
We hacked a ragged grave in the unfriendly earth
And fired a ragged volley over the grave.

You could tell from our listlessness, no one much missed him.
This is a quiet sector of a quiet front.
There is no poison gas and no HE.

But when they shelled the other end of the village
And the streets were choked with dust
Women came screaming out of the crumbling houses,
Clutched under one arm the naked rump of an infant.
I thought: how ugly fear is.

This is a quiet sector of a quiet front.
Our nerves are steady; we all sleep soundly.

In the clean hospital bed my eyes were so heavy
Sleep easily blotted out one ugly picture,
A wounded militiaman moaning on a stretcher,
Now out of danger, but still crying for water,
Strong against death, but unprepared for such pain.

This on a quiet front.

But when I shook hands to leave, an Anarchist worker
Said: 'Tell the workers of England
This was a war not of our own making,
We did not seek it.
But if ever the Fascists again rule Barcelona
It will be as a heap of ruins with us workers beneath it.'

W. 1936

Diary Letter from Aragon (Third Quarter of 1936)

Darling, I'll explain why in a minute, but just at the moment I'm spending whole days at the front with nothing to do, and so I am writing you an immense letter: if it wasn't so hot here I'd try and get my ideas and impressions sorted out, but I can't, so I'm writing everything down just as it comes out . . . First of all, a last will and testament. As you know there is a risk of being killed. Statistically not very great, but it exists all the same. First of all, why I am here? You know the political reasons. There's a subjective one as well. From the age of seventeen I was in a kind of way tied down, and envied my contemporaries a good deal their freedom to bum about. And it was partly because I felt myself for the first time independent that I came out here. But I promise this is the last time I shall leave you unnecessarily. Maybe that the Party will send me, but after this I will always be with you when I have a chance . . .

Well, all that's said. At the moment I am on top of a hill at the front in Aragon. A complete circle of rocky mountains, covered with green scrub, very barren, with a few fields in between. Two kilometres away a village held by the enemy. A grey stone affair with a big church. The enemy are quite invisible. An occasional rifle shot. One burst of machine-gun fire. One or two aeroplanes. The sound of our guns sometimes a long way off. And nothing else but a sun so hot that I am almost ill, can eat very little, and scarcely work at all. Nothing at all to do. We lie around all day. At night two hours on the watch – last night very fine with the lightning flickering behind Saragossa, miles away. Sleeping in the open with a single blanket on the stones – last night it rained, but just not quite enough to get through the blanket. How long we are to be here I don't know. And now comes the catch – I came up to the front and Richard was left behind. Enlisted here on the strength of my Party card. There was one little Italian comrade with some broken English. Now he's been sent off. So I'm here and the only communication I have is with the very broken French of a young Catalan volunteer. And so I am not only utterly lonely, but also feel a bit useless. However it couldn't have been expected that everything would go perfectly as it did to here. This loneliness, and this nervous anxiety from not knowing when or how to get back, and not yet having been under fire, means that inevitably I am pretty depressed. Even thought of using my press ticket to get home, but it would be too ridiculous to come out here to fight and go back because I was a bit lonely. So I am here provisionally until the fall of Saragossa whenever that is . . .

In the morning – it was a Sunday – before it was yet hot, the bells of the enemy village of Perdiguera sounded very slow and mournful across the distance. I don't know why, but that depressed me as much as anything ever has. However, I'm settling in now. Last night we began to make ourselves more comfortable – dug little trenches to sleep in and filled them with straw. So long as I am doing anything, however purposeless, I feel fine. It's inactivity that just eats at my nerves. But the night before last I had a dream. One of the toughest people when I was small at school was the captain of rugger, an oaf called D—. I was in the same dormitory and terrified of him. I hadn't thought of him for years, but last night I dreamt extremely vividly about having a fight with him and holding my own, and I think that's a good omen. I don't know how long we stay on this hill, but I am beginning to settle down to it ...

Now a bit about the political situation. That isn't easy to get straight, particularly as I haven't yet heard anyone explain the position of the Party (and the militia here I am with are POUM – left sectarian semi-Trotzkyists). But roughly this. The popular front tactics were worked magnificently to begin with. They won the elections. And under the slogan of defence of the Republic, they enabled us to arm the workers when the Fascist revolt started. Up till then the position is quite clear. But now in Catalonia things are like this. There is a left Republican Government. But, in fact, the real power is with the workers. There are 50,000 or more armed workers in Catalonia – and in the Barcelona patrols they are organized in the following proportions: 325 CNT (Anarchist), 185 ERC (left Republican), but this means simply the civil guard and the *guardia de asalto*, the police; 145 UGT (Soc.– Com.); 45 POUM. Thus the Anarchists predominate. Seventy-five per cent of industry is already socialized – and mostly worked by the Anarchists. In order to prevent a Fascist outbreak, every night splits, unpopular bosses, and known Fascists are taken for a ride. Assisted by the militia, there is a peasant war raging in the countryside and thousands of Kulaks and landlords have been killed. The Anarchists appear to be preparing to attack the Government after the fall of Saragossa. That would be disastrous. The only possible tactics for the Party are to place themselves at the head of the movement, get it under control, force recognition from the Government of the social gains of the revolution, and prevent at all costs an attack on the Government – unless the Government actually begin to sabotage the fight against Fascism. That may be what the Party is doing. But I have a fear that it is a little too mechanical in its application of People's Front tactics. It is still concentrating too much on trying to neutralize the petty bourgeoisie – when by far the most urgent task is to win the Anarchist workers, which is a special technique and very different from broad Seventh Congress phrases. But I don't really know ...

In Barcelona one can understand physically what the dictatorship of the proletariat means. All the Fascist press has been taken over. The real rule is in the hands of the militia committees. There is a real terror against the Fascists. But that doesn't alter the fact that the place is free – and conscious all the time of its freedom. Everywhere in the streets are armed workers and militiamen, and sitting in the cafés which used to belong to the bourgeoisie. The huge Hotel Colon overlooking the main square is occupied by the United Socialist Party of Catalonia. Farther down, in a huge block opposite the Bank of Spain, is the Anarchist headquarters. The palace of a marquis in the Rambla is a CP headquarters. But one does not feel the tension. The mass of the people are oblivious of the Anarchist–Government trouble brewing, and simply are enjoying their freedom. The streets are crowded all day, and there are big crowds round the radio palaces. But there is nothing at all like tension or hysteria. It's as if in London the armed workers were dominating the streets – it's obvious that they wouldn't tolerate Mosley or people selling *Action* in the streets. And that wouldn't mean that the town wasn't free in the real sense. It is genuinely a dictatorship of the majority, supported by the overwhelming majority. Not yet in Soviet form – the elections to the committees aren't on the basis of localities or factories but representatives of organizations. That narrows the basis a bit, but not much, as a huge majority of the people are organized.

Going into action. Thank God for something to do at last. I shall fight like a Communist if not like a soldier. All my love. Salute.

Up till now this letter has been very miserable. For this reason. I came out with the intention of staying a few days, firing a few shots, and then coming home. Sounded fine, but you just can't do things like that. You can't play at civil war, or fight with a reservation you don't mean to get killed. It didn't take long to realize that either I was here in earnest or else I'd better clear out. I tried to avoid the dilemma. Then I felt so lonely and bad I tried to get a pass back to Barcelona. But the question was decided for me. Having joined, I am in whether I like it or not. And I like it. Yesterday we went out to attack, and the prospect of action was terribly exhilarating – hence the message on the top of the page. But in the end we went back without doing anything. But I am settling down, picking up scraps of the language and beginning to feel happy. I think I'll make a good fighter, and I'm glad to be

here. And since they won't let me go, it means that I don't feel
useless or in the way, as if I were I'd be sent back. So I'll probably
be here two months, and I will learn a hell of a lot. There is a 70
per cent chance of getting back uninjured and 90 per cent of
getting back alive; which is, on the whole, worth while – and
even if it wasn't, I'd have to stay . . .

Altogether I've passed the worst days of mental crisis, though
all the physical hardship is to come. But I think I'll bear up. I've
got a kind of feeling, rather difficult to explain, that my person-
ality, I myself, was beginning to assert itself again. For days I've
been shoved about from place to place, lost and anxious and
frightened, and all that distinguished me personally from a unit
in the mass obliterated – just a unit, alternately worried, homesick, anxious, calm, hungry, sleepy, uncomfortable in turn – and
all my own individuality, such strength as I have, such ability to
analyse things, submerged. Now that's beginning to be different,
I am beginning to adapt. Probably I'll be swept off my feet again
when the first action starts. But now I, John Cornford, am beginning to emerge above the surface again and recognize myself
and enjoy myself, and it feels good.

The army is a curious mixture of amateur and professional.
There is practically no shouting and saluting. When somebody is
told to do something, he gets up to do it all right, but not in a
hurry. Officers are elected by acclamation, and obeyed. About half
the troops are more or less in uniform, in blue or brown overalls
and blue shirts. The rest are more or less nondescript. I myself am
wearing a pair of heavy, black, corduroy trousers (expropriated
from the bourgeoisie), a blue sports shirt, and that alpaca coat,
rope-soled sandals, and an infinitely battered old sombrero.
Luggage, a blanket, a cartridge case (held together with string) in
which there is room for a spare shirt, a knife, toothbrush, bit of
soap, and comb. Also a big tin mug stuck in my belt. But most
are a good bit smarter than that.

What is new is the complete feeling of insecurity, new for me,
but most workers have it from the day they leave school. Always
in all my work before there has been the background of a secure
and well-provided home, and friends that I could fall back upon
in an emergency. Now that is no longer here, I stand completely

on my own. And I find that rather difficult at first. But I shall manage. Just now, for instance, I have unlimited opportunity to write. And I have plenty of things which for years I've wanted to write. But I can't get them together in my head, things aren't straight enough: all I can put down are my immediate subjective impressions, and I can't think about Birmingham or anywhere else. Oh, for the objectivity of a Nehru. I'll learn: I am learning. But it's going to be something of a testing-time.

8.12.36.

Darling,

There is an English comrade going back, and this is my first chance of an uncensored letter. Remember that a good deal is not for publication. Excuse incoherences, because I'm in hospital with a slight wound and very weak. I'll tell you about that later.

I'll assume none of my letters have yet got through, as I've had no answers. First of all about myself. I'm with a small English group in the Machine-Gun Company of the French Battalion of the First International Brigade. Luckily we are the best company, the machine gunners; and in the best section of that, a Franco-Belgian section.

Now, as to the English blokes. Amongst the good blokes, Bernard, who is political delegate, replacing me because I did not speak enough French to get things done. He's been ill, and suffers terribly from the cold, but has borne up really well. John Summerfield [*sic*], tough and starting like me with no military training has become a good soldier, and a good scrounger which is very important in a badly equipped army. David Mackenzie, a Scots student: age 19: first-class rifle shot and machine gunner: intellectual and writes good verse. A very good guy is Edward Burke of the *Daily Worker*. Ex-actor, looks like a sap, always loses everything, but has a queer gift for understanding machinery, became a good machine gunner in no time, was put *pro tem* on a trench gun, promoted to section leader he did well on a really nasty bit of the front line.

We had about a month's training at Albacete and La Rada. We English did badly, we were a national minority very hard to assimilate, mucked about between one station and another, starting work on one kind of gun and then having it taken away from us, taking part in manoeuvres which those that didn't speak

French couldn't understand. When we at last got down to work with the machine gunners our training was interrupted almost before we started, and we were switched through to the front. That was early in November. We were put in general reserve in the University City, thought we could rest and take it easy. The first morning we were heavily shelled with 75s. I did quite well that day. The section leader, Fred Jones, was away, and so confident that all was quiet that he hadn't appointed a successor. I took charge on the moment, was able to get all the guns – we then had four – into position, and rescued one which the gunmen had deserted in a panic. But there was no attack after all.

Then in reserve in the Casa del Campo: a big wood, ex-royal forest, rather Sussexy to look at: but behind to the right a range of the Guadarama, a real good range with snow against a very blue sky. Then a piece of real bad luck. Maclaurin and three other Lewis gunners were sent up to the front. The French infantry company they were with was surprised by the Moors. The Lewis gunners stayed to cover the retreat. Mac was found dead at his gun, Steve Yates, one of our corporals, an ex-soldier and a good bloke, was killed too. Another, wounded in the guts. It's always the best seem to get the worst.

Then for the first time up to the front. We advanced into position at exactly the wrong time, at sunset, taking over some abandoned trenches. The Fascists had the range exact and shelled us accurately. Seven were killed in a few minutes. We had a nasty night in the trenches. Then back into reserve. The main trouble now was the intense cold: and we were sleeping out without blankets, which we had left behind in order to carry more machine-gun ammunition. Worse still to come; we had to make a night march back. There was a lorry load of wounded behind us. The lorry driver signalled, but wasn't noticed and got no answer. The four lines were so indeterminate that he thought we were a Fascist column and accelerated past us. Someone put up a wire to stop the car. The wire was swept aside, caught Fred Jones by the neck, hauled him over the parapet and killed him. Fred was a really good section leader: declassed bourgeois, ex-guardsman unemployed organizer, combination of adventurer and sincere Communist: but a really powerful person and could make his group work in a disciplined way in an army where there wasn't much discipline. That day the French redeemed their bad start by a really good bayonet attack which recaptured the philosophy building. We were in reserve for all this.

Then a spell of rest behind the lines. Back at the front in a really comfortable position in the philosophy and letters building. This was our best front line period. Comfortable, above all warm, and supplies regular. A great gutted building, with broken glass all over, and the fighting consisted of firing from behind barricades of philosophy books at the Fascists in a village below and in the Casa de Velasquez opposite. One day an anti-aircraft shell fell right into the room we were in. We were lucky as hell not to be wiped out completely: as it was there were only three slightly wounded, I gathering a small cut in the head. After the night in the rather inefficient but very nice Secours Rouge Hospital, where the amateur nurses wash your wounds like scrubbing the floor, I came back, feeling all right, but must have been a bit weak from loss of blood. Then came two heavy days' work trench-digging in the frozen clay. The afternoon of the second day I think I killed a Fascist. Fifteen or sixteen of them were running from a bombardment. I and two Frenchmen were firing from our barricades with sights at 900: We got one, and both said it was I that hit him, though I couldn't be sure. If it is true, it's a fluke, and I'm not likely to do as good a shot as that again. Then back again into reserve. The first day we were there, David Mackenzie and I took a long walk towards the Guadarama. When I came back my wound began to hurt again: this morning I was very weak, a kind of retarded shock, I think, and am now in hospital for the time being.

Well, that's how far we've got. No wars are nice, and even a revolutionary war is ugly enough. But I'm becoming a good soldier, longish endurance and a capacity for living in the present and enjoying all that can be enjoyed. There's a tough time ahead but I've plenty of strength left for it.

Well, one day the war will end – I'd give it till June or July, and then if I'm alive I'm coming back to you. I think about you often, but there's nothing I can do but say again, be happy, darling, and I'll see you again one day.

Bless you,
John

To Margot Heinemann

Heart of the heartless world,
Dear heart, the thought of you
Is the pain at my side,
The shadow that chills my view.

The wind rises in the evening,
Reminds that autumn is near.
I am afraid to lose you,
I am afraid of my fear.

On the last mile to Huesca,
The last fence for our pride,
Think so kindly, dear, that I
Sense you at my side.

And if bad luck should lay my strength
Into the shallow grave,
Remember all the good you can;
Don't forget my love.

From *Crusade in Spain*

Interest in the Irish Brigade was now growing fast, and when, on November 27, a third and still larger party of volunteers – eighty-four in all – left for Liverpool and Lisbon, thousands gathered at the North Wall and each man was cheered as he walked up the gangway. Before leaving, the volunteers were presented with Rosaries, Agnus Deis and other religious emblems, the gift of the Right Rev. Monsignor Byrne, Clonmel, Dean of Waterford.

Seventeen counties were represented in this party, the largest contingent coming from Tipperary. Referring to their departure, the Right Rev. Monsignor Ryan, Dean of the Archdiocese of Cashel, preaching after Mass the following Sunday, said: 'They have gone to fight the battle of Christianity against Communism. There are hosts of difficulties facing the men whom General O'Duffy is leading, and only heroes can fight such a battle. Those at home can help the cause with their prayers. The Rosary is more powerful than weapons of war. In the presence of Our Lord Jesus Christ let us promise that we will offer one decade of the family Rosary daily for poor suffering Spain; for the Irish boys who have gone out to fight the desperate battle that is threatening desolation all over the world. Let us pray that the destruction of civilization may be averted, that Christ may live and reign, and that Communism and the power of Satan on earth may be brought to naught.'

At Liverpool this party was joined on the *Aguila* by a number of young Irishmen from London and Manchester, and again a large crowd assembled at the quay.

Those who travelled on this occasion included Rev. J. Mulrean, chaplain, and the following volunteers who became officers:

Charles Horgan, Cork, who has had a splendid record in the IRA and National Army; Thomas Cahill, Tipperary, who was an active member of the Irish Volunteers and underwent a hunger strike with me in Belfast Gaol, was a Captain in the National Army and later joined the Garda Siochana; and Eamon Horan, UDC, Tralee, who had long service in the IRA and National Army.

The departure of volunteers became a regular Friday feature, as parties had left on three consecutive Fridays, so again on the 4th December a big crowd assembled on the Dublin quays to wish God-speed to an expected contingent. They were disappointed however, as more elaborate plans were in mind for the next week-end, when the fourth and largest party, over a hundred, set sail. They arrived in Dublin carrying Papal, National and Spanish flags, and wearing Sacred Heart badges sent from various Irish convents.

While Saturday's report of the departure of the fourth contingent from Dublin was being read in the newspapers, young men from every county in Ireland were moving westward to embark on a special ship from Galway Bay. Close on five hundred left Galway under cover of darkness in the small hours of Sunday morning to board a ship specially chartered to sail direct to Spain. Soon after this contingent had left Galway pier in a tender, many more volunteers arrived only to find they had missed the boat. They returned in buses to their homes to sail at a later date.

So secret were the arrangements kept that only those directly concerned knew of the departure until the last moment. It is related that Galway hotel proprietors were startled when they were knocked up at 1 a.m. and looking out on Eyre Square, the chief thoroughfare of Galway, found it blocked by buses and hundreds of private cars. Only a few minutes before, the spacious square had been deserted. Quickly the hotels were thrown open and after short meals the unexpected visitors left again to board their buses and cars. This time the entire fleet of vehicles made in the direction of the pier. Within a few minutes the tender *Dun Aengus*, which had been under steam for over an hour, threw open her gang-ways.

It was only then that those citizens of Galway who had left their beds to investigate the mystery of this strange invasion learned that they were witnessing the first departure for Spain of a draft of the Irish Brigade on a large all-Ireland scale. The volunteers hurried aboard the *Dun Aengus*, while on the pier and the surrounding thoroughfare now black with people, young women and old wiped tears from their eyes to smile at departing brothers, husbands, sons, and sweethearts.

The *Dun Aengus* drew off from the pier with three shrill blasts on her siren at 2.15 a.m. Then, as handkerchiefs waved and voices from the darkness were raised in farewell, somebody on the pier began singing 'Faith of Our Fathers'. A thousand voices took up the hymn. From the tender there floated back to the pier that solemn strain. Then the 'Soldier's Song' which re-echoed back more faintly from the receding tender.

Amongst those on the quayside to see the men off were Rev. T. Fahy, Professor, University College, Galway, and Rev. J. O'Donohoe, C.C., Galway.

Swiftly the lights of the *Dun Aengus* retreated into the blackness of the harbour, soon to be lost to the sight of those remaining behind, and then the stillness was broken by the roar of all types of motor engines as the buses and cars swept through Galway again, making homeward to Cork, Dublin, Belfast, Clonmel, various towns in Kerry, Limerick, Wexford, and other parts of the country.

When the tender had got out in the bay, the wind rose and there were squalls of heavy rain. The men on the unsheltered upper deck were soon wet through, and those below began to suffer from sea-sickness. On the whole they bore the hardness of their lot cheerfully, especially those on the open deck, who, although drenched through and shivering with the intense cold, never murmured.

At about 5.30 a.m., when no sign of the ship had been seen, Captain Goggins, of the *Dun Aengus*, decided there was no use in further cruising around, and the tender was hove to in a more sheltered position to await daylight. For a couple of hours there was silence aboard the little vessel, except for the steady tramping backwards and forwards of the men on deck, who kept up a ceaseless patrol, looking for the vessel that was to bring them forth on their great adventure.

Dawn broke with the wind rising and the rain coming in sleety squalls. Before night had fully cleared away, all who could get on deck turned their eyes seawards in eager search for what all were calling 'the mystery ship'. There was no sign of her however, and hearts sank again. Doubt as to whether their adventure would ever materialize began to enter even the stoutest hearts, and there was talk of putting back to Galway.

The *Dun Aengus* again put out towards the open sea and no sooner had she rounded Black Head than a large vessel was sighted steaming close in to the shore. The *Dun Aengus* immediately swung about and guided her farther back into the bay. It was almost 11 a.m. before the big ship and the little one came alongside each other. Then there was the troublesome task of making them fast in the rising gale, but at last this was accomplished, and the two vessels were fast moored to each other.

Rope ladders were let down the side of the bigger vessel, and the volunteers forgot their coldness as the spirit of their great undertaking again flared up in them. Soon they were scrambling actively up the ladders, carrying their attaché cases and other belongings. Dixies, full of hot soup, were awaiting them, and when they had taken this they were hurried below, where arrangements had already been made for them. As only one man at a time could climb up the swaying rope ladder, and as the vessels were swinging heavily in the gale, trans-shipment was a lengthy and dangerous task, but was completed safely about 3 p.m.

Some thirty-five of the men now re-embarked on the *Dun Aengus*, leaving nearly five hundred of their comrades aboard. The lines were cast off, the little vessel's hooter blew three times as a salute from the men aboard her to their gallant comrades, and then she steamed back to Galway.

The gale continued during the greater part of the troopship's journey to Ferroll, a Spanish seaport, and the volunteers endured much further hardship *en route*. On reaching Ferroll bay they were transferred for the night to the *Domino*, the ship on which La Cierva had intended the brigade should travel. Here they enjoyed their first comfortable night's rest and the first good meal since leaving their homes almost a week before.

Next morning they entrained on a twenty-four-hour journey to Salamanca. There they had a great reception, were met by military bands and marched through the streets to the City Hall, where dinner awaited them. They were welcomed by the Mayor, high military and church authorities, and many of the principal citizens. After enjoying generous hospitality the volunteers entrained on the last lap of the journey to their headquarters at Caceres. The

Military Governor, Civil Governor, Mayor, Judges, other leading citizens and their Irish comrades who had previously reached there awaited the arrival of the train. Every house in the city was decorated in honour of the brigade, and although the volunteers were almost worn out from the effects of the journey they were constrained to march through the streets so that the waiting thousands who lined the route to welcome them to Caceres might not be disappointed.

The departure of the men from Galway, while attended by many discomforts, was a successful achievement. The seven hundred volunteers who travelled to Passage East on the night of January 6 would, I believe, gladly have suffered even worse if they had met with the same success. Instead they suffered intense disappointment from the non-arrival of the ship which was to take them to Spain.

Early in the morning of January 7 a ship was to arrive at Passage East, a fishing village seven miles from Waterford city. Throughout the night the quiet country roads were lighted by beams of motor-car lights, and at midnight the little village of some fifty houses were thronged with men. Unlike Galway, Passage East seemed more or less to expect them. All roads leading to Waterford were patrolled by the Guards, all cars were stopped, the numbers taken and the drivers asked for their licences. In some cases they were questioned as to where they were going and whence they were coming.

The time of their ship's arrival was not known to the men, and as the hours rolled by they remained in high spirits, and paraded the streets singing popular songs to the strains of bagpipes. They continuously scanned the river mouth for sign of the lights of a ship, the villagers joining in the eager watch. The local people, though most hospitable, had not the means to cater for such an influx of visitors and soon all available refreshments were gone.

That January day broke bright and sunny, and the volunteers continued their watch cheerfully enough. When a coal boat came slowly up the river they rushed to the pier to find their hopes frustrated. Hungry and tired they were greatly chagrined when told at about 11 a.m. that the ship was not coming. They remained hopeful until the transport had actually arrived to bring them back to their homes after their all-night vigil, and manfully expressed their willingness to spend even another night under the same conditions, if they could get to their comrades in Spain.

The people of Passage East felt the disappointment almost as keenly as the volunteers themselves and their kindness and hospitality on the occasion will not soon be forgotten.

In Spain the military authorities had made all preparations for the reception of this contingent which was to form the second or reserve bandera of the Irish Brigade. I was afterwards informed that the ship was commandeered hurriedly by the navy for service at Malaga on the day it was to leave for Ireland. The Admiral in charge of the zone apparently was not in a position at the time to notify general headquarters at Salamanca. Such are the exigencies of war.

Letters from Spain

The following letters were published in *From Spanish Trenches*

Socoro Rojo, Albacete, Spain, January 3, 1937

My dear Gerald:
It's time I thought of writing you – but the trouble is to find a quiet corner in this country. Every place is full, everybody is rushing about. Anyway, here I am. We arrived here the 16th of December, five hundred and fifty strong, of which three hundred and fifty are from Ireland, fifty being from Belfast, sixty Liverpool-Irish, and as you know New York, Philadelphia, and Boston are well represented. The Irish lads who had enlisted at the start of the hostilities and who were attached to the French and British companies of the International Brigade are being transferred to the Irish Battalion.

We are in excellent form, having been in intensive training and it has done us a lot of good. I have sent one Irish unit to the front on December 28th, and there is another in the making. But you must remember that all our years in the IRA were to good purpose; these lads are well trained and they will never let us down. Those who come home from this scrap will be of good use in Ireland soon. Quite a lot of our crowd were in the IRA right up to their departure; this will be the making of them.

And you should see the International Brigades. There isn't a country that isn't represented and there is great camaraderie, in spite of it all. The trouble is, there aren't enough guns in the country. Thousands of Spaniards are not yet armed.

The people are 90 per cent against Franco. I've been among the peasants at villages. They have enough to eat, for the first time in their lives. Food and clothes are cheap – and, strange to say, plentiful. Cigarettes are terrible, but I'm always hearing they have good ones in the next town. (I fear I'll never reach that 'next' town.) The unit entered Madrid defence trenches, University Section, on December 28th, for the heaviest bombardment experienced so far, and the men behaved wonderfully. Thomas Patten from Achill County, Mayo, and Patrick Berry from Northern Ireland were killed on December 29th. Since then we have eight wounded and one missing.

I am now pressed for time as I have interviews with the French press and making arrangements to speak over the Madrid radio.

I go to school – to the kids of Madrid. They get a great kick out of my Spanish, and always I'm reminded of that bundle of mischief of yours back in Dublin – and I get lonesome.

I will write you soon again, in the meantime, send me all the news and remember me to all the crowd. Good luck.

Frank

Socoro Rojo, Hospital de Sangre, Elda, February 17, 1937

Dear Helen & Gerald:
The above address should be enough to let you know that I am off the Active List for a little while. I got a bullet through the left arm a few days ago, on the South Madrid front. It's not serious and I'm not confined to bed. I count myself lucky: it was the fourth day of a pretty tough fight, and anyway, I have escaped for a long time, haven't I? As I went out on a stretcher I heard the Yanks come in – so expect news from them soon.

I got five letters from you – mostly together – after I came back at the end of January from Madrid. I got Helen's letter enclosing that *brilliant* 'New York Post' cutting about myself just as I was going up the line. I guess I'll pick up more news in a day or two. I'm here in a sunny climate, where there are actually baths and barbers – so I'm not too badly off.

Why can't I write oftener? Well, I certainly could have written postcards – but probably I wasn't in the humour. I'm sorry to have to refuse to write those newspaper articles: I have had similar requests from London and Dublin – but the censorship here is sensible: you go up the line as a soldier, or you stay behind as a correspondent. And if you stay behind, what can you write of? I guess I could get special permission, if I tried, but then I'd have to omit mention of places, dates, and units – so it wouldn't be worth the trouble. And anyway, what did I come out here for? To be another O'Duffy, directing his men from the rear – would you like me that way? Would I like myself?

Which reminds me – why must the *Post* and other papers talk of this 'blood feud' between O'Duffy and I? We would be out here, if there never was an O'Duffy. We smashed his attempts to set up his dictatorship in Ireland – and, as *you* know, he came here to find the career that he could not get in Ireland. We came here to fight Fascism; it's just an accident for us that O'Duffy happens to be here fighting for it. And, the pity is that the vast majority of those whom he enticed into Franco's camp are just fools to think they are 'Fighting for the Faith'. I've seen how Franco and his German and Italian masters 'Fight for the Faith'. The bodies of babies cluttered in a schoolyard after an air-raid, breadlines of women blown to bits, working-class houses razed. And you heard of the bull-rings of Badajoz and other towns which the Fascists took? And the women who are turned over – one to every twenty Moors? That's the kind of Faith *they* fight for, it . . . well – to Hell with it!

I'll write you in a few days. I've lost some of my best, including Kit Conway who led No. 1 Company since the start. Another boy is with the Americans and I await news. Regards to all the crowd.

Frank

February 11, 1937

Dear Gerald:
I've had some days' rest (during which I didn't write you!) and I'm feeling fit now. I'm pretty well acclimatized. I can even roll a cigarette (of the world's worst tobacco) and my throat stands up to it. I lost my voice for a week, when I first came, but now I keep free from colds. The days, as a rule, are brilliantly sunny; it freezes at night. Rain is rare – but even so – the roads are like those of Flanders. And you can't believe what Spanish lorry-drivers will chance, until you come here. I tell you I'm more afraid of them than I am of aeroplanes or even machine guns.

Not one of my boys let me down. Every man justified his selection. And when this war is over, I'll be able to tell just what they did, and the difficulties under which they did it. Kids some of them were – lads not nineteen years old, who told me they were twenty-four – and they were heroes. Down in Andalusia, someone spread the story that O'Duffy's men were opposite us. When the order to go over came, you should have seen our lads charge. 'Up the Republic!' 'To hell with the Fascists!' – the old war cries rang out all along the line. (Of course, O'Duffy and his men were doing police work in Salamanca that day.) One incident of that fight is typical: Jack Nalty of Dublin was caught in machine-gun fire. He has three bullets in his chest and his right arm broke. He picked up his rifle and slung it over the good shoulder, caught up the broken arm, and walked three kilometres to the field hospital. 'Others need stretchers more', he said. Of course, a man with such an iron constitution is alive and on the mend today.

Who'd think that a sensitive chap like Frank Edwards could stand up to this kind of war? Yet, none better than he.

Frank

February 5, 1937

Dear Friends:

I read in the *Irish Press* that 'the Wild Geese have flown again'; I read in the *Irish Echo*, New York, of the 'tragedy' of men like me coming out here. The type of canned nationalism that inspires such talk is THE tragedy I deplore. They ignore the changes in world politics, they would have us ignore the Great Danger until it is on our shores. 'We serve Ireland only', they cry, but they would have us wait until it would be too late to make effective use of our services. Catalonia recognizes that it must not wait until Franco reaches its borders. Is Ireland to commit the error Catalonia avoids?

Is the *Irish Press* comparing the Wild Geese to O'Duffy's hirelings? The Wild Geese were honest-minded men who went out to fight against their country's enemy. (Incidentally, their fate should have forever killed the slogan: 'England's enemy is Ireland's friend'.) To compare O'Duffy's dupes with them is an insult to national tradition. Does O'Duffy go to fight against even 'England's enemy'?

What mistakes – yes, tragedies – are caused by failing to face facts. Not ten per cent of O'Duffy's forces in Spain are Fascists;

the rest of them are just dupes who go to 'fight for the Faith'. The *Irish Press* refused to say that, for it fears to tackle the pro-Fascist Irish Hierarchy, yet to avoid alienating Republican opinion, it has to shadow-box with O'Duffy. And there is no paper to champion truth and justice unequivocally. How can we let the world know that the lives of Conroy and Coady, Meeham and Boyle, have not been wasted, that their deaths are not 'tragedies' that need not have happened? Honour to those who died for the freedom of the Irish people; honour even greater to those who die here for the freedom of ALL HUMANITY. No 'wild geese' were these lads. You remember how I warned them, before they left home, what their life here – as long as it would last – would be like. You remember how I discouraged every suspicion of adventurism. You know how they could have stayed at home and be regarded by their friends as 'soldiers of Ireland'. They chose to come here asking neither for pay nor preferment, coming because they believed it was their duty to come to participate in this decisive fight against Fascism. And, for my part, while it would be wrong to accuse me of bringing them here, I would never regret having done so. Our 50,000 who died in the Great War were sacrificed uselessly; no life given here is given in vain.

And look at it from the purely selfish viewpoint. Which is better: that some of us should die here, or that thousands should die at home? For if Fascism triumphs here, Ireland's trial will soon be at hand.

Frank Ryan

A Letter from Spain

The following letter appeared in *From Spanish Trenches*

American Hospital No. 1, Socoro Rojo, Albacete, Spain,
February 27, 1937

Dear Sally –
Here's more of the adventures that befell ... Landed in Port Bou from Paris, sitting up in the train. Was of course seen off by a delegation, among them John Langdon-Davies, the English writer, *'Behind the Spanish Barricades'*. More about him later. At Port Bou, the Spanish Border – got in 8 a.m. tired and hungry – the scenery on the way down was beyond words or descriptions – snow-capped mountains – sparkling sea (Mediterranean) and gay coloured grounds and villages. At the port we were met by a very handsome Spanish Captain – whom we all took to and he on the other hand, said he felt very ill and needed nursing – you know the old story. So –, after a lunch of a variety of foods and liquors and of course, a toast with champagne again. (Gee, you should see us drink wine – we demand it now!) After a heavy lunch and no sleep – with the little tavern very crowded – the problem of sleep came up – where was the town going to put up some 17-odd people. We were put up in grand style, though. They opened the railroad station hotel for us – the most modern building in the town – even a bathroom between two rooms (no hot H_2O). Nevertheless, everyone pitched in, making our beds – even the chief commandant.

So to bed and did we sleep. We were wakened at nine o'clock. (By the time we got to bed it was three or four – time doesn't seem to matter here. Lunches and dinners take two–three hours – tell that to Blumey.) We had supper and took walks up the mountain paths, all very nice, etc. The next a.m. about eleven – big touring

cars came and took us to Barcelona. What cars. Some had in-
signias – must have been a count's or some big shot, at one time.
Then some more swell views and scenery and arrived at Barcelona
about eight at night. Nice hotel – I think I sent you some cards
from there. We stopped at Hotel Oriente, a good enough place.
Stayed for about five days, where things happened. Met J.
Langdon-Davies, got his snapshots – took us touring about town
(all this time the big cars and chauffeurs were at our disposal so
that we saw a good bit of the town). Saw a command perform-
ance of a dance festival – finished at two a.m. Folk dances.

Were we tired. What struck me funny: Imagine the officials of
New York City taking visitors to the CAMEO. Well, we were.
We were taken to see WE ARE FROM KRONSTADT – and had
box seats. Are you laughing?

By the way, J. Langdon-Davies threatened to put us in his next
book. Met lots of boys on leave in Barcelona – took in dances,
walks, etc. People sit in cafés all day – meet, have business, in fact
even children are brought in to have coffee (undrinkable), milk
etc. On to Valencia, again in cars. We saw a lot of Spain, speeding
through towns. Valencia not as interesting as Port Bou, but nice.
Met Dr Bethune, swell guy very busy. Stopped at a place called
Hotel Inglis, where nobody spoke English. This certainly was a
seething place – all sorts of reporters – who were forever curious
about us – men who came to sell or buy things – we even had a
hotel SIREN – probably a chorus girl at one time – waiting for a
boy friend or something. Anyway, we went to a CHARITY bullfight! And she was in our party. Were we stared at – she looks like
Jean Harlow. The bullfight is not a pleasant thing to watch – none
are really fought any more nowadays, though. This one we saw
was a fancy dress and comic fight – so we all had a laugh.

About this time I understand telegrams were sent out, about us
being in Madrid, which is wrong of course. Our leader and Head
Nurse did go out to see about a site for the hospital. We stayed in
Valencia three or four days.

Then on to Albacete – a seething military town – where I guess
I can't say too much in a letter. Make note and I'll try to recall
facts. We travelled to Albacete in big trucks and our ambulances.
The nice, comfortable touring cars were gone from now on. No
more grand style. The Americans had made their splash – so what.

We met a Lady Hastings in Barcelona, who was with the English Medical Unit and she told us what a good impression we made. Nice woman. She was ill. We took turns taking care of her.

Then to our destination – again I'll just mention the name – *El Romeral* – not even on the map. Make another note, especially about travelling down to El Romeral . . . I'll tell you about it. We found a building which just about suited us. Of course no running hot and cold water or toilet or shower. Another note: I'm going to soak next time I reach a bath tub. So we started unpacking and unloading our stuff. We had the whole town about us.

I'm writing this in the kitchen at 4 a.m. Yet again I'm on night duty, but this time I don't mind it. We have some Spanish women in to help us. I don't overwork – but we are busy – and do we need trained help. Do you know when the other Unit is coming over? I'm going around the hospital to make the rounds now. We have an upstairs and a downstairs and we have a staff house across the lane. Two nice Englishmen with an ambulance were attached to us and one of our MDs is trying to play matchmaker. Wow – chilly and clear around here. We're very high above sea level. The days are nice but – oy – the nights are cold. You should hear me jabber away in Spanish, with a vocabulary of about fifteen words, and hands – I just about get along. Just brought in food from our storehouse. I go around with a big batch of keys and give materials to our little Spanish night cook. Maurice is sitting opposite me and buttering bread for the patient's breakfast. By the way, reading matter is important here. The only paper we get is the *English Daily*, and the latest is February 10 – any sort of reading matter but soon!

Love and regards to everyone, thanks for the note to Grandma —

Ray

Jef Last

Battle Accounts from Spain

These accounts were published in *From Spanish Trenches*

Madrid, November 18, 1936

The reasons for our retreat at Getafe are deeply rooted, and perhaps they are partly inevitable in a struggle like this, where an army has not been built up systematically over a period of years, but has in truth been improvised by the proletariat. On top of that come the specific political circumstances in Spain. The contrast between the Anarchists and the Communists and the fear of both groups that the other might make a grab for power has been the reason for naming officers everywhere not because they were composed of the best military material, but because they were those who could best be trusted from the political point of view. While the fight was going on promotions were made on the basis of proven bravery, which is, however, in many cases, quite different from military clearsightedness or organizational ability. Our Captain, for example, is a most charming boy of twenty who has had one and a half years of schooling, worked in a factory at the age of nine, participated in his first strike at eleven, got his first jail sentence at fifteen and who ever since did wonderful work in the illegal Youth Movement. He is brave, has a good disposition, a lot of good will, but in reality he is nothing but a big child, without authority or military foresight. That our men are brave, one and all, was proven sufficiently at Naval Peral and on other occasions, but in the first place they are big children, who never look ahead, and in the second place they are so anarchistic and anti-militaristic in their deepest being, that they greet every effort to bring more military discipline into the troops with suspicion. It is true, of course, that the political commissars have done good work here, and the unity of command is constantly being enforced more rigidly, but they are still very far away from being a red army. In addition to all this, our company had the bad fortune to get replacements from the village, men who had never been under fire before.

At eight o'clock in the evening, the order came that we were to advance and until two o'clock in the morning there was singing and laughing as though they were going to a party instead of to the trenches. I must add to this, that all drinking was forbidden on such occasions in the barracks, so that there can be no question of drunkenness. As far as that is concerned, the boys will warn you themselves: 'Careful, when you have been drinking, you can't shoot straight.'

At two in the morning our buses departed and at the first grey light of morning we replaced the First and Fourth companies in the trenches. These trenches themselves belong to the fortifications of Madrid. They have been constructed in all haste by the women, the boys and the workers who are too old to carry arms, in their spare time. From the military point of view, they are completely inadequate, so narrow that the officers cannot pass through freely. They have no ridge to rest the arms on, on which one can also put cartridges. They are without drainage in rainy weather, and worst of all, they have no dug-outs where the men can seek shelter against wind and cold. So here again we find typical improvisation.

When the sun went up, we found out that there was a second line of soldiers about three hundred yards ahead of our position in the field.

It was beautiful weather, almost summer, the batteries were silent and we almost had the feeling of being in the country on a little outing – for our health. I studied Spanish industriously from a little handbook which I had bought. A squadron of planes bombarded the first line, but left us in peace. Only the commissary functioned badly. That whole day and the next one we got nothing to eat but some dry bread and a piece of sausage. In the afternoon a car came by with some women from the World-Committee. They told us that the first line was pretty much demoralized because of the bombardment. They distributed a few bottles of Cognac. I had a long conversation with two nurses from the

Scottish Ambulance Unit, who do some swell work. The night was freezing cold, but we had found some straw in a barn and slept fairly comfortably under our blankets. It was hilly, so I was not able to see the line to the right of the road. Since it seemed the next morning as though the day would pass again in complete calm, our captain went to Madrid to get blankets and clothes for the men.

At eleven o'clock, suddenly, intense rifle fire started in the first line, and towards one we saw the troops from that line fall back in a fairly orderly manner. We brought them to a stand. The officers ordered them back into our trench. This was the first big mistake. Because of this, the trench became overfilled, with demoralized forces at that. What should have been done, of course, was to have them form in a third line behind ours, as a protection for the village. At about two o'clock, the big play started. The enemy opened up a big bombardment on our line, which lasted for more than two hours without a let-up. In addition to that, five tanks, or rather armoured cars, rode up and down along the highway and peppered us incessantly with machine-gun fire. We ourselves had only an armoured train at our disposal, and a junky armoured car on the road, both of which had to draw back pretty soon. Our machine guns dated from the Middle Ages and hitched constantly. It was remarkable that regardless of all this, the enemy's fire did but little damage in our trench. What was much worse was that our boys were constantly firing when there was even no enemy in sight. (The armoured cars were immune to our bullets, of course.) On top of all that, most of them shot without taking aim, so that the bullets would often hit the ground no more than thirty yards from our line. As a result munitions began to run short everywhere towards evening and many guns became unclear. I tried, as much as I could, to hold the firing, in which I succeeded fairly well in our section, but my voice, of course, did not reach much farther than a hundred yards. Then came the attack. As the tanks were not able to break through on our sector, they went to the right of the highway and there they succeeded in breaking through the lines in two places at about four o'clock. At that moment a panic ensued on the extreme right wing and one of the companies ran for dear life. That one company dragged along the others: especially those soldiers who had no ammunition any more or whose guns did not function. They left the line without any order. The officers commanded them to hold their positions, but a feeling of comradeship evidently kept them from shooting at the fugitives, although the retreat might have been stopped that way. The breach became wider and wider and then the retreat started to the left of us, too. In my section I held the men as long as I could with words and sometimes by threatening them with my gun. We held out a quarter of an hour longer than the others, perhaps, but at last I was all alone in the trench with our *alvarez* (second lieutenant), who had come back when I called him a coward. '*Somos solos*' [We are alone], he said. At that moment the enemy was at about three hundred yards. I saw that nothing could be done so I ran with him in the direction of Getafe. At a railroad crossing we found a few officers and for a few minutes we formed a second line of defence with them, but that position became impossible to hold also. We saw the lines of the Fascists coming towards us slowly against the sinking sun. My throat was dry as leather. All out of breath, we dragged a box of ammunition along the road. Pretty soon we had to leave that behind in order to carry a wounded man. His blood streamed over my hands and he was constantly wailing: 'An auto, an auto'. At last we found an ambulance; it had become completely dark in the meantime. I rested up in a house half-way to Madrid. Perhaps a half an hour later we were chased out by an alarm. On the road stood a company of our Assaltos. (These are not volunteers, but regular troops.) I asked them something and evidently they took me for a spy or for a Fascist, who had walked too far ahead by accident. This was the most horrible moment of that night, because they stood there, guns raised to shoot me. Luckily I could prove with my papers that everything was okay. I attached myself to them and marched back in the direction of Getafe where we occupied a position on the road with about a hundred men. There we lay the entire following morning, without reinforcements and with no other food than the raw tomatoes which grew in the field. I thought: 'This will be the end if they attack.' Notwithstanding this, the exhaustion had been so great that I fell asleep in a ditch along the road. I awakened by being shaken by someone and at once I saw the kind, good-hearted face of our Sergeant Rubio before me. He had come back to the line of fire, searching for me. I think that never in my life have I been so happy. With him I found our company back in Madrid.

November 24, 1936

So we are at the front again, but such a front. You could not imagine anything more fantastic, hardly eight minutes' walking distance from the 'Cuatro Caminos' subway station. Transportation of our company to the front was extremely simple this time: we just took the subway. But at the same time you will be able to understand how terribly dangerous the advance of the Fascists was. It literally brought them to the gates of Madrid, even though it was only in the form of a wedge, so that their front is very narrow here.

Our company is housed in a deserted roadhouse. When they have relief periods from the firing line, our militiamen play with the marble game, or they turn on the electric piano, and practise bullfighting with crazy-looking overcoats, using some cow horns mounted on some sort of a little wagon as their antagonist! In front of us lies University City, where the Republican government was building a model city with tremendous hospitals, schools, student houses, stadiums, and parks, partly to provide work for the unemployed. It was meant as a fortress of culture, and human endeavour, but Franco has made a fortress of the hospitals and university buildings, from which he destroys culture and life in Madrid. It is from this city that we are dividing the enemy away systematically but slowly, and here the International Brigade is doing especially marvellous work.

December 10, 1936, Frente de L'Estacion de Goya

The position which we occupy here – the Goya Station Front – is in one of the suburbs of Madrid. It consists of a group of tenements. Holes have been broken through the walls, in order to connect them by trenches. When there is no fighting, all those who have no sentinel duty live and sleep in these houses which offer a fairly good protection against gun and shrapnel fire. Since it is getting colder right along, we make a fire in a bucket on the cement floor. We have to be very careful that the smoke is not visible to the enemy, because they would take us under fire immediately. So we close doors, windows and chimney, with the result that the room is so full of smoke that you can cut it. At night we sleep in that same smoke, in all our clothes, shoes laced and cartridge belt around the waist. You can understand that this did not help my bronchitis much. My voice is practically gone, especially since I have yelled too much giving orders during night fighting in the last few days. Yesterday I felt so rotten, that I went to see the doctor. He gave me a can of condensed milk and told me to drink it with some cognac, as hot as I could stand it. In addition to that I was relieved from duty for the night and put in my eight hours for the first time in I don't know how long, without my clothes on and under a few decent blankets. The next morning I felt much better, but Pepe told me to stick around the telephone which connects us with headquarters. He would take my place in the front line. You owe it to this comparative house-arrest that I am writing.

I was just talking over the telephone and while I am looking at the instrument it is almost as though it were the symbol of all the shortcomings which we will have to conquer before we arrive at the big offensive and the final victory. When the enemy – four weeks ago now – broke through our lines first at Getafe and then at Villa Verde I thought for just one moment – and I was not the only one who thought of this – that everything was lost. I had seen the disorganized companies being decimated by the machine-gun fire of low-swooping Heinkels. From villages and stations which we passed the flames flared high into the air, then the buildings would cave in under shell fire. Moorish cavalry sabred down whatever they met. They chased our troops way back to the Princesses Bridge and the Franceses Bridge, which cross the Manzanares. I maintain that it was the women who saved Madrid in those despairing days. They chased the men, who had fled to their homes, back to the front, or they picked up the guns which the men had thrown away in their haste and themselves defended the city behind barricades which had been thrown together hurriedly. It soon became evident that the fleeing of the militiamen was not the result of cowardice, but could only be considered as a typical panic. They who had fled in the past few days streamed back to their companies and not only showed resistance, but started the counter-offensive, under circumstances many times more difficult.

They succeeded – with enormous sacrifices and unlimited bravery – in definitely stemming the advance of the enemy; even in winning back several of the important positions. I repeat what I have already written: our militiamen are the finest and bravest human material you can imagine, providing they are well led. In many ways they are just like children, extremely susceptible to psychic contagion when strong leadership is lacking, or if the officers lose their heads. When they come to their senses later they are ready to show the most crazy courage because they are ashamed of themselves and want to make up for it. The days of Getafe and Villa Verde are also the days in which boys like Col captured enemy tank after enemy tank, with nothing but a few hand grenades. That Saturday Franco announced over the radio that he would drink his coffee in Madrid the next day. Radio-Lissabon described how he had triumphantly entered the city on a white horse. In Avila the blood-tribunal, which was to take over the reign of the city, had already been named. Foreign correspondents were forbidden to follow the army, Franco wanted to be alone when he settled with the inhabitants of Madrid. Mola counted on a repetition of Badajoz and announced the penalty of death for anyone who might be found with weapons . . . That was four weeks ago. In the meantime Franco's coffee has become cold! All of them miscalculated because they did not understand the proletariat and because they did not know that even though this proletariat may make mistakes, it learns from those mistakes; that you can beat it down, but that it will get up again every time, that it can fall back for a moment, but then only to resume the battle with so much more courage and conviction. In their haste they bumped their heads into a bloody mess, against the renewed heroism of the people of Madrid.

To come back to that telephone.

Our position partly depends for its defence on an armoured train which can come from Madrid within a few minutes in case of a heavy attack. In order to be able to call this train at a minute's notice, a field telephone was installed in all haste. When it was installed and when the workmen had gone back it turned out that a contact was missing somewhere, so that it would not work. For more than three days we were there before a repair man at last came who re-established the contact. During all that time the men amused themselves royally with the telephone ... which did not work. The captain, the *alvarez*, the sergeants, and everybody who came into headquarters, played telephone. They called up their fiancée, their mother-in-law, they ordered a supper with champagne in the city, or they held fabricated conversations with Mola and Queipo de Llano, whose hides they covered with insults. To me the telephone seemed the reflection of their greatest worth as well as of their greatest weakness; their joyous lack of worry, which always keeps them gay and full of good humour, but through which they also, only too often, neglect the most necessary action at a moment when there still is time!

The enemy lies in a trench at about eight hundred yards from us. This trench runs from the military hospital to the Estremadura highway. Opposite us they occupy a little village and we can very clearly see the holes in the houses, where they have mounted their machine guns. The artillery base, which puts us under fire for several hours every afternoon, must be just beyond that. They shoot badly and most of their projectiles explode one hundred yards behind our lines on the cemetery, where they seem to begrudge the dead their rest. Or is it possible that the Fascist motto 'Spain, Awake!' is meant for them too?

Still the war has pretty badly damaged the workers' houses, which together with the trench form our line. Everywhere holes have been hacked into the walls. We shoot through them when there is an attack. The moon looks in through the broken tiles in the roof, the windows are broken and replaced by boards which keep the light out. In the evening, the flame of a wick floating in turbid oil makes the dark shadows of the broken furniture look spooky. From the wall a bridal couple stares at us from a gold frame which is almost hidden by cobwebs. A broken gramophone is proof of a modest attempt at prosperity. Two of the boys are busy cutting up an old high chair for firewood.

A bunch of books are swept together in a corner. Everything is filthy, dusty, broken and neglected. In the houses a little way up you can hear the hoarse howling of the hungry dogs, who were left behind.

We have already been living in these ruins twelve days. Everything we touch is filthy, even the water from the well is muddy and leaves grey dregs in our mugs. It is too cold to wash with decently. The stoop in front of our house – the only piece of road which is not in the line of fire – is unapproachable because of the excretions of one hundred and forty soldiers. For twelve days we haven't been out of our clothes, three times we have thrown the enemy back after a night attack, every day we stand at our posts for eight hours, most of us don't even have decent shoes, and at no time during these two weeks have we had a hot meal, since the field kitchen can't get through.

Yet during all these weeks I have not heard a single complaint. At night, when we sit around the fire with tears streaming down our faces, the comrades tell stories! Tyl Eulenspiegel or Ali Baba and the Forty Thieves. There is a lot of singing, too. Nobody doubts our victory. Yesterday a bullet shattered the shoulder-blade of our little Manuelo. Thomas has been hit in the thigh by a splinter of shrapnel. '*Que suerte*!' say the comrades. 'What luck. Not a single one of us killed in this whole week!'

Often they ask me: 'Tell us again, *teniente*, why did you really come here?' I shrug my shoulders: 'Well, boys, you ought to know that story by now, because your battle is our battle, too!' 'Yes,' they say, 'we know that, but he over there comes from the village, you must explain it carefully for him once more!' I get my map and point out how France is surrounded on all sides by the Fascists if they should come to win in Spain. With Spain to bolster it, Germany can shut off England from its colonies. That will be the moment when a new world war will have to break out, under the most favourable circumstances for Fascism. For that reason we are not only defending Spain, but Democracy and even the borders of the Soviet Union!

They look at me with shining eyes and say: '*Que lucha*! Boy, what a battle!'

Several times during the last few weeks we have witnessed aerial combats. The fleet, which went in the direction of Madrid over our positions, was the largest I have ever seen. Thirty-nine gigantic bombers, protected by twenty pursuit planes. They don't take the trouble any more these days to bombard the trenches, knowing how extremely difficult it is to hit a narrow line like that. Without bothering about the troops, they take a straight course for Madrid, which offers them a much surer target. The town, which has but little charm once one is in it, looks, as seen from our position, like a phantasmagorical fairy city on the hills. Then the planes approach, the earth rumbles from the dull sound of the explosions and five minutes later the whole town has disappeared in dirty brown clouds of dust and smoke; even the skyscraper of the telephone company is hidden by them. Our men lie in the trench, helpless. Nobody speaks; they ask themselves: 'Didn't those bombs fall on our quarter – are my wife, my mother, my brother still alive at this moment?' They won't know until our company has had its full two weeks at the front and returns to the ruins of Madrid on leave. Irrespective of this I have not seen a single man whose determination was shaken by this terror. On the contrary, every bombardment makes their hate of Fascism and their will to conquer flame up.

'That is,' says Fermin to me, 'because we have known ever since the start that there was no other choice but death or victory. Every one of us is a volunteer and knows what he is fighting for. We are a backward people as far as knowledge is concerned, but they cannot deceive our hearts!'

That Fermin was right became evident several days ago when the enemy threw another one of their propaganda packages behind our lines with tens of thousands of throw-aways. Of course, nobody thought of forbidding the men to pick up or read the leaflets. On the contrary, officers and men ran like hares to get hold of one. Then – did we laugh! It turned out to be quite a merry afternoon! I remember the illiterate Juan Antonio from the Fourth Platoon who had it read to him three times over, by three different people, as though he could not believe it. He looked at me questioningly: '*Que tonterías*! [what foolishness]. Is it possible that they are that dumb?'

Indeed, the mixture of impudence, cynicism and fantastical lies which not only fill these papers but are heard in the radio speeches of Franco and that drunken Queipo de Llano, too (we often hear them over Radio-Burgos or Radio-Seville), is so obviously in direct contradiction to the truth that even the simplest illiterate lad can see through these lies because of his own practical knowledge.

Why is it that their propaganda is so clumsy?

It is because those who write this have never known the people and themselves have come to believe in the picture of fear and prejudice which they have painted. For them indeed 'the people' is synonymous with 'stupid Red rabble' and their sickly imagination ascribes to them all the brutality which they fancied in their sadistic dreams. How could they, who themselves have never suffered, be able to understand the everlasting tenderness and the commiseration, born of sorrow, animating the soul of the people? How could they, whose whole life has been dominated by the pursuit of money and power, be able to understand that the people have other motives which drive them to battle than just greed? How could they, who build their propaganda ministries on the systematic lies of big-business advertising, be able to understand the primitive urge for candour which still exists in the unsophisticated farmer? The propaganda leaflets of Franco would have worked very nicely with the bourgeois public of Holland; his mistake was that he distributed them among the working people.

Repeatedly the boys read one sentence to me, their voices shaking with indignation: 'Spaniards, while you go hungry, your government pays most exorbitant salaries to foreign adventurers who, with their weapons, wish to make your country into a Russian colony.' Other boys scoffed: 'Say, José, when we get to Madrid I guess you will treat, since we know now that you are a millionaire!'

Our boys know that Franco started this battle with Moorish mercenaries and with the foreign legion, in whose uniform many a German and Italian Fascist hid himself.

Our boys know too that we stand at the same little wicket with them, officers and men alike, to get our monthly three hundred pesetas. Our boys know that we don't have any 'recruiting stations' and that those who come here from other countries come voluntarily and often with the greatest trouble, without any promises and without any compensation over and above what is given to any Spanish labourer who joins the militia.

That accounts for the love, the admiration and the fondness that they bestow on us foreigners, and which often makes us ashamed of ourselves.

The Spanish people are a people of story-tellers; even now, when we sit around the smoking wood fire in the evening, they are already weaving legends around the International Brigade. In the stories of the comrades, the fighters of the International Brigade become half-Gods, figures like the Cid or like the heroic knights who once routed the Moors from Spanish soil. The raconteur speaks with such respectful admiration of these heroes of the International Brigade that sometimes he seems to forget that he himself has been at the front for more than five months now. Still it has to be admitted that the boys of the International Brigade have indeed always given the example of bravery, sacrifice and discipline on the most threatened front.

A few days ago Domela said to me: 'Haven't you noticed that we get larger rations at night lately?' 'Yes,' I answered, 'the fare evidently is getting better.' Domela shook his head, 'If anything the fare is getting worse, but they give us more than the others.' And that night we got a double portion of ham again. We went to the captain to complain, but he just made a very mysterious face, 'Don't let that bother you, everything is okay!' We protested energetically that it was not OK. It seemed that the militiamen had met while we had been to the academy at night and had decided 'that the two foreigners should have double rations, because the rations that we got right now, since no hot food is getting through, are less than adequate!' Need it be said that we henceforth refused to accept double rations at the expense of others, much as we appreciated their good intentions?

I notice that this letter is getting excessively long. The militiamen look over my shoulders as I write. But still one more thing: in co-operation with our political commisar, we have organized several classes for illiterates, and even political recitals. Much to our disgust these evenings are all too often interrupted because of an aerial attack or because of other unpleasant movements of the enemy. But it is wonderful to see how much the militiamen care for all this; they do everything they can to support us in every way. This afternoon I went to practise map reading again with the corporals and sergeants. They should also know how to make a small sketch. It is about time for me to start gathering the necessary material so I will close this letter.

Christopher Caudwell

Last Letters from Spain

From the *News Chronicle*, June 28, 1937.

Extract from a letter, December 9, 1936
I expect it will be a surprise to you, but I am leaving for Spain the day after tomorrow. You know how I feel about the whole mad business of war, but you know also how I feel about the importance of democratic freedom.

The Spanish People's Army needs help badly; their struggle, if they fail, will certainly be ours tomorrow and, believing as I do, it seems clear where my duty lies . . . I am going out as a driver in a convoy of lorries and we shall make the journey by road through France.

Postcard from Perpignan, December 17
Just arrived at frontier. Convoy had engine trouble all through France. Spain tomorrow. *Salud!*

Extract from a letter, December 30
Just a line to let you know that we delivered the lorries safely at (*name censored*) and have now been drafted into the British Unit of the International Brigade. At the moment, we are at a training centre, but do not expect to stay here long.

My letters will be very sketchy from now on, and do not be surprised if you do not hear from me at all for a fairly long time.

Extract from a letter, January 7, written to the brother of a fallen comrade in the International Brigade
I am writing to you because I have only just heard the news of your brother's death – though I gather that it must have been known to you soon after it happened.

I want to pass on the sympathy with [*sic*] your mother and you that all the English-speaking battalion here feels; and above all I want to tell you of the tremendous pride and admiration the whole International Brigade feels for those few English comrades, including your brother, who were with the Thaelmann Battalion of the Brigade from the very start.

In (*name censored*) I met the German under whose command your brother served soon after the casualties had occurred, and although he was a reserved kind of man, he was so moved by them that he was going up to every Englishman to explain in his broken English what admiration the whole Battalion felt for them. (*Name censored*) asked the same man why the casualty rate among the English portion of his unit was so high, and he answered, 'Because every one of them was a hero.'

I think you can understand what that means, coming from the commander of the Battalion which played such a vital part in the early days of the Madrid fighting.

Extract from a letter, January 14, from Albacete

Our training is almost over now. It has been extraordinarily interesting; the International Brigade in its composition and organization is so entirely different from any ordinary army.

Our commandant is thoroughly at home in this Spanish fighting, which is about as different as possible from that of the Great War; a very extended front, continual flanking movements and a very mobile type of fighting.

At Madrid, of course, there is a certain amount of digging-in. A feature of this war is the tremendous use of machine guns – far eclipsing the last war, so I am told. In this connection we are handicapped by shortage of ammunition due to the Arms ban. We are also short of artillery and aeroplanes.

English recruits are coming out fairly well now and we are already forming an English battalion. Of course, we are tremendously outnumbered in the Brigade by the Germans and the French and the Italian sections.

Extract from letter, January 30, from Albacete

We expect to move off very soon.

We've been here so long now, waiting for new drafts to arrive to bring us up to battalion strength – that I am almost beginning to feel an old soldier, and already act as machine-gun instructor to our group.

England seems centuries away, and we are yearning to get to the Front. No rifles yet – the arms shortage is acute here – but we should get them very soon now and will then move off.

Extract from a letter, February 7, from Albacete
This is only a short note, written in haste. I may not find time to write again for some time. You will understand why. So until I write again, all the best to you both.

Chris

Five days after writing that letter he was killed in action outside Madrid. One of his comrades, himself wounded, wrote this letter describing how he died:
On the first day Chris' section was holding a position on a hill crest. They got it rather badly from all ways, first artillery, then machine-gunned by aeroplanes, and then by ground machine guns. The Moors then attacked the hill in large numbers and as there were only a few of our fellows left, including Chris, who had been doing great work with his MG, the company commander – the Dalston busman – gave the order to retire.

Later, I got into touch with one of the section who had been wounded whilst retiring, and he told me that the last they saw of Chris was that he was covering their retreat with the advancing Moors less than 30 yards away. He never left that hill alive, and if any man ever sacrificed his life that his comrades might live that man was Chris.

When I come out of hospital I will try to obtain further details for you, but I am afraid it may prove a little difficult, as out of the 600 men of his battalion who went into that engagement less than 200 are now left.

André Malraux

'This is War'

From *Collier's Magazine*, May 29, 1937

It is the Epiphany, the feast of the Three Kings, the great festival of the children of Spain. In the morning when I came to the War Ministry all the streets were filled with armoured cars. They have been passing by all day long, while one hundred kilometres away the International Brigade and the columns of militiamen captured, lost, and recaptured the Teruel cemetery. It is the first children's feast since the birth of the new Spain, and the trade unions have wanted to give them a celebration such as they have never had before. For a week the workers have been busy all night making cardboard figures taken from the animated cartoons which the children have been clamouring for, and, in addition to the traditional cake fortresses, the old bulls, the kings and the playing-card characters, twelve-foot figures of Mickey Mouse and Felix the Cat have on this occasion invaded Valencia.

My car is taking me back from the War Ministry to the front. It is three o'clock in the morning. In the starlight that breaks through the clouds one senses the tall buildings around the great square, grounded in the night like the prows of old Spanish galleons. The blue wartime lights, like the blue lights of deep-sea fishes, cast a faint glow over the square and the shadows of Mickey Mouse figures are swallowed up by the asphalt that is wet from the last brief shower. When the automobile reaches the broad boulevards that encircle Valencia we are stopped by the heavy traffic. We turn on our headlights for a moment: all the characters that people the dreams of children, from the early dreams of Christianity to those of American children, from the Magi to Mickey Mouse, are there in a jumble; and between their legs some of the thousands of children who have come for the feast of the Epiphany have sought refuge from the rain that may start again any moment and have fallen asleep.

Here and there for miles we come upon these great phantoms of childish dreams abandoned in the night, as if the genii of all races were to come here to fetch them for the dreams of all the children who sleep. On each base, around their legs, the dimmed automobile lights reveal in passing a cluster of children, calmly asleep – stretched out like the wounded of Teruel a little farther on, on the same ground.

The dull explosions from the cannon of Teruel, that seem imperceptibly to shake the earth, seem at the same time to shake these frail phantoms above the serene slumber of all the motionless children, their arms relaxed in gestures of the dead.

A battalion of militiamen is leaving for the front. They are heading towards the Prado, and the loud strains of the Internationale draw nearer. When they are almost immediately below my window, at the moment when the singing should be loudest, it subsides, only to pick up again a little farther on, on a lower note, muffled. I go to the window; a blind man, holding his white cane out in front of him, is walking down the middle of the street. None of those adolescents on their way to the battle front has dared to push him aside, and he advances against the current of the marching militiamen who go around him on both sides, and stop their singing. After they have passed him and gone on a little way their song breaks out, in a more sober strain. The blind man continued forward, throwing back his shoulders as almost all blind men do, distressed by this crowd which he cannot see, and which is silenced by his presence – and, surrounded by an empty circle as by the respectful terror with which the blind men of old were regarded, not understanding and wanting to escape, he walks faster and faster; and the militiamen swerve aside before he touches them, as though to let Destiny pass by.

I saw him again. The Moors were in Carabanchel – at the gates of Madrid. Those of us who had fought in the infantry and were used to hearing the tom-tom of the Moors at night opened the windows to listen; but the wind was coming from Madrid, and we could hear nothing in the rainy night, not even the rattle of machine guns. After nine o'clock the patrol of the thoroughfares was extremely strict, and the streets were almost wholly deserted.

From the top of one of the big hotels, no doubt for the benefit of the police, a searchlight periodically swept the street. Suddenly before me, in the vast flood of light, appeared two enormous hands, hands fifty feet long, that vanished into the night. The police and the militiamen no doubt knew the blind beggar and had let him pass. He was without a cane and was protecting himself with his groping hands; he was barely visible in the beam from the searchlight, but his outstretched hands, trembling like those of a god of the night, seemed to be seeking the living and the dead with a frightful maternal gesture.

On the outskirts of a village between Madrid and Talavera the dynamiters were awaiting the enemy tanks.

Messengers would come and give them the warning signal. For the time being there was nothing to do but wait. They were in a deserted bar, telling each other stories.

'I took part in the retreat with Gorde and Sabranek. They are both miners in the country where they come from; they were assigned to the company at our rear back of the village. At that time there weren't any dynamiters. They had both been machine gunners in the army, and so they were put on the machine guns. The first day of the attack their company of machine gunners was detailed to hold a small wood. Hell was popping right and left, when they suddenly noticed that their two flanking companies had been pushed back and that they were surrounded by Moors. There was nothing to do but to take to their heels and try to get through; make a three-hundred-yard dash, stop, fire a roll, make another three-hundred-yard dash. So off they went, jumping like rabbits, taking their Hotchkiss with them. After the first three hundred yards they stopped and began to fire. It was Gorde who was at the gun. He shot his roll. The Moors were falling in their tracks, just like in the movies, but they were bound to catch up to them.

' "Beat it!" shouted Sabranek. The other continued to tinker with his roll.

' "Beat it, for God's sake!" He continued to tinker with his roll, sitting 'way back in the saddle, and then opened fire. The Moors once more began to go down. Exasperated, Sabranek let go with his booted foot and kicked him in the pants again and again. The other got up, hesitated a moment. And again Sabranek kicked him in the tail. Then with both arms Gorde grabbed his machine gun and took to his heels, running full speed right into the enemy, with Sabranek behind him still yelling at the top of his lungs. And they both disappeared over the ridge held by the Moors, like Laurel and Hardy. I can't get over seeing them again here. I thought they'd been killed.'

Others, outside, are sitting or lying down with their horse blankets wrapped round them, giving the effect of a Mexican army, minus the sombreros. The flames at intervals light up the faces, as in engravings of the Napoleonic wars.

'Pedro was in the Asturias in '34 with Gonzales Peña. We were fighting with one bullet to every five men. When the cartridges were empty the women gathered them up, put them in their salad baskets, and the baskets went off in a truck to be reloaded with bullets. The enemy planes chased the armoured trains that scurried into the tunnels, waited till the planes went back to refuel, and then made a dash for another tunnel. And so on. The peasants were fighting all around Miejes. It was the last day. Nothing more could be done. But they needed three hours to prevent the outer flanks of the Moorish guard which was advancing like a crescent towards Miejes from closing together, and to evacuate all who could be evacuated.

'There was still quite a bit of dynamite that came from the mines. But nothing to make bombs with. No copper, no steel. The Moors were advancing. In a little peasant hut the committee was deliberating. The Moors were advancing. A strange rumbling was beginning to make the walls tremble. It was not an earthquake: the walls were trembling, but not the ground. And it was not cannons: it was a dull, but multitudinous sound, like thousands of muffled drums. Pedro went outside, and the moment he opened the door the noise of machine guns, like the ripping of cloth, could be distinctly heard in the room beneath the rumble that was growing louder and was as mysterious as ever. Suddenly a cow appeared in the main street, hesitated, passed in front of the central committee shack and fled down the other end of the street. A bull ran after her, with the jerky, nervous gallop of the *corrida*. And when Pedro saw a rabbit scurrying towards him, he understood.

'To encircle the town, the Moors were advancing as for a round-up. Game and cattle, thrown back on Miejes by machine-gun fire, were beginning to pour in among the peasant huts on the outskirts, towards the centre, and it was the sound of thousands of hoofs that was making the ground shake. The cattle were coming down the mountain with the rumble of great herds, returning from pasture. And now, seemingly rising from the ground, the sound of bells could be heard.

'The animals all carried bells – the heavy, deep-sounding bronze bells of mountain cattle, like those of the Moslem herds. In a moment tables, chairs, boards, objects of all kinds were thrown out through the windows of the hut or brought from nearby houses. The rumble was growing louder: the cattle were coming. The materials gathered for the barricades were feverishly piled up. From all sides the peasants were converging for the building of a new barricade – the barricade against the cattle herd.

'The herds were stopped. One by one the peasants unfastened or tore off the heavy bells, which sixty dynamiters transformed into bombs. And they began to take their places in all the hollows in the rocks along the path of the Moors.

'For more than three hours they held them off by hurling cow-bells from the hollows. The fighting population scattered into the interior of Spain or crossed the frontier into France. Fifty-eight dynamiters were killed.'

'I was in Talavera,' said another. 'We were being bombarded by their planes as we had never been before. Around Saragossa there are holes like those in the valley of the moon; here there were twenty-five-pound bombs all over the place – unexploded. During the bombardment only one out of ten went off. It was an amazing sight. The Fascists were bombarding almost entirely with light bombs. No doubt they had no heavy ones left. The bombs came out of their holes like handfuls of grain, fell right on us, and here and there one of them would burst, as if by accident. It was as if the Fascists were bombarding us with enormous darts. On the embankment of the road where our trucks passed they must have bombarded us fifteen times, in small squadrons of five to nine; on both sides the bombs were piled up as if they were there ready to be carted away. They had fallen on top of each other and had not exploded.

'It was rather odd. When a few don't explode it's more or less natural; but with so many it was uncanny. Some of our men had been aviation mechanics; they had often helped with loading the bombs on their planes. They began to unscrew the percussion fuses to examine the bombs. The first one turned round, excited as a windmill, holding out a little slip of typewriter paper to show the second one who, no less excited, was holding a similar slip. It was the message of the Portuguese workers: "This bomb will not explode".'

The messengers had just arrived. It was the signal for action. The dynamiters scurried off with their bombs. I thought of an Annamite I had known several years back who had been killed in his first elephant hunt: the animal was charging, and it had seemed to my friend that a man was so slight a thing before this great mass that he had dropped his gun and run; the elephant had killed him with one blow of his trunk. So slight a thing before the mass that was coming down on him . . . The men continued to advance to the firing line, one behind the other, their bombs on their backs or under their arms. We heard what sounded like distant motors. And with our eyes fixed on the broken crest of the hill in front of us we waited for the first armoured car to appear.

'There's a peasant who wants to talk to you. He's come over from the Fascist lines.'

I follow him to where the peasant is standing, surrounded by aviators who are questioning him. His answers come reluctantly. As I approach I see his face in full profile – the long, dark, lean profile of the Spanish peasant: of the men who fought Napoleon; to complete the illusion one has merely to imagine the visored cap he is wearing replaced by a knotted kerchief.

'You say you want to speak to me?'

'No. I've come to speak to the commander of the air squadron.'

'That's him,' the aviators tell him.

The peasant is suspicious. My outfit – the planes will be leaving in half an hour – bears no insignia of rank.

'Can you give the word for the planes to take off?'

The pilots stand round him, some friendly, others suspicious; he comes from the enemy lines. I draw him aside. He has been sent to me by the People's Front of Leon. The Fascist planes are in the vicinity of his village. He has just gotten through the lines and has gone to notify our people in Leon; they have immediately sent him to me.

I have one of the men get a phone connection through to the People's Front headquarters in Leon to check the story, and come back to the peasant.

'Where are the planes?'

'In the woods. The Fascists have made clearings under the trees where they can keep them out of sight.'

'What's the field like?'

'Where they take off?'

'Yes.'

He makes a drawing. Long and narrow.

'The soldiers have been working since yesterday to make the field wider.'

'How does it run?'

He thinks for a moment.

'East and west.'

'And the wood?'

'To the east.'

This means that the enemy planes have to take off from east to west. The wind, which is very strong, comes from the east, and it is undoubtedly the same in Olmedo. The enemy planes would have a hard time taking off from the field which the peasant has described.

'How many planes are there?'

'There were twelve large ones and six small ones last night. We managed to find that out through some of our boys.'

We have only four planes at our disposal. If the peasant is telling the truth it is worth attempting to surprise the enemy camp. If he is lying the enemy planes will be able to take to the air before we discover them, and we will not return. A telephone operator comes, bringing the answer from Leon. The man does, in fact, come from Olmedo, but the Leon people don't know those in Olmedo. It is up to us to decide what to do.

'It's near Olmedo,' he repeats.

I show him a map; as I supposed, he is unable to read it.

'Take me to Olmedo,' he says: 'I'll show you. I can guide you right to the spot.'

'Anyone in your family been killed by the Fascists?'

'No. Take me in your plane.'

In such a situation spies are likely to betray themselves – in aerial warfare enemies cannot choose their victims. Olmedo is an hour and a half away. Our planes hold enough fuel to last five hours.

'Have you ever been up in a plane?'

'No.'

'Aren't you nervous?'

He didn't quite understand.

'Aren't you afraid?'

'No.'

'You think you will recognize the way?'

'From Olmedo, yes. I know the country better than a dog.'

We have no pursuit planes, but the sky is overcast and we may be protected by the clouds.

The three other planes that follow us in triangle formation disappear from minute to minute in the clouds that grow increasingly dense as we approach the Sierra. The inverted plough-shares of the highest crests rise above the great expanse of piled-up snow; up there the enemy scouts are awaiting us with rockets that will warn their pursuit planes. But no doubt the sea of clouds is compact on the other side and separates the scouts from their observers. We fly amid the clouds, emerging from time to time so as not to crash into the mountains – as sperm whales come to the surface to breathe. Above us and the enemy scouts, far above the subterranean agitation of war, is a wonderfully clear sky of autumn morning. An almost biting cold finds its way into the plane; these combats that were to have lasted only a few weeks settle on the invisible earth like wounded men in their beds, and in the wind that strikes our faces winter once more passes its hands over the old face of war.

The clouds draw nearer. The peasant looks at me. I know that he is thinking: 'How am I going to guide you if I can't see anything?' But he asks nothing. I yell into his ear:

'We'll cross above Olmedo.'

He looks at the Sierra, looks below him and waits. In each plane the crew commander, his eyes on the crest rising above the clouds, watches for the rockets.

We are now above the Sierra. On the other side the sea of clouds forms a compact mass.

We navigate by the compass, but the compass does not record

the drift caused by an oblique wind. If we are carried twenty to thirty kilometres out of our course the enemy planes may have a chance to take off. I will try to reconnoitre the country without completely getting out of the clouds, rise again to pick up the other planes, rectify our course, and head for Olmedo. Then it will be up to the peasant to show the way.

We have passed the Sierra; we are over enemy territory. Now any accident to the motor is fatal. The Moors have a special predilection for wounded aviators. Beneath the radiant sky, buried under the clouds, lie torture and death. Behind us the other planes, still in triangular formation, follow us with the comradeliness of two arms of the same body.

We are approaching Olmedo. The clouds, the sky, still the same serenity . . . We enter the clouds. As soon as the mist envelops us it seems as if the battle were beginning. The plane descends slowly, so as to stay within the clouds as much as possible; at the fighting posts the machine gunners and the bombers are now on the lookout. And the pilots and I watch the compasses and the altimeter with more intensity than we ever watch a human face.

The altimeter drops: 800 – 700 – 500 – 400 – 375 – 350. We have not yet pierced through the blanket of fog. If we continue to drop and we are not exactly over Olmedo (which is probable) we are going to crash – there are hills throughout this region.

We begin to take on altitude again. Before dropping I have observed that the sea of clouds was punctured here and there. We shall wait, circling over the point where we are, till a rift appears below us.

Our plane loses all contact with the earth. Until now we have been advancing, our eyes and our minds always turned to what lay before us, fascinated by what we were approaching; for the first time now we must wait. The planes circle above the bank of clouds that extends beyond the distant crests; but the clouds advance with a movement that gives the illusion of being the movement of the earth itself, and it seems as if men, earth, destiny, flow away with that immensity that is gliding beneath us, while high up, beyond the world, the planes circle with the fatality of stars.

Yet at the same time the old savage instinct of the bird of prey has taken hold of us. With the centuries-old wheeling flight of hawks we circle as we wait for a break in the clouds, the eyes of all the crew looking downward as though we were on the lookout for the entire earth and expected it presently to appear in a sudden rift. And it seems as if the whole landscape of clouds and mountain peaks is turning with the slowness of a planet round our motionless machine.

A cloud darker than the rest, and greenish in hue, approaches. It is the break. Like a worn and dirty map, the earth begins to appear.

Olmedo is not immediately below us, but a few kilometres to our right, russet because of its tiles, like an old smear of blood on the shredded surface of the clouds. My plane beats its wings – the combat signal – and we swoop downward.

All heads are stretched forward, parallel like those of ancient bas-reliefs. We are above the church; below us, the houses rush past at full speed like a herd in flight.

The peasant looks, his whole body tense, his mouth half open, and tears zigzag down his cheeks, one by one; he does not recognize anything.

Some distance away large puffs of shell smoke appear, like fragments of the clouds from which we have just emerged. The enemy anti-aircraft guns are beginning to fire. The battery is no doubt close to the enemy camp, but there is no trace of smoke on the ground. We have two minutes at the most. The peasant said that the field was north of Olmedo. I put the signal on the command dial square north; no one in the other three planes is aware that we don't know where we are going.

For a brief moment I bank the plane 90 degrees. Our path is parallel to the main street of Olmedo. I point it out to the peasant: 'There's the church. The street. The Avila road.'

He recognizes all that in passing, but can't get his bearings for the direction we have to take. What will he be able to recognize when we no longer have even the buildings? Below the immobile upper half of his face from which the tears are flowing his chin quivers convulsively.

The Fascist pursuit planes are surely getting their motors started. The first one that takes off will show us the field; but if its attack allows the others time to leave the ground, none of us will return. It is now a question of seconds.

There is only one resort: give the peasant an angle of vision that he is used to. Perpendicularly he does not recognize the country;

on the ground – horizontally – he would recognize it at once. We must get a view as close as possible to that which one gets from the ground. I shift the course a few points off north and drop to thirty metres.

The machine guns rattle, but that doesn't matter. The anti-aircraft guns have ceased firing – we are too low, below their range. Soldiers and farm animals scurry off frantically below us like snow shooting sideways from a snowplough. If one could die of looking and seeking, the peasant would die. He catches hold of my arm, points with a taut, crooked finger which he does not manage to straighten at a large publicity billboard, black and pale yellow under the low sky. And he pulls me to the right, with his whole might, as though I were the plane. I put the command signal east. The peasant shouts. None of the men turns his head. The peasant yells, but does not speak, and with his finger which is still crooked points to a wood.

'Is that it?'

He answers yes with his whole head and shoulders, without relaxing his outstretched arm. And there, next to the wood, is the oblong field which he had drawn for us before our take-off. A pursuit plane and a bombing plane are out in the open. The propeller of the pursuit plane is in motion.

We are approaching in the very direction in which it must take off. In order not to be brought down by our own bombs, we take on altitude, and in a few seconds we will again become targets for the anti-aircraft shells. As we pass over the field we drop a few light bombs – enough to cut the path of the pursuit plane and prevent it from taking on speed. We circle and turn back, dropping a string of light bombs. It's impossible to aim, but our blind firing cuts the path of the Fascist plane. We drop bombs as we pass over the wood, where a cluster of figures is trying to push the bombing plane. We bank as we did a while ago above the clouds and come back. As the field comes into sight again, the pursuit plane is lying on its side: a heavy bomb from one of our planes must have struck close by.

At full speed the four wheeling planes in oblique formation pass again one after the other over the wood and rise towards the shells which are beginning to form a barrage – as though we were deliberately going to meet them. Our bombs fall on the wood, where we can make out nothing. Undoubtedly the pursuit planes from the nearest enemy aerodrome, advised by telephone, are already in the air. Our machine-gunners watch the sky, the pilot and the bombers keep their eyes on the ground; the round continues.

We are suddenly jolted as by an air pocket. Has a shell just burst close by? There is no puff of smoke near us. But down below, from the wood, a thick, black smoke begins to pour, which I immediately recognize: gasoline. Directly or indirectly, we have struck the enemy depot. Still we see nothing of what we are bombarding. The enormous smoke begins to rise as if subterranean beds were burning beneath the quiet wood that looks exactly like all the others in the late morning. A few men come running out of the wood – and, in a few seconds, hundreds of them, in the same headlong animal flight as the flocks of cattle a while ago. And the smoke, which the wind beats down as if the sky would fling every trace of war back towards the wretched world of men, begins to spread. Beside me, shivering with joy and cold, the peasant stamps his feet in the fuselage.

Madrid is being bombarded. I am following a man who lugs a manuscript as big as himself. People rarely write on paper of that size, and such a large manuscript naturally interests a writer. I stop the man:

'What is that manuscript of yours?'

The sound of aeroplane bombs reaches our ears.

'It isn't a manuscript,' he answers gently. 'I'm changing the wallpaper in my apartment.'

The Reporters

Professional journalists brought a wider, often more cynical perspective to the war than did the volunteers. Yet even the reporters became immersed in the war's apocalyptic horror. Jay Allen, a stringer for *The Chicago Tribune*, saw Badajoz immediately after the massacre in the bull-ring and he writes in the phrenetic, out-of-breath way witnesses have when telling a mad tale. Cecil Gerahty, a pro-Franco correspondent for the *Daily Mail*, begins in smug tones – it helps to be with the winning side – but soon the terror and panic of the war breaks through. Gerahty is also a true scavenger of war: he goes beyond the parasitic reporter role and he begins picking up more than information, actual loot.

Alexander Werth, the famous continental correspondent for *The Manchester Guardian*, saw the war in wide historical perspective (at one point he compares a scene in Barcelona to one during the Russian Revolution). But finally Werth puts aside his cosmopolitan air and remarks, 'The human side of these people is unforgettable.'

Unfortunately, reporters agree to the journalistic and/or sensational demands of their newspapers. Arthur Koestler stands apart from the other reporters in that he did not really go to Spain as a newspaper man (his press card was a cover for his Comintern activities) and also, he wrote almost all his articles for the *News Chronicle* when he returned to England after his release from a Nationalist prison. As a result, he could see the war from inside what he calls 'the Apocalyptic flood', and he could connect its meaning to his own deeply personal experience, his 'Dialogue with Death'. Koestler's Spanish experiences so obsessed him and changed his life that the *News Chronicle* account is the first of his four versions about it: *Spanish Testament*, 1937; *Dialogue With Death*, 1941; and the Spanish section of *The Invisible*

Writing, 1954. (Ed. Note: Koestler's 'Captain B' is Jerrold's friend, Luis Bolin, and the 'Paris music-hall programme' was, in fact, a set of pornographic pictures – See *Dialogue With Death*.)

Jay Allen

'Slaughter of 4,000 at Badajoz'

From *The Chicago Tribune*

Elvas, Portugal, August 25, 1936

This is the most painful story it has ever been my lot to handle. I write it at four o'clock in the morning, sick at heart and in body, in the stinking patio of the Pension Central, in one of the tortuous white streets of this steep fortress town. I could never find the Pension Central again, and I shall never want to.

I have come from Badajoz, several miles away in Spain. I have been up on the roof to look back. There was a fire. They are burning bodies. Four thousand men and women have died at Badajoz since Gen. Francisco Franco's rebel Foreign Legionnaires and Moors climbed over the bodies of their own dead through its many times blood-drenched walls.

I tried to sleep. But you can't sleep on a soiled and lumpy bed in a room at the temperature of a Turkish bath, with mosquitoes and bedbugs tormenting you, and with memories of what you have seen tormenting you, with the smell of blood in your very hair, and with a woman sobbing in the room next door.

'What's wrong?' I asked the sleepy yokel who prowls around the place at night as a guard.

'She's Spanish. She came thinking her husband had escaped from Badajoz.'

'Well, didn't he?'

'Yes,' he said, and he looked at me, not sure whether to go on. 'Yes, and they sent him back. He was shot this morning.'

'But who sent him back?'

I knew, but asked nevertheless.

'Our international police.'

I have seen shame and indignation in human eyes before, but

not like this. And suddenly this sleepy, sweaty being, whose very presence had been an added mystery, took on the dignity and nobility that a fine dog has and human beings most often have not.

I gave it up. I came down into the filthy patio, with its chickens, rabbits, and pigs, to write this and get it over with.

To begin at the beginning, I had heard dark rumours in Lisbon. Everybody there spies on everybody else. When I left my hotel at 4 p.m., August 23, I said I was going to Estoril to try my luck at roulette. Several people noted that down, and I hope they enjoyed their evening at Estoril.

I went to the Plaza de Rocio instead. I took the first taxi. I drove around and around and finally picked up a Portuguese friend who knows his business.

We went to the ferry that crosses the Tagus. Once on the other side we told the chauffeur, 'Elvas.' He looked mildly surprised. Elvas was 250 kilometres (about 150 miles) away.

We streaked through an engaging country of sandy hills, cork oaks, peasants with sideburns, and women with little bowler hats. It was 8.30 o'clock when we pulled up the hill into Elvas, 'the lock nobody ever opened'. But Elvas knows humiliation now.

We entered a white narrow gate. That seems years ago. I have since been to Badajoz. I believe I was the first newspaperman to set foot there without a pass and the inevitable shepherding by the rebels, certainly the first newspaperman who went knowing what he was looking for.

I know Badajoz. I had been there four times in the last year to do research on a book I am working on and to try to study the operations of the agrarian reform that might have saved the Spanish Republic – a republic that, whatever it is, gave Spain schools and hope, neither of which it had known for centuries.

It had been nine days since Badajoz fell on August 14. The rebel armies had gone on – to a nasty defeat at Medellin, if my information was correct, as it sometimes is – and newspapermen, hand-fed and closely watched, had gone on in their wake.

Nine days is a long time in newspaper work; Badajoz is practically ancient history. But Badajoz is one of those damned spots the truth about which will not be out so soon. And so I did not mind being nine days late, if my newspaper didn't.

We began to hear the truth before we were out of the car. Two Portuguese drummers standing at the door of the hotel knew my friend. Portugal, as usual, is on the eve of a revolution. The people seem to know who 'the others' are. That is why I took my friend along.

They whispered. This was the upshot – thousands of Republican, Socialist, and Communist militiamen and militiawomen were butchered after the fall of Badajoz for the crime of defending their republic against the onslaught of the generals and the landowners.

Between 50 and 100 have been shot every day since. The Moors and Foreign Legionnaires are looting. But blackest of all: The Portuguese 'international police', in defiance of international usage, are turning back scores and hundreds of republican refugees to certain death by rebel firing squads.

This very day (August 23) a car flying the red and yellow banner of the rebels arrived here. In it were three Phalanxists (Fascists). They were accompanied by a Portuguese lieutenant. They tore through the narrow streets to the hospital where Señor Granado, republican civil governor of Badajoz, was lying. Señor Granado, with his military commander, Col. Puigdengola, ran out on the loyalist militia two days before the fall of Badajoz.

The Fascists ran up the stairs, strode down a corridor with guns drawn, and into the governor's room. The governor was out of his mind with the horror of the thing. The director of the hospital, Dr Pabgeno, threw himself over his helpless patient and howled for help. So he saved a life.

The day before the mayor of Badajoz, Madronero, and the Socialist deputy, Nicelau de Pablo, were handed over to the rebels. On Tuesday forty Republican refugees were escorted to the Spanish frontier. Thirty-two were shot the next morning. Four hundred men, women, and children were taken by cavalry escorts through the frontier post of Caia to the Spanish lines. Of these close to 300 were executed.

Getting back in the car, we drove to Campo Maior, which is only seven kilometres (about four miles) from Badajoz on the Portuguese side. A talkative frontier policeman said:

'Of course we are handing them back. They are dangerous for us. We can't have Reds in Portugal at such a moment.'

'What about the right of asylum?'

'Oh,' he said, 'Badajoz asks extradition.'

'There is no such thing as extradition for a political offence.'

'It's being done all up and down the frontier on orders of Lisbon,' he said belligerently.

We cleared out. We drove back to Elvas. I met friends who are as much Portuguese as Spanish, and vice versa.

'Do you want to go to Badajoz?' they asked.

'No,' I said, 'because the Portuguese say their frontier is closed and I would be hung up.'

I had no other reason. The rebels do not like newspapermen who see both sides. But they offered to take me through and back again without complications. So we started. Suddenly we drove out of the lane on to a bridge that leads across the Guadiana river into the town where Wellington's troops ran amok in the Peninsular wars, where now is just another tragedy.

Now we were in Spain. My friends were known. The extra person in the car (myself) passed unnoticed. We were not stopped.

We drove straight to the plaza of Badajoz. Here are my notes: Cathedral is intact. No, it isn't. Driving around the side I see half a great tower shot away.

'The Reds had machine guns there and our artillery was obliged to fire,' my friends said.

Here yesterday there was a ceremonial, symbolical shooting. Seven leading republicans of the Popular Front (Loyalists). Shot with a band and everything before 3,000 people. To prove that rebel generals didn't shoot only workers and peasants. There is no favouritism to be shown between the Popular Fronters.

We stopped at a corner of the narrow Calle de San Juan, too narrow for traffic. Through here fled the Loyalist militiamen to take refuge in a Moorish fortress on a hill when the descendants of those who built it broke through the Trinidad gate. They were caught by the Legionnaires coming up from the gate by the river and shot in batches on the street corners.

Every other shop seemed to have been wrecked. The conquerors looted as they went. All this week in Badajoz, Portuguese have been buying watches and jewellery for practically nothing. Most shops belong to the Rightists. It is the war tax they pay for salvation, a rebel officer told me grimly.

The massive outlines of the Alcazar fortress showed at the end of the Calle de San Juan. There the town's defenders, who sought refuge in the tower of Espantoperro ('Frightened Dogs'), were smoked out and shot down.

We passed a big dry goods shop that seemed to have been through an earthquake.

'La campaña,' my friends said. 'It belonged to Don Mariano, a leading Azanista (follower of Manual Azana, President of Spain). It was sacked yesterday after Mariano was shot.'

We drove by the office of the Agrarian reform, where in June I saw the chief engineer, Jorge Montojo, distributing land, incurring naturally the hatred of the landowners and, because he was a technician following strictly bourgeois canons of law, the enmity of the Socialists, too. He had taken arms in defence of the republic, and so —

Suddenly we saw two Phalanxists halt a strapping fellow in a workman's blouse and hold him while a third pulled back his shirt, baring his right shoulder. The black and blue marks of a rifle butt could be seen. Even after a week they showed. The report was unfavourable. To the bullring with him.

We drove out along the walls to the ring in question. Its sandstone walls looked over the fertile valley of Guadiana. It is a fine ring of white plaster and red brick. I saw Juan Belmonte, bullfight idol, here once on the eve of the fight, on a night like this, when he came down to watch the bulls brought in. This night the fodder for tomorrow's show was being brought in, too. Files of men, arms in the air.

They were young, mostly peasants in blue blouses, mechanics in jumpers. 'The Reds.' They are still being rounded up. At four o'clock in the morning they are turned out into the ring through the gate by which the initial parade of the bullfight enters. There machine guns await them.

After the first night the blood was supposed to be palm deep on the far side of the lane. I don't doubt it. Eighteen hundred men – there were women, too – were mowed down there in some twelve hours. There is more blood than you would think in 1,800 bodies.

In a bullfight when the beast or some unlucky horse bleeds copiously, 'wise monkeys' come along and scatter fresh sand. Yet on hot afternoons you smell blood. It is all very invigorating. It was a hot night. There was a smell. I can't describe it and won't describe it. The 'wise monkeys' will have a lot of work to do to make this ring respectable for a ceremonial slaughter bullfight. As for me, no more bullfights – never.

We came to the Trinidad gate through these once invulnerable fortifications. The moon shone through. A week ago a battalion of 280 legionnaires stormed in. Twenty-two live to tell the tale of how they strode over, climbed over the bodies of their dead, and, with hand grenades and knives, silenced those two murderous machine guns. Where were the government planes? That is one of the mysteries. It makes one quake for Madrid.

We drove back to town past the republic's fine new school and sanitary institute. The men who built these are dead, shot as 'Reds' because they sought to defend them.

We passed a corner.

'Until yesterday there was a pool blackened with blood here,' said my friends. 'All the loyal military were shot here and their bodies left for days as an example.'

They were told to come out, so they rushed out of the houses to greet the conquerors and were shot down and their houses looted. The Moors played no favourites.

Back at the plaza. During the executions here Mario Pires went off his head. He had tried to save a pretty fifteen-year-old girl caught with a rifle in her hand. The Moor was adamant. Mario saw her shot. Now he is under medical care at Lisbon.

I know there are horrors on the other side aplenty. Almendra Lejo, rightist, was crucified, drenched with gasoline, and burned alive. I know people who saw charred bodies. I know that. I know hundreds and even thousands of innocent persons died at the hands of revengeful masses. But I know who it was who rose to 'save Spain' and so aroused the masses to a defence that is as savage as it is valiant.

Anyway, I am reporting Badajoz. Here a dozen or more rightists were executed every day during the siege. But —

Back in Elvas in the casino I asked diplomatically:

'When the Reds burned the jail, how many died?'

'But they didn't burn the jail.' I had read in the Lisbon and Seville papers that they had. 'No, the brothers Pla prevented it.'

I knew Luis and Carlos Pla, rich young men of good family,

who had the best garage in south-western Spain. They were Socialists because they said the Socialist Party was the only instrument which could break the power of Spain's feudal masters.

They harangued the crowd that wanted to burn the 300 rightists in the jail just before they entered, saying they were going to die in defence of our Republic, but they were not assassins. They themselves opened the doors to let these people escape.

'What happened to the Plas?'

'Shot.'

'Why?'

No answer.

There is no answer. All these people could have been allowed to escape to Portugal three miles away, but they weren't.

I heard Gen. Queipo de Llano announcing on the radio that Barcarota had been taken and that 'rigorous justice' was dispensed with the Reds there. I know Barcarota. I asked the peasants there in June if, now that they were given land, they would not be capitalists.

'No,' indignantly.

'Why?'

'Because we only get enough for our own use, not enough to be able to exploit others.'

'But it's yours.'

'Of course.'

'What do you want from the republic now?'

'Money for seed. And schools.'

I thought then, 'God help anybody who tried to prevent this.'

I was wrong. Or was I? At the casino here, which is frequented mostly by landowners and rich merchants, I ventured to inquire what the situation was before the rebellion.

'Terrible. The peasants were getting twelve pesetas for a seven-hour day, and nobody could pay it.'

That is true. It was more than the land could stand. But they had been getting from two to three pesetas from sun-up to sun-down before. Twenty Spaniards with red and yellow ribbons in their buttonholes sat around the casino and from the fact that they were here I assumed they did not feel Franco had yet made Spain quite safe.

On the moon-drenched streets there was a smell of jasmine, but I had another smell in my nostrils. Sweet, too horribly sweet.

On the foothill in the white plaza by a fountain, a youth leaning against the wall with his feet crossed twanged his guitar and a soft tenor sang a melting Portuguese love song.

At Badajoz in June boys still sang beneath balconies. It will be a long time before they do again.

Suddenly through the square shot a car with a red and yellow flag. We halted. Our drummers came to meet us.

'They are searching the hotel.'

'For whom?'

'Don't know.'

We shall go away, as soon as it is light. People who ask questions are not popular near this frontier, if it can be called a frontier.

'On the Heels of Atrocities'

From *The Road to Madrid*

To get a pass to go to Torre Hermosa it was necessary to go to general headquarters at Caceres, where a senior member of General Franco's staff was always helpful and sympathetic to me. I explained to him that I had heard that advances were being made in the region of Torre Hermosa and that atrocities were being continually discovered of which I should like to have first-hand information. He was then kind enough to give me a pass, worded in such a way that I knew I should be able to join any of the columns in that neighbourhood without much difficulty. In order to be as near the front as possible for the next morning's start I decided to sleep at Merida, where I should also be able to get more detailed information from the local Falange.

Dining that night at the 'Parador' there, I was lucky enough to meet the chief of the local Falange, a very interesting young Spanish doctor who was working in a German hospital when the Civil War broke out but had returned to Spain in order to take part. He was the first real Falange I had met, and he was really keen on his work of organizing, and struck me as being a type of man that is going to be very useful to the new Spain which is bound to arise from the present struggle.

He told me to call on him at his office first thing in the morning, when he would give me a pass for Oliva, which he anticipated would be captured in the early hours. I collected the pass about eight o'clock, and a few minutes afterwards crossed the old Roman bridge and turned to the left into the mountains.

Shortly before arriving at Oliva the road passed a very large house standing in park-like grounds which I thought would be worth a visit, since the Reds had spent the night there and, having retired in the early morning, might have left something interesting. Walking round that large silent house was a curious experience. The stillness seemed unnatural, and as I strolled from room to room, making my way through broken furniture, heaps of books, and remnants of food lying everywhere, I began to feel definitely shaken. The sight of a bed piled with crumpled blankets made me wonder if by chance someone who had overslept or was wounded was lying quietly there.

I went carefully through some of the smaller books in the hope of putting a keepsake in my pocket, but actually the only thing I took away was an old English family Bible which I thought would be an appropriate present for my small son, and a revolver which I gave to my chauffeur. On the walls I noticed an interesting document signed by members of the United States Congress in the eighteenth century, and I am still regretting that I did not take it from its broken frame and keep it.

The Reds had left no papers of any interest, but while turning over a heap of odds and ends on the ground floor I came across what looked like an empty carbide-tin, which I picked up only to discover that the end was carefully bound round with insulating tape and was attached to an electric cable. This was sufficient for me, and I crept carefully out of the house without touching anything more.

Before I left the grounds I noticed one room, possibly a stable, that could be entered only from the outside, and I decided to give it a quick look over. I stepped into the comparative darkness, to see that it was empty except for some heavy planks of timber. As I turned to leave, however, there was a loud bang behind me, which made me leap into the air, but which I discovered was caused only by a cat jumping on to one of the planks.

I arrived at Oliva a few minutes after it had been taken. The dead bodies at the entrance to the village were being collected for burial, and as I entered the little square I was just in time to witness the proclamation of martial law. A Falange, with a couple of armed men, a bugler, and a standard-bearer, was reading from a document. The principal order it contained was the demand for the handing-in of all arms, which could only be carried with permission, failure to obey being punishable by death.

As usual there were very few inhabitants remaining and the audience consisted merely of some half-dozen townspeople.

At this time I began to hear the sound of distant gunfire, and I gathered from some of the troops that the column had gone on and was at that moment beginning an attack on Guareña a few miles distant. I determined to join these troops, trusting more to my pseudo-Spanish uniform and the Spanish appearance I had cultivated rather than my pass. Half an hour later my car had mingled with transport wagons and troops on the road entering Guareña.

I left the car by the cemetery wall and joined some troops who were marching in on foot. Our route lay straight to the centre of the little town, which in normal times had a population, I should imagine, of from eight to ten thousand.

It was very hard to gather exactly what was happening as firing was taking place in a great many streets, including the one we were going down, and as far as I could see no one part of the town was safer than any other.

On these occasions the townspeople remaining are nearly always anti-Reds, and to avoid trouble the custom is to leave the doors of their houses open and fly a white flag, which may consist of anything from a dishcloth to an under-garment. These white emblems were showing almost everywhere, but on one house that we passed the soldier next to me, noticing that the door was shut, hammered on it with his fist, shouting a warning to the inhabitants to open it.

Instead of the door being opened a couple of shots came through the shutters, hitting the poor fellow in the stomach. The wound was fatal, and he died before we could carry him to medical help.

I found a very little of this sort of thing was sufficient, and seeing that the church was not far away I thought a view from the top of the tower would not only be interesting but decidedly safer than the streets. The scene in the church was very picturesque. Some fifty horses were stabled inside with their nosebags on, while on the floor were soldiers who had dropped asleep before they had had time to settle into any sort of comfortable position. The church was absolutely wrecked, no pictures or statuary unbroken, but a shaft of sunlight streamed through the doorway and lit up the horses, making a very attractive picture.

I climbed the winding stairway to the tower, and from there I was able to gather a more or less comprehensive idea of the proceedings. The only organized resistance still going on was at the railway station, where about a hundred Reds were entrenched, awaiting, as I was afterwards told, the arrival of an armoured train to relieve them. Here the firing was brisk on both sides, and guns were being got into position to help blow them out.

It was some time before I grasped the cause of loud crashes which were occasionally heard. Then I saw soldiers smashing doors with the butt ends of their rifles while they carried out a systematic house-to-house search. After a short time only the firing at the station remained, the only noise from the town being the occasional breaking-in of a door.

I descended again into the town and made my way to the square, which seemed to be developing into some sort of headquarters. On the way I noticed some bloody footprints leading from a closed door, so I fetched a civil guard and asked him to break it down so that we could see what had happened inside.

The scene within was almost too dreadful to describe. The floor was swimming with blood, and everything in the house was wrecked. Lying by the bed was the body of an old lady of seventy-six, her head half chopped-off and her poor broken arms lying unnaturally as if trying to reach the bodies of her son and grandson, who were lying beaten to death beside her. I could find no trace of a gunshot wound on either of them, but they were both terribly disfigured by blows which had rained on them from head to foot.

In the half-light of the shuttered room I could hardly keep my feet on the bloody floor as I groped my way back to the open air.

In the street again two men, their eyes looking half insane with hysterical fear, seized me by the hand explaining volubly that they had just been released from prison. They seemed to be unable to grasp for sure that they were talking to friends and not foes, and were panicking for a friendly voice and safety. They told me that they had been in prison for weeks expecting death at any moment and had only just been released. They were very anxious to get somewhere where there was no risk of meeting their late enemies or of being mistaken for Reds by any of the soldiers who were clearing up the town. I could quite understand their anxiety, as the soldiers who had just witnessed scenes such as I have described were in no mood for half-hearted measures with any of the perpetrators they could lay their hands on.

I saw a large building on which was chalked '*Casa del Pueblo*', in other words the town hall of the Red occupation. This struck me as a glorious opportunity to get hold of evidence of their methods. I found a back door open and made my way in. Above all I was struck by the dreadful fuggy smell. Several of the rooms were dormitories packed with bedsteads which had been stolen from the shops. Banana-skins, olive-stones, remains of ham, and egg-shells were everywhere. There is something peculiar about this smell. One gets it in the churches that have been occupied by the Reds as well as their houses, but in this building it seemed to be concentrated and left me with the impression that I should never be near a real Anarchist again without my nostrils warning me of his presence.

I soon found the desk of the Red president. Paper was still in his typewriter, and he had evidently been typing when the alarm took place as the orders for the current day were begun. I have beside me as I write a large meat-chopper which was on his desk, and which was possibly the actual weapon or a similar one to that used on the poor old lady. There were a thousand printed copies of a list of twenty-eight names, headed 'Should the following be placed at liberty?' A space on which to put a cross as in a ballot paper was in front of each name – literally a ballot of death.

Some of the documents were headed 'THE REPUBLIC OF GUARENA', bearing witness to the influence of Russian agitators. On the door was an amusing paper which stated that danger approaching by various roads would be signalled by the church bell in the following way: one toll indicating one road, two tolls another road, and so on.

Beside the desk were suitcases filled with loot such as jewellery, silver, cutlery, and small arms. In my nervousness I am afraid I must have slipped an old Cordoba silver cigar-case into my hip pocket, as I found it there some time later.

Not having much time to spare, I stuffed what papers I could lay my hands on into my shirt and went back to the street.

As I retraced my steps to the Square I saw a weeping mother supported by some of her neighbours, crying out for vengeance. Her own daughter had been dragged away from her literally by the feet to probably an unspeakable death at the hands of the retreating Reds.

From time to time shots and screams betokened another capture. On one of these occasions I saw a woman trying to get at the prisoner and being held back screaming that he was the man who had murdered her husband.

By eleven o'clock the town itself had been cleared up and all the prisoners safely secured. Ten of these had been caught red-handed at their dreadful work, and were shut up handcuffed in the building that was being used as town hall. They were to be shot at twelve o'clock, so I interviewed the officer in charge and asked if I might question them before this took place. He raised no objection, so I had them brought to me one at a time.

The first man I spoke to was a rough-looking customer at the best of times, but it was soon clear that he was still very drunk and had no idea of the predicament he was in; in fact he still thought he was enjoying last night's party when he was shot. The second man was a schoolmaster. I explained that I merely wished to give him the opportunity of letting the world know what ideals he was about to die for, explaining that I had no influence whatever as regards his fate. He insisted on trying to argue that he had nothing to do with the dreadful crimes committed, but as the result of patient questioning it became quite apparent that his callousness, even from his own admissions, was such that he could watch the most dreadful kind of murder without feeling it his duty to interfere. When finally they were shot I believe he was the only one for whom I had no feeling of regret.

Among the others was one man who interested me particularly In appearance he was something a little above the average peasant. I should think he was probably a small freeholder who raised cattle. I asked him how on earth he had got himself into this position, and he explained that everybody had told him that (although he realized it was a very dreadful thing to have to do) the killing of landowners and capitalists would lead to a wonderful and happy new Spain. When I asked him who had given him this information he seemed to have been more particularly affected by the wireless than anything else. He explained that night after night they listened to the recital of triumphs of the Red forces everywhere. It was fresh news to him to learn that the anti-Reds were in the neighbourhood at all. When I asked him what radio he listened to I found that he had never realized that it was just somebody talking to him through a machine. He looked upon it as something of an oracle, the voice of God, that could not be wrong. The whole thing struck me as being terribly pathetic.

I asked him, as he had now lived for several months under the regime of these people, what sign of the promised good times he had observed, to which he replied, 'Nothing – nothing but terrible things.' He had no desire to escape his fate. He had the stoic Spanish indifference to death, his attitude being rather that he had backed the wrong horse and could not grumble at losing his stake. He went off to his death with less fuss than I make going to the dentist.

Alexander Werth

Dispatches to *The Manchester Guardian*

The Road to Barcelona

December 21, 1937

In crossing the frontier into Catalonia we did not notice anything very unusual. No doubt the red star – the Soviet star! – on the caps of the carabiniers and *asalto* guards – the latter mostly Communists, some of whom were actually wearing the famous leather jacket popularly associated with the Ogpu – might have suggested to some travellers that they were entering another Soviet State, but actually these guards are under the orders of the Negrin Government, whereas not much more than six months ago the whole North of Catalonia was ruled by the Anarchist syndicates, and the black-and-red flag of the FAI and the CNT flew on every public building. But the country beyond the frontier looked just like a continuation of the rich Roussillon Plain, with its vineyards, its flocks of sheep, its peasants ploughing the fields lined by long rows of cypresses. It was a warm day, and in the small towns women were sitting on their doorsteps, playing with their children or knitting. The children looked healthy and well dressed. A large number of lorries were coming in from France, mostly laden with chassis or with complete motor-cars; others carried small but substantial-looking cases marked 'Le Havre'.

We discovered the first signs of abnormal conditions when we stopped at Gerona, with its beautiful cathedral marked 'National Monument' and with one of its churches turned into a military hospital. At Gerona we could get no lunch. One hotel had been requisitioned for the Air Force, and through the window we could see the dining-room, with its ceremoniously folded napkins; but the other hotel had not provided lunch for any visitors. In the dark hall the old woman in charge merely shook her head. So we sat in the sunny square outside the 'Bar Express', on the river embankment, sipping a doubtful vermouth. The local inhabitants also sat round tables drinking their vermouth or a black liquid that looked like coffee. Among them were many young civilians of military age. Nobody ate anything and nobody smoked. Cigarettes are almost non-existent in Spain, except among the troops. Two oranges were displayed in a shop window in solitary glory. Nearly all windows were pasted over with strips of brown paper – an anti-air-raid precaution. 'Immortal Gerona' had been bombed once or twice. On the other side of the square there was a public building decorated with the Spanish red-yellow-and-purple and the Catalan yellow-and-red flags, and on the wall were painted the hammer and sickle and the words 'A Fascist at large is a spy in action'. Along the river front were two competing bookstalls – one Anarchist, with books by Bakunin, William Morris, and Kropotkin, and the other Communist, with pamphlets on Stalin, the Soviet Union, and Leon Blum, and postcards with portraits of Galan and Hernandez, the two leading Spanish Communists, in an orgy of Republican flags. The newspapers the people outside the café were reading were printed on dirty grey paper. At the other end of the town were several streets recently renamed after Garcia Hernandez and the 19th of July (the suppression of the military rebellion in Barcelona).

Driving on to Barcelona we went through a vast beech and pine forest, and then took the road along the sea. The Mediterranean, without any ship in sight, was a dazzling pattern of blue and gold. We passed several bathing resorts; it was like any road on the Riviera. Everywhere the food shortage was apparent. In one small town we tried to buy some green apples we had noticed in a window, but in vain. Not only was food scarce, but its delivery was most irregular; on some days a great deal could be bought, on others nothing at all. This faulty distribution largely paralysed the official rationing system. Manufactured goods, on the other hand, were plentiful: there was no lack anywhere of shirts and ties and socks, and hair oil and perfume; and even soap, unobtainable a few months ago, was plentiful though expensive. Outside Barcelona, whose hundreds of smoking chimneys we could see miles away, there are miles of allotments, and we passed scores of donkey-carts and mule-carts filled with cabbages and salad going to town. We also passed a funeral procession with a regular black hearse with a yellow crown, but without any cross or other religious marks, and followed by some fifty working people, but without any sign of a priest.

Just outside Barcelona we saw the first double-decker bus, almost exactly like a London bus, but painted in the Anarchist colours of black and red and with 'CNT' (the Anarchist trade union federation) painted in white on the radiator. The buses and trams, and many other things besides, are still run by the Anarchists in Barcelona. We entered Barcelona from the east, through a grimy working-class district. The tobacco-shops had notices pasted on their windows saying that there was no tobacco. Outside the food-shops there were long queues of women, some of them looking distinctly bad-tempered. The tram-cars were overcrowded, with human 'bunches of grapes' clinging on to the footboards and buffers – a sight strangely reminiscent of St Petersburg in 1917. The vast bull-ring, where they still have bullfights ('only the bulls are badly fed, and aren't much use', I was told), marks the border between the east end and the centre of Barcelona. There is perhaps more absurd architecture along the Ramblas of Barcelona than in any other town in the world – houses looking like wedding-cakes, houses with domes and cupolas and mounted by eagles, houses in the 'style moderne' of 1900, with metal ivy railings, and shell-shaped balconies, and 'stalactite' porticos, and tiled fronts, dotted with little blue flowers. We stopped at the Hotel Majestic, near the Plaza de Cataluña, one of the few big hotels commandeered by the Government, the rest having been turned into hospitals or trade union headquarters. The windows were pasted over with zigzags of brown paper, and there were many bullet-holes in the walls and shop-windows along the street – a memory of the Anarchist rising of last May, 'the tragic days of May 1937' as the Anarchists themselves call them. It was night now, and the streets were pitch black except for the lighted tram-cars and the dazzling lights of passing motor-cars.

In Republican Spain – Barcelona – Life In a Troubled City Still 'Bourgeois'

December 24, 1937

Except for the Cathedral and one or two other churches 'of artistic value' all the churches in Barcelona have been destroyed; and although by a recent decree several thousand priests have been 'reinstated', it does not mean much in practice. They are allowed to say Mass in private houses, but anti-clerical feeling is still so strong in Barcelona that the authorities hesitate to allow Mass to be said in any public place of worship. The same applies to the other towns; it is true that Presbyterian and other Protestant services are tolerated both in Madrid and in Barcelona; but the only Catholic service I heard of was that held at the Basque Legation at Valencia. But none has been held in the Basque Legations either in Barcelona or in Madrid.

Barcelona is not a pleasant city. Unlike Madrid, with its wonderful unity of spirit, it seems tormented by doubts and contradictions. The memories of the May rising, when 5,000 people were killed in street fighting, are still fresh; in the wide luxurious ramblas of Barcelona walls and windows are riddled with bullet holes, and although by moving to Barcelona the Negrin Government has made Barcelona more 'war conscious' than it was before, there is still much political tension below the surface. It is a city of contrasts. 'In Madrid,' an Anarchist remarked to me, 'one says "comrade"; here one still says "señor". Barcelona is still dreadfully bourgeois.'

The wide avenue in front of the Basque Legation is crowded from morning till night by pitiful Basque refugees. Food is, generally, scarce; and yet by paying exorbitant prices – fifty pesetas – one can still dine luxuriously in one or two Barcelona restaurants. And round the corner from the Basque Legation with its refugees you hear at night while the streets are pitch dark the shrieking and bellowing of a jazz band. For the night life of Barcelona goes on. The hall is crowded with young officers in suspiciously spotless uniforms and well-groomed young men with perfectly creased trouser legs, and good-looking women with bare backs and shoulders. 'Valencia!' (oh, irony!) the trumpet blurted. 'Valencia!' the saxophone wailed in reply. An old, old jazz tune.

And the couples on the floor and the men at the bar roared the refrain of 'Valencia' as though it meant nothing more than an old, old jazz tune. But a tough-looking man in uniform, looking at the well-groomed men with the creased trousers, could be heard growling: 'Fascists ... machine gun ...'

Interviews with Dr Negrin and Señor Companys

December 28, 1937
The Premier's office in Barcelona occupies a large private house in the Pasea de Gracia which once belonged to a banker who is now on 'the other side'. The entrance, which is guarded by two soldiers with fixed bayonets, is decorated with a religious panel in blue and golden majolica. In the courtyard there usually stands a large limousine, flying the Republican flag. It looks an efficient, up-to-date office. The day I called there they were unpacking several large cases of American dictaphones. Negrin's office, with wood-panelled walls, a horseshoe desk with a row of telephones on one side, modern lighting, and soft leather armchairs, is like that of an important American businessman.

Nothing is more refreshing than a talk with Negrin. He joined politics late in life, and still looks more like a lecturer in biology than like a professional politician. He smiles kindly through his horn-rimmed glasses, and when he speaks (in excellent English) he speaks with quiet assurance and self-confidence ...

We also saw Señor Companys, the President of Catalonia, that day. He received us at his official residence in the Rambla de Cataluña, a sumptuous building, protected by Catalan guards in red and yellow – slightly 'Ruritanian' – uniforms. Companys is quite different from Negrin – a wily Mediterranean politician, whose vivacious manner and exuberant French reminded me of Veniselos. He hotly denied the report that he had gone to Brussels to enter into contact with the rebels. 'That I, the man who proclaimed the Republic and spent fifteen years of my life in Alfonso's gaols, should do such a thing,' he cried, 'no, never!' Apart from that he made no statement for publication ...

Madrid

December 29, 1937

We stayed in the Hotel Victoria, some five minutes' walk from the Puerta del Sol. Most foreign visitors stay there now. The windows of the Victoria face east (the best direction) and south (the second best). For, in Madrid, with the shelling coming mainly from the north and west, there are degrees in the security (or insecurity) of houses, just as there are also parts of the towns – said to be largely inhabited by Franco sympathizers – which have suffered far less than others. No place, however, is as perfectly safe as the underground vaults of the Bank of Spain; and it was in this exclusive place that we attended the luncheon that General Miaja gave in honour of Mr Attlee, Mr Noel-Baker, and Miss Wilkinson. The famous soldier, enormously popular in Madrid, looks like a kindly old bishop.

The first night in Madrid, groping our way along a dark, narrow lane littered with debris – for there had been some shelling that morning – we went to see Ernest Hemingway, one of the three remaining tenants of the Hotel Florida, whose 'modern comfort' we had seen advertised on the way up to Madrid that day. The Florida forms the angle of two of the principal Madrid avenues, and the side facing north-west is almost completely wrecked. The room Hemingway occupies is on the first floor in the south-east corner of the hotel, the only 'relatively' safe room in the place. Hemingway, with his exuberant Douglas Fairbanks laughter, loves movement, action, and human courage. He is immensely popular both in Madrid and in the trenches. He takes a boylike joy in collecting all the bits of shell that have landed in the Florida, and labels them lovingly according to the number of the room which they had wrecked. One of the 'duds' that had landed in the Florida has now been turned into an electric lamp on Hemingway's desk, with a lampshade painted by an anti-Fascist artist.

That night there were two other people in Hemingway's room. One was 'John the Greek', who spoke a boisterous New York-Greek jargon and who had not yet fully recovered from the shock of being buried by a shell which had at the same time killed five of his comrades in the International Brigade. The other was a young

American poet, Evan S., shot through the thigh at Brunete, a delicate consumptive boy, quiet and modest. He was going back to the front, against 'doctor's orders'. To these two, as to many others, Hemingway was like a father. Some days later I saw Hemingway again at Chicotes Bar, in the Gran Via. There were crowds of soldiers around him; everybody in Spain seemed to know him. Chicotes Bar figures in *The Fifth Column*, the play about Madrid which Hemingway has just completed. (The 'Fifth Column' is that which, in Franco's own words, was waiting inside Madrid to join the other four as they entered the capital.) The proprietor of Chicotes is 'on the other side', and the place is run by the waiters.

It was cold and sunny the next morning, and we went down to the Puerta del Sol. It is a sort of Piccadilly Circus of Madrid, and, like Piccadilly Circus, undistinguished by any outstanding monument or building. A big yellow block of offices on the north side had been completely gutted by a bomb; nothing was left but the bare walls, with the sky showing through the glassless windows. But the other houses seemed moderately intact or had, rather been patched up. Franco has a predilection for the Puerta del Sol. Last New Year's Eve, on the stroke of twelve, twelve shells landed there – an example of rebel humour.

That morning, however, the tram-cars jingled and the motors hooted as they would anywhere else, though the place was barely a mile away from the enemy trenches. On the bookstalls along the pavements there were large piles of the seven or eight daily papers published (on rather grey paper) in Madrid. There were some blank spaces – the work of the censorship – in the Anarchist paper. The shoe-cleaners were doing a brisk trade on the north side of the Puerta at the foot of the wrecked yellow house, and we got the best shoeshine in the world for our sixty centavos. We went into a café where crowds of people sat drinking wine and vermouth and some eating nasty-looking bits of raw mule flesh. All the shops except those selling foodstuffs were well stocked. In the wine stores there were respectable arrays of bottles, including genuine French champagne at twenty-five pesetas; and there must be enough shirts and shoes and ties and handkerchiefs – some in Republican and even Anarchist colours – to last a generation. But food-shops look rather miserable; for instance, a famous grocery store to which we went, in the Calle Alcala, had little to show except bottles of wine and one big bag of rice, part of its contents wrapped up in little half-pound parcels, and innumerable bottles and jars of Worcester sauce, mustard, and pickles!

Madrid is supremely war-conscious. In the food queues there is far less grumbling than in Barcelona, where grumbling is often deliberately stimulated by *agents provocateurs*. In Madrid such tactics do not work. Madrid is also strangely cheerful. Ten thousand people have been killed by bombs and shells, but people do not speak of the dead; everybody will prefer to tell you of his own 'miraculous' escape. It makes for optimism. So also does the important fact that children, at any rate, are getting enough to eat. These healthy children playing in the streets of Madrid are a truly happy sight. And what is more cheerful on a fine day than the wide, sun-lit avenues of the Prado and the Castellan, where one still sees some old horse-cabs standing in a rank; Madrid is a clean city, and the rubbish carts are active every morning. In the wide eastern avenues – finer almost than the Champs Elysées – the Prado Museum is closed to visitors, the best pictures having been taken to Valencia and other places and the rest being carefully stored in the basement; the statues in the streets are carefully covered up with brick masonry, with a little Republican flag flying on top of these strange pyramids. The large building on the General Post Office is badly damaged by bombs and shells, but people continue as usual to drop their letters into the boxes. And, strangest of all, the Zoo goes on as before and is open to the public on Sundays. The lions still get meat, but the lady zebra was seized with panic during a shelling and battered her head fatally against a stone wall, and there are a few other little anomalies. The hippopotamus – or so at least the story goes, for Madrid is full of jokes – developed a skin disease after being fed for weeks on bird seed, and the cockatoo, I am told, is the most unpopular creature at the Madrid Zoo, for he had learned to imitate the noise of exploding shells.

How the Middle and Upper Classes Live in Madrid

December 30, 1937

One may wonder how the 'ordinary' person lives in Madrid after a year's bombing and shelling and privation. Having had the good fortune of being able to visit some private houses, I shall describe a couple of typical cases.

In the Calle Atocha we called on a 'middle-class' Spanish family to whom I had an introduction. The house was a large seven-storey block of flats, and since lifts are not allowed to work in Madrid we had to climb all the way, for they lived on the top floor. Like all stairways in Madrid, it smelt of rancid oil. The man to whom I had a note was an artist. But the door was opened by a delicate little dark-skinned woman, with a strained, careworn look on her face. No, she said, her brother was not in Madrid; he had left some months ago for Murcia, where he had a job with a trade union organization. She herself was working with a cinema firm in the Calle Atocha. She also had another brother in Madrid. 'But he is a bit more nervous than I am,' she said, 'and, on account of the shells, he doesn't like coming home at night. So he lives near his office. Nor does he like this flat, which he thinks is a little too exposed.' She took us on to the balcony. Right below us, half a mile away, with nothing between, were the rebel trenches, from which, with a dry noise, a little flare of smoke would go up every few minutes.

'You must be brave to live here,' I remarked. 'You might as well live on top of the Telefonica building.' 'Why?' she said. 'What's the good of moving? I like this little house of ours. We've got all our furniture, and my brother's belongings are here. And look at this,' she said, pointing to a whatnot filled with porcelain, 'everything completely intact!' 'What do you do when the shelling starts?' 'Oh, nothing; I just stay here. What's the good of running downstairs? A shell might hit me while I was running down the stairs, and the people would then just say, "Serves her right for being a coward!" So it's better to stay where you are. Don't you think so?' The girl had a typically Madrid mentality. She had lately joined the Communist Party, and believed firmly that Madrid would never be captured by the Fascists. 'If they couldn't capture it a year ago, how can they possibly capture it now?' How often had I heard that refrain!

'Oh, it is no use denying it,' she said, 'it is tiring, terribly tiring; and we know the war must go on for another three years. And we do not get much to eat. Beans and split peas, and a little rice, day after day. And no cigarettes. But we stick it, and we shall stick it; and, except for the Fascists, everybody in Madrid feels exactly the same.'

'How many people in Madrid, would you say, are Fascist?'

'Oh, quite a lot; twenty-five per cent, I should say, though many of them have gone away in the last few months – to Valencia, to Barcelona, to other places which are more "comfortable". Murcia is full of Fascists.'

The Government has to keep an eye on the 'Fascists', and although there are frequent arrests and house-searches among potential members of Franco's 'Fifth Column' – can one blame the Government for it? – there is no Terror in Madrid today and no 'atrocities'. Until this spring, before the Government was in proper control, there was a great deal of private and semi-private terrorism in Madrid and many fearful things happened. People would be dragged out of their houses by unknown men, and their bodies would later be found somewhere outside the town. But the Negrin Government has put an end to all this.

No doubt people of the middle and upper classes in Madrid, incapable of adapting themselves to new conditions, or unwilling to do so in the expectation of an early rebel victory, are having a thin time; and old people of that class suffer great hardships, though a considerable amount of relief has been organized for them, chiefly with the help of the various Consulates and Legations, mostly South American, but also some others. So long as this relief, which also includes evacuation to rebel territory, is dictated by purely humanitarian motives and is not calculated to keep the 'Fifth Column' going it deserves nothing but praise.

Here is a concrete example of how a man who a year ago was in danger of being murdered by terrorist gangs is now living normally again. Señor N. is an elderly man, something of a literary dilettante, who never took any part in politics, but who, through his family connections, could be ranked as a member of the aristocracy. Worse still, having been the member of a Conservative club (which was enough to make him a 'Fascist' in the eyes of the terrorists), he believed himself to be in serious danger of being murdered. His friends abroad tried a year ago to help him to leave Madrid, but for some reason he remained there. When I called at his house I found that he was not in. The door was opened by an old woman – a housekeeper or a 'nanny' – who, judging from the way she talked about her master, must have been in the family for a couple of generations. The house was tidy and well furnished, though the floor just above it had been wrecked by a shell. Oh, Señor Alfonso was very well, she said, thank you. Unfortunately he had gone to Barcelona and wouldn't be back for a few days. He had gone there to buy the raw material for the shoe polish he was now manufacturing. It wasn't easy, she said, but he was making ends meet.

'Have you enough food?' I asked, as a matter of course. The old woman's answer was sublime. 'Yes, would you like some?' she asked sympathetically. And, in spite of my grateful refusal, she urged me to sit down, as she would make me 'a nice cup of tea'. And outside, at some distance, a machine gun was going pat-pat-pat.

Through Madrid's Devastated Areas to the Front

December 31, 1937

Few parts of Madrid have escaped bombing or shelling, but the actual 'devastated areas' of Madrid are in the west, on the hill around the Royal Palace, and in the north-west around the University City, through which the 'front' still runs. Both devastated areas are within fifteen or twenty minutes' walk from the Puerta del Sol. Armed with passes signed by Señor Prieto, the War Minister, in person, we set out for the . . . 'front' one morning.

. . . The whole area around the Royal Palace, which has been turned into a sort of fortress overlooking the rebel plain below, forms a . . . piece of 'devastated Madrid'. The Opera House, now used for storing army material, behind the Royal Palace, and all the houses around it are badly damaged by shells. The wide avenue along the front of the hill on either side of the Royal Palace and the adjoining streets are barricaded. The statues of the Spanish kings are used as supports for these barricades, with the royal bodies half-cemented into them. There was a great deal of rifle and machine-gun firing that evening when, conducted by a guard who had been impressed by our Prieto passes, we went down the wide barricaded avenue which runs, south of the royal park, down to the Casa de Campo, a wood on the other side of the Manzanares River. We were taken through the wood to the battalion commander's headquarters in a building that looked like a farmhouse. But nobody would deal with us there, and we were sent to another house at the other end of the wood. It was strange to walk through this peaceful wood, over a thick carpet of brown and yellow leaves, with a shell whizzing over us from time to time and the rifle fire, a few hundred yards away, becoming more and more active.

The little white house to which we were taken was like a game-keeper's lodge. We presented our Prieto passes and were taken into a small room, where we were told to wait. And as the door opened and we were shown in we heard an extraordinary thing: 'King's Park, 1; Dunfermline, 3; Montrose, 1; Dundee United, 2;' – London broadcasting the football results, while outside the rebels were firing shells at Madrid. It was an expensive wireless set, and the little room itself was expensively furnished with heavy drawing-room chairs covered with crimson silk – no doubt from the Royal Palace. At the desk, dressed in khaki, sat a slim young officer, with dark hair and a fresh scar on his forehead, taking notes. There was a large desk in the room, and above it, a pair of antlers, and a clock, and a bottle of wine on it, with two glasses, and various objects were hanging on the wall – an old sword and a mandolin and a framed picture of Napoleon's retreat from Moscow and a crudely coloured print of that meek-looking man President Azana, with his goggles and puffed cheeks. In a corner there was a pile of brown army pullovers. And the wireless wailed:

> *You are my lucky star,*
> *I'm lucky in your arms,*

drowning the noise outside.

Farewell

January 1, 1938
Our car was nearing the French frontier. Those two poplars and
the hill beyond were France. I have known many people who at
that moment felt like crying '*Vive la France*!' Instead I turned
round and had a last look at Spain. And I thought of the small
female figure looking down on the rebel lines from her lonely little
flat in Madrid; and I remembered the soldiers in the dug-out and
how they stroked the wounded paw of their friend, the little red-
haired mongrel. The human side of these people is unforgettable.

'Koestler's Own Story'

From the *News Chronicle*, May 23–28, 1937

I: Malaga Was in Danger

Twenty days after my arrest I received my first message from the outside world. It was a ball of screwed brown Spanish cigarette paper, flung through the spyhole of my cell in the prison of Seville.

Unfolding it, I found a few lines scrawled in childish handwriting with many spelling mistakes. It ran:

> '*Comrade:*
> We know that you are here and that you are a friend of the Spanish Republic. You have been condemned to death: but they will not shoot you. They are too much afraid of the new King of England. They will only kill us – the poor and humble (*los pobres y humildes*).
>
> 'Yesterday again they shot seventeen in the cemetery. In our cell, where there were 100, there are only 73 now. Dear Comrade foreigner, we three are also condemned to death, and they will shoot us this night or tomorrow. But you may survive and if you ever come out you must tell the world all about those who kill us because we want liberty and no Hitler.
>
> 'The victorious troops of our government have reconquered Toledo and we have also got Oviedo, Vitoria and Badajoz. And soon they will be here, and will carry us victoriously through the streets. Further letters will follow this one. Courage. We love you.
> *Three Republican Militiamen*'

No further letters followed. As I learned later, two of these men were shot the same night and the third, whose sentence was commuted, was sent to the penitentiary for thirty years.

I never forgot that letter. I learned it by heart; every word is etched in my brain. It has literally become part of my body, for half an hour after I received it the inspection guard came into my cell. I had no time to tear up the paper and had to eat it.

I swore never to forget those '*pobres y humildes*'. I swore then and there that if ever I got out I would tell the world.

Since then I have been myself a prisoner for three months without news of the efforts that had been made by friends abroad to secure my release. Every time I was summoned from my cell I expected to be shot. Every time I lay down to sleep on my iron trestle, covered with a straw palliasse, I expected to die the next day.

Not until I reached Gibraltar from La Linea a week ago did I know for certain that I was safe. I find it still difficult to believe that I am in England, shaved and clean and – free.

But first I have to tell of the taking of Malaga where I was captured and the long story of my imprisonment began.

In the middle of January the second division of the insurgent army, commanded by General Queipo de Llano and reinforced by approximately 50,000 Italian infantrymen, started the fatal offensive.

On the 25th the news became alarming. The rebels, we heard, had conquered Marbella on the Gibraltar road and Alhama on the Granada road – two strategic positions. It seemed that Malaga might fall any day.

On Tuesday, January 26, I left Valencia to find out what had happened and what was going to happen. I travelled by car, accompanied by a Norwegian journalist (Mrs Gerda Grepp), a Polish journalist (Mr Winter) and a chauffeur on the staff of the Spanish Ministry of Foreign Affairs.

We have passed through Alicante on the night of the 27th and reached Almeria in the south on the 28th. Here my diary of the last days of Malaga begins.

These notes, originally composed of about twenty typewritten pages, were confiscated when I was arrested in Malaga; but in the prison of Seville I was able to reconstruct them while the dates were still fresh in my memory and so smuggle out a second version hidden in my underclothing.

I leave unaltered these notes on the agony of a threatened city and of the strange behaviour of the people who lived and died in it. This although I realize that they contain some sharp, even bitter, criticism of the Republican authorities, who were partly responsible for the tragedy of Malaga.

But I swore on the memory of my three militiamen to tell the whole truth, and I am keeping my promise. Perhaps, even, it may have a useful result.

Thursday, January 28, Almeria. Got up, still oppressed by talk yesterday with KST (a volunteer officer in the International Brigade) at Murcia. He said during the Italian tank attack at Prado front forty-two German Republican volunteers (some of them mutual friends) had been massacred in trench because they did not get order to retire in time. Useless and senseless hecatomb. Red tape and negligence everywhere.

10 a.m. – Saw British consul in Almeria, Campbell; following Spanish custom palavered, standing without being offered a seat. Nevertheless was nice and helpful. Says Malaga will be terrible butchery. City believed able to defend itself to last man; says all foreign consuls have left Malaga because of permanent air and sea bombardments. But British warships still in harbour – so still some hope of escape, if cut off.

Conversation cheered us up. These British consuls in forlorn Spanish cities are like pillars in the Apocalyptic flood: dry and solid.

At noon continued towards Malaga. Road becomes worse and worse. Flooded over at several points by streams of water coming down from the Sierras. Wonder how lorries with troops and ammunition can pass. As a matter of fact, they don't pass; the road, the only road, connecting Malaga with Republican Spain is absolutely deserted. Is Malaga already abandoned? Yet, we do not meet refugees either. It's ghostly.

Motril, 3 p.m. – Dirty little fisher-town. No one knows where headquarters are. Finally we find them in the municipal school.

Fresh search for military commander. At 4 p.m. we find him – an exhausted-looking youth with a five-days' beard, a former postmaster and member of Prieto's right-wing Socialist Party.

Shrugs shoulders in reply to our questions about absence of troops and arms supplies on road. Says, 'Three days ago twenty lorries arrived in Almeria with ammunition. They asked the local Syndicate to carry the load to Malaga because they had to go back.

'But Almeria Syndicate refused, claiming it needed its own cars for food supplies, and that the Valencia cars had to carry the load to Malaga. So the twenty lorries returned to Valencia and the munitions – badly needed – lingered somewhere in Almeria, and Malaga has no munitions. The Fascists may come in any time they like. Maybe you will meet them when you get there.'

Mrs Grepp is taking notes, only to tear them to pieces five minutes later. You can't cable such things, as a war correspondent.

'By the way,' says the Commander, 'you can't go on to Malaga. The bridge beyond Motril is broken. The road's flooded. You'll have to wait till the rain stops.'

'So Malaga is practically cut-off from the world?'

'As long as the rain lasts – yes.'

'And how long has it been raining now?'

'This is the fourth day, and then a week ago we had another wet period of ten days.'

'And how long has the bridge been broken?'

'Four or five months.'

'Then why, for God's sake, don't you repair it?'

Fresh shrugging of shoulders. 'We get no material or specialists from Valencia.'

The apathy of this man exasperates me.

'Don't you realize that Malaga is a strategic point – perhaps the key to the war in the South, and that its fate depends on this bridge? I call this criminal negligence.'

The ex-postmaster gives me a long, untroubled look.

'You foreigners are always very nervous,' he says paternally.

'We may lose Malaga, and we may lose Madrid and half Catalonia, but we shall still win the war.'

There is a good deal of oriental fatalism in the Spanish manner of conducting the war on both sides: that is one reason why it drags on so long.

Other wars consist of succession of battles: this one of a succession of tragedies.

A little later we carry on despite the broken bridge. It costs us a detour of about 10 miles through practically impassable field paths, the last mile through a stream bed in 10 in. of water. Our light car gets through where a heavier vehicle would be bogged.

We arrive at Malaga about sunset. First impression:

A city after an earthquake. Darkness, entire streets in ruins; a pavement deserted, strewn with shells, and a certain odour which I knew from Madrid; fine chalk dust suspended in the air mixed with shell powder and – or is it imagination? – the penetrating smell of burnt flesh.

The straying lights of our headlamps glimmer on piles of debris and yet more debris. *Pulvis et nihil* – Madrid after the great bombardments was a health resort compared with this town in agony.

In the Regina Hotel unpleasant-looking but good-humoured militiamen are spitting on the marble pavement and eating the only available food – fried fish. We are the only guests of the hotel; the waiter tells us that this very afternoon a neighbouring house was destroyed by a 500-kilo bomb, killing fifty-two in this house alone.

The other waiters are gathered round the table discussing the bombardment and everyone's attitude during it: Bernardo hiding behind the table, Jesus looking out of the window and Dolores, the cook, crossing herself fifty-seven times before she fainted.

I take a stroll with Mrs Grepp. But the darkness is so menacing that we quickly return shivering and very uneasy. The porter looks at the sky full of stars and comments: 'Fine air raid weather tonight.' His daughter lost both her legs in the bombing of yesterday and he wonders whether the bridegroom will take her without legs.

Go to bed full of bad presentiments, trying to persuade myself that it is all fancy. I finish my notes, writing quite illogically in scribbled letters across my diary: 'Journey's end – *le voyage sans retour.*'

And so it proved for me and for many hundreds.

II: The Agony of a City

No bread for breakfast, nothing but black coffee; the food supply of the town broken down by the same irresponsible negligence like the munition supply.

All the morning busy visiting offices: Propaganda Department and Civil Governor's house: meeting everywhere good will but hopeless red tape and disorganization.

After lunch, air-raid alarm; later, interview with Colonel Villalba, military commander of the Malaga forces. Admits frankly that things are going badly, but says, ten days ago, when he was appointed, they were still worse.

I inspected first the most exposed front: the coast road, Malaga–Marbella–Gibraltar. I found no trenches, no fortified positions, nothing but two militiamen in a mile's distance from the enemy's positions sitting on a milestone and smoking cigarettes. 'Where are your troops?' I asked them. 'Somewhere in the barracks,' they said. 'If the Fascists were to attack us we would see it and have plenty of time to warn them; why should they sit out in the rain?'

Visiting systematically the different sectors of the Malaga front: the roads to Marbella, Alfernate, Antequera. Everywhere the same impression; no second defence line, no arms, no munitions, a few improvised trenches or stone barricades, absolutely useless against a possible tank attack.

Last night, after a relatively quiet week, Queipo de Llano started his final offensive against Malaga.

The attack began, very surprisingly, in the sector Ardales–El Burgo; and – still more surprising – it was hit back. Watched the fighting from a hill. Awful butchery. Spoke to a deserter, Antonio Pedro Jimenez, from Dos Hermanos, near Seville. Says, in Dos Hermanos there is a newly established munition factory, built and run by Italians; says, all through the night ten to twenty lorries are carrying Italian infantry to Malaga front.

Late afternoon visited headquarters, asked Commander Alfredo G. how things are going on. Says: '*Ça va mal*,' enemy attacking simultaneously all sectors. Asked how long he thinks the town may resist. Says three days maximum. Can't get any message through censorship.

Rebel cruisers *Canarias*, *Baleares*, *Almirante Cervera*, and three smaller rebel warships bombarding all day over the coast north and south of Malaga. Where is the Republican fleet? Invisible. The rebels are uncontested masters of sea and air. No food, no munitions. First symptoms of panic in the town. Learn that Civil Governor L. A. deserted to Valencia. Last wire-line destroyed near Motril. Try to get through by Marconi cable via Gibraltar, but don't know whether my messages arrive in London.

At night Commander Alfredo comes to have dinner with me at the hotel. Says Alfernate and Ventas de Zefareya lost: that means the end. Mrs Grepp (Polish journalist) says she will leave tomorrow. Then I shall be the last Mohican of the world Press.

Several air raids during the morning. Without news from London since Thursday, so feel sure my messages don't get through. Went to Civil Governor's office, trying to find out whether I could use radio for SOS message telling the world that Italian troops are going to capture Malaga. But at the Governor's office everybody lost his head. Went to headquarters with same intention, but Villalba is invisible and has left order that '*la Presse*' – *la Presse, c'est moi*! – is not allowed to cable anything about the military situation except optimistic propaganda stuff. Army people always believe that if they call a defeat a victory it is a victory and the dead will stand up. They believe in the magic effects of propaganda lies like bushmen in the prayers of the witch-doctor.

In the meantime, Mrs Grepp got ready to leave. An official

takes her in his car to Valencia. I have just time to scribble a few words on a piece of paper, which she should phone from Valencia to London, to the Foreign Editor of the *News Chronicle*: 'Malaga lost. K staying.'

At 2 p.m. the exodus from Malaga begins. The road to Valencia is a flooding stream of lorries, cars, mules, carriages, frightened, quarrelling people.

Impossible to know what is going on the fronts. At 4 p.m. I leave in my car for Velez. The sight is simply frightful. The militiamen of the routed army – bearded, exhausted, starving – linger in the cafés, in doorways, public buildings, lie sleeping on the pavements. There is no order, no more command, complete chaos.

As soon as we get back to Malaga, stopping at headquarters, my chauffeur, who has got the contagion of the panic, declares categorically that he won't stay any longer. As a matter of fact, I have neither the right nor the power to hold him back; I only ask him to take my luggage from the hotel to Sir Peter Chalmers Mitchell's house, as Sir Peter has invited me to stay with him if the situation becomes critical. Ten minutes later chauffeur and car disappear on the Valencia road, with them the last possibility of getting away.

It is dawn now. I feel very lonely, abandoned, and sit down on the staircase of headquarters. Commander Alfredo comes along and sits down beside me. After a while he says: 'This is probably our last night. The road will be cut off in a few hours, and they will kill us like rats in a trap.'

'What are you going to do if they come in?'

He taps his revolver. 'I have still got five cartridges. Four for the Fascists, the fifth for myself.'

I have the uneasy feeling that he is acting as in a show, and the absurd idea comes to me that Alfredo and all the others, including myself, are children, playing Walter Scott heroes and unable to imagine the reality of death.

It is completely dark now; and the uninterrupted grumbling of cannons and coughing of machine guns behind the hill.

Alfredo takes me to the officers' casino. I fill my pockets with dry bread and two bottles of cognac. Then I stagger through the dead-dark city to Sir Peter's house, with the Union Jack planted on the white roof.

(I had paid my first visit to Sir Peter two days after my arrival in Malaga. He was, after the Consul's departure, the only Englishman in Malaga.

'I am going to stay,' he told me, 'when the rebels come in. If they know that I am here – a foreign observer – it may have some attenuating effect and even prevent a second Badajoz. And, besides, if they don't shoot me, I wish to give evidence afterwards to the world on the Malaga tragedy.'

I told Sir Peter that I had come with the same intention, and he invited me to stay in his house.)

Breakfast air raid at 8 a.m. The noise of artillery and machine guns doesn't stop any more. Later on, another air raid. Lola, Sir Peter's housemaid, suffers an hysterical attack.

After lunch – lunch is an exaggeration – went down to town. Since yesterday the physiognomy of the town completely changed; no more tramways, all shops closed, groups at every corner and all faces covered with the grey spider's-web of fear. Just while passing Caleta Bridge a squadron of six rebel planes pass very low above our heads, sowing murder. I look for shelter beyond the bridge; there are two militiamen drinking cognac, one singing the 'Internationale', the other, in low voice and with a stupid smile, the hymn of the Falange (the Spanish Fascists). I feel how the contagion of fear gets me, too.

Get in to headquarters; it looks like a night asylum; sleeping, unhuman-looking men on the desks and floors. While waiting to be received by Colonel Villalba, an exhausted sergeant staggers in and is conducted immediately to the chief commander. I enter with him.

'What news?' asks Villalba.

'They are coming with fifteen tanks down the Colmenar road.'

'How far are they?'

'An hour ago they were five miles from the city.'

'Resistance?'

'None. Our people threw away their rifles and dispersed in the Sierra.'

'Thank you.'

The sergeant puts himself below a table and falls immediately asleep. Villalba has a short, whispered conversation with some of his staff officers. An order is issued to an adjutant and they leave the room rather hurriedly.

I stopped Villalba. 'What do you want?' he says nervously. 'You see that I am in a hurry. I can give you the following statement: The situation is difficult, but Malaga will defend itself.'

'Where are you going?' I ask him. But he is already out.

I rush to a window and look down. Villalba and his staff officers get into a car. Everybody is looking rather embarrassed. The car leaves the courtyard.

'Where did he go?' I ask an officer whom I know.

'He deserted,' the officer says, calmly.

'It was his duty to leave,' says another one. 'We will be cut off in an hour, and he is the commander of the entire southern sector: so he had to leave.'

'How can he command if we are cut off?'

'He deserted,' repeats the first.

'Who is the chief now?' I ask.

'The chief?' Everybody looks surprised. Nobody knows.

I passed to another room. There is Commander Alfredo sitting behind a typewriter. It is all like a bad dream. I note, that he is using the red half of the ribbon. I read:

'To whom it may concern. This is to certify that Commander Alfredo G. is leaving on an important mission to Valencia. Authorities are requested to let him pass.'

'You too, Alfredo?' I ask him.

He blushes. 'And you, too. I take you in my car. It is all over.'

That is no more Walter Scott. It is rather James Joyce.

In the courtyard we find X, a mutual friend. He is ill, high fever, coughing and spitting.

'Come,' says Alfredo, 'it is all over.'

'Go to hell. I stay,' says X.

'Villalba left too. We take you by force,' says Alfredo, tears in his eyes.

'Go to hell,' says X. (He is dead now. Eighty per cent of the persons mentioned in this story are dead.)

We step into Alfredo's car. Alfredo's mother is in the car and Alfredo's sister and some other women, and all are crying and sobbing.

When the car starts I remember Sir Peter; during the last hour I have completely forgotten him.

'We must take my English friend,' I say to Alfredo.

'Impossible,' says the chauffeur. 'The Fascists are on the New Road; his house is cut off.'

'But I left him an hour ago!'

'They came in since. Don't you hear the machine guns?'

I am hesitating. We reach the city barrier. The crowd of refugees stares at us, privileged owners of a car, with envy and hatred.

I have a sudden attack of deep disgust and something like a nervous breakdown.

'Stop,' I say to the chauffeur, 'I want to go back.'

'Don't stop,' says Alfredo.

I jump out of the car. Alfredo gesticulates. The car disappears in the crowd.

It is dawn again. I walk slowly to Sir Peter's house. The Fascists are not yet in.

They came in only the next day.

III: At the Mercy of Franco

Since my return to London I have received several letters and personal visits from relatives of British people who are detained for political reasons in Franco's prisons.

They have all asked me not to publish anything that may annoy the rebel authorities, fearing that those unfortunates who are at the mercy of the rebels, would have to pay for it.

Now, as a matter of fact, my liberation was not due to an act of grace on the part of Franco, but was the consequence of an exchange – a simple business transaction, with human lives as the merchandise.

I have, therefore, no reason to be thankful to Franco, nor any moral obligation towards him, not to tell the truth about how they treated me and my fellow-prisoners.

It seems, further, rather unlikely that an objective exposure of facts could influence the fate of other prisoners; first, because both sides are equally interested in effecting exchanges – until now about 2,000 prisoners have been exchanged by the intermediary action of the British authorities – and, secondly, because any reprisals against prisoners on one side would induce similar measures on the other side. Their fate is mutually bound by a tragic chain.

Nevertheless, being aware of the grave responsibility which the above-mentioned circumstances induce, I feel obliged to satisfy the demands of mothers and wives who are still suffering the same hell of anxiety and dread which my wife suffered until a few days ago.

With the agreement of the editor of the *News Chronicle*, I have decided, therefore, to delete from my articles anything that may 'annoy the rebels' – a task not easy to accomplish.

I shall say nothing about the details of my arrest, about how my fellow-prisoners and I were treated in the prison of Malaga, Seville, and La Linea. Being at last physically free, I have had to learn that liberty is a very relative thing.

But I feel sure that the hour when this nightmare of a war will end and when I regain my entire liberty is not very far off now – and I have the firm hope that it will end in such a way that the Spanish Republic will also regain its liberty.

I told you in my last article how those who were responsible for the defence of Republican Malaga deserted the helpless city on Sunday, February 7, 1937.

Since then the Valencia Government – as a message announced only yesterday – has decided that the men responsible for the fall of Malaga will be tried and punished.

Following are extracts from my diary of the day when the rebel troops entered Malaga, and I was staying in the house of Sir Peter Chalmers Mitchell.

Monday, February 8

8 a.m. During breakfast observed through glasses, rebel cruisers, flying the yellow-red-yellow Bourbon flag, entering the port of Malaga. Waiting for the beginning of the bombardment; but they don't shoot.

8.30 a.m. Rebel aeroplanes revolving over us in the sky. But they don't drop bombs.

9 a.m. Usual hour for beginning of the artillery bombardment. But not a single detonation. Sunshine and dead, ghostly silence.

10 a.m. A wounded militiaman, unarmed, trembling, and half-dead, passes before the house, asking for water and cigarettes. While I give him a light, his arms and feet are trembling.

'Is the road to the town still free?' he asks.

'Yes – still free.'

'They will not kill me?'

'They will not kill you.'

'Are you sure that they will not kill me?'

'I am sure that they will not kill you.'

'God bless you, señor.'

And he staggers on. (I wonder whether they did kill him.)

11 a.m. Rebel cruisers and planes continue their peaceful promenade in the waters and airs of still Republican Malaga.

Sir Peter and I decide to go to town, to find out what is happening.

Immediately after we leave the house an invisible machine gun in the neighbourhood starts barking; the road is under fire. We run back; a refugee family enters the garden. We greet them, as we are accustomed, by raising the fist – the usual greeting in Republican Spain – but they don't move their hands. We ask them where the rebels are, and the woman says, whispering. 'The Nationalists are everywhere, in the hills – here, there. Since morning there has been a white flag on the tower of the Civil Governor's.'

So it is over. Malaga has surrendered.

And I remember Colonel Villalba's last statement before he stepped into his car: 'The situation is difficult, but Malaga will resist.'

I have a water-glass full of cognac.

1 p.m. An officer, wearing the grey steel-helmet of the Italian Army, appears on the road leading to Colmenar just opposite our house.

He looks around and fires a revolver-shot to the air. Immediately after about 200 infantrymen in perfect order come down the road. They sing Mussolini's hymn, the *'Giovinezza'*.

Passing before the house they salute us, and the house-people, yesterday still diligently raising their fists, now raise their arms in the Roman Fascist greeting with the same Spanish effusiveness. They seem perfectly at their ease, but, as they consider us foreigners as half imbeciles, the gardener warns Sir Peter and me to change our attitude too, 'because we have a new Government now'. It is tragic-comic and humiliating.

After a certain time, as more and more troops pass and greet us – we are all gathered on the balcony as if we were reviewing a military parade – after a certain time Sir Peter and I have to raise our arms too. We avoid looking at one another.

3 p.m. A company of Italian infantry occupies the neighbouring hill.

4 p.m. A clamour of hurrahs and clapping comes from the town. The rebels have entered Malaga.

4.30 p.m. Cars with the Bourbon flag circulate over the roads. Tanks are coming down from Colmenar. The detonation of shots comes in regular intervals from the town. Someone among the house-people puts forward the suggestion that, as the fighting is over, these shots may mean 'the beginning of the executions of the Red criminals . . .'

I am burning some compromising papers. Introduction-letters of the Spanish Embassy and of well-known politicians in Valencia.

It is definitely over. We are at the mercy of Queipo de Llano. Unhappily, I know him from before.

Tuesday, February 9. Arrested at 11 a.m.
The history of the arrest of Sir Peter Chalmers Mitchell and of myself is attached to a chain of extraordinary coincidences, which confirms the old proverb that life is the best novel-author.

I have to go back to the past. In August, 1936, one month after the civil war started, I visited, as a special correspondent of the *News Chronicle*, Lisbon and Seville and was received by General Queipo de Llano.

Like all journalists, I had to keep in close contact with Captain B, head of the Press Department of the Burgos Government. In consequence of an argument with a Nazi correspondent and some German war-pilots in the hall of the Hotel Cristina in Seville, I was denounced to Captain B as a notorious and incorrigible Left Wing Liberal and preferred, therefore, to leave for Gibraltar, rather precipitately.

Never again was a Liberal correspondent allowed to enter rebel territory; and Captain B swore, as I was told later by a French colleague, 'whenever he gets hold of K to shoot him on the spot'.

It was precisely Captain B who got hold of me in Malaga.

Now, Captain B happened to have a cousin living in Malaga; and this cousin – let us call him Señor B – happened to owe his life to Sir Peter, who saved him from the Anarchists.

Señor B owned the garden and the house neighbouring Sir Peter's garden and house. Señor B was a member of the Fascist 'Falange', and when the Fascist revolt was crushed in Málaga in July, 1936, he came to Sir Peter's house, asking for protection and shelter.

Sir Peter installed Señor B on the upper floor of his house, in the same room which I afterwards occupied, and Señor B handed him over his documents in an envelope, which Sir Peter locked in his writing desk.

Next day an Anarchist patrol came to the house.

They did not want to trouble Sir Peter, knowing his sympathetic attitude towards the Republican government; but they wanted to see the documents of the Señor living upstairs.

Sir Peter had to hand over the documents. The Anarchist chief, a young boy, opened the envelope. The first thing he found was a membership-card of the 'Falange'; the second, an illustrated programme of a Paris music-hall. He seemed very pleased with both discoveries.

Sir Peter had one of his usual happy inspirations.

'Look here,' he said in his softest voice, 'we'll make an exchange: you keep the programme and I'll keep the card.'

The Anarchist who, as I have said, was very young, was first indignant, then amused, and finally, out of sympathy with Sir Peter, he agreed.

Some days later Señor B, with the help of Sir Peter and of the British Consul in Malaga, escaped to Gibraltar.

His luggage remained in Sir Peter's house, his house was transformed into a military hospital.

Señor B returned the day after the rebels conquered Malaga and dropped in to Sir Peter's house to fetch his luggage, on Tuesday, February 9, at 11 a.m., at the very moment when his cousin, accompanied by two other officers, arrested me, his revolver pointed on my neck.

So I was saved – for the moment at least – by an old programme of a Paris music-hall.

If this story had happened in a film it would have been a bad film.

IV: Inside a Rebel Prison

As I told you, I was arrested on Tuesday, February 9, at 11 a.m. by Captain B from the Burgos Press Department. While my hands were being tied, and, following the custom on such solemn occasions, the revolvers of Captain B and two other officers were pointed at me, Sir Peter Chalmers Mitchell entered the room.

I was convinced that Captain B was going to shoot me on the spot. Sir Peter was very pale, and I thought he might collapse – he is a man of seventy-three.

Again I had the feeling that it was all a bad dream and that it didn't concern *me* at all. It was a kind of merciful psychic narcosis, which Nature always provides in critical moments. I heard myself saying, to my own astonishment: 'Look here, B, if you are going to shoot me, take me upstairs; don't do it in Sir Peter's presence.'

Afterwards I often wondered – I had all the time in prison to deal with such problems – whether these words, which maybe saved my life, were induced by consideration for Sir Peter or just by the motive to gain time. Maybe it was a mixture of both; but I think the second predominated.

In the meantime Sir Peter was arrested, too, but his hands were not tied.

Then Señor B, Captain B's cousin, dropped in to fetch his luggage. Although Señor B, a member of the Fascist Falange, owed his life to Sir Peter, who had saved him from the Anarchists (as I related yesterday), he seemed rather pleased at the scene which he found in his benefactor's house.

The two Bs and Sir Peter had a short conversation in the next room. Sir Peter obviously was pleading for me, but just as obviously without much success.

I was not allowed to approach them. 'What is going on?' I shouted through the open door. They came out, and Sir Peter said, very quietly and with a tender look, 'It seems all right for me but not for you.'

Anyhow, they did not shoot me on the spot.

They took us to a car. When we passed the Italian troops beyond the hill they seemed not unwilling to lynch us; but Captain B persuaded them that it wouldn't be nice to do that.

We were taken to the police station. Captain B went out and we had to wait in the car with the two other officers.

We waited two hours. The sun shone: it was very hot. I don't remember what we talked about, and I suppose most of it was nonsense; everything is nonsense when facing the imminent reality of being shot. But I remember Sir Peter reciting to me these verses of Swinburne which he knew I liked very much and which appear on the front page of his recently published memoirs.

> *Pray thou thy days be long before*
> *thy death,*
> *And full of ease and kingdom:*
> *seeing in death*
> *There is no comfort and none*
> *aftergrowth,*
> *Nor shall one thence look up and*
> *see day's dawn*
>
> *Nor light upon the land whither I*
> *go*
> *Live thou and take thy fill of days*
> *and die*

> *When thy day comes; and make*
> *not much of death*
> *Lest ere thy day thou reap an evil*
> *thing.*

Then we separated.

They took me into the police station. There I had to wait for another two hours. I don't want to speak about what I saw and heard there, for the reasons which I mentioned yesterday.

Some time in the afternoon – I had lost all sense of time – Captain B came back and gave orders to search me thoroughly.

To be searched was just the thing which I feared more than to be tortured or beaten. I had a treasure in my pocket, the most useful thing in the circumstances: a morphine syringe with a reserve needle and a quantity of morphinae hydrochloridum; sufficient to get anyone out of all troubles of the Spanish Civil War.

Sir Peter had obtained two such syringes from a medical mission in case anyone of his household should be wounded in an air bombardment and no medical help was available.

In the last critical days he had handed me over one of the syringes, as we both disliked the idea of being captured alive. All this may appear somewhat romantic and exalted; but in abnormal situations human reactions are abnormal, too, and a civil war is just the most abnormal and mad thing which human fantasy can imagine.

Now they searched me. While waiting in the police station I had managed to hide the syringe among my cigarettes and to push the needle in the lining of my jacket hoping to be able to make use of it in an unobserved moment.

But the soldier who searched me, drawing his hand along my jacket, suddenly pricked himself with the needle.

'What's that?' he asked. I showed him the needle and he and his companions all retreated panic stricken, thinking it was some murderous poisoned instrument – Spaniards like reading detective stories just as we do.

In all despair I had some little satisfaction in seeing these warriors childishly frightened, and I couldn't help appreciating the insane humour of the situation. '*Galgenhumor*' the Germans call that – the laughter under the gibbet.

They emptied my pockets and confiscated everything. I still had some Catalan money, which has no value in rebel territory. 'This you may keep,' one of the soldiers told me rather good-humouredly. 'You may pay your ticket with it when you undertake your journey to heaven tonight.'

I asked them to leave me my fountain pen.

'You won't need it in heaven,' they said.

They put me into a lorry; five soldiers, their rifles in their hands, took their places behind me.

It was already dark; and once again I was convinced that the moment had come when they were going to shoot me.

I am afraid that I repeat myself, but the fault is in the facts: for three months every new situation, every opening of my cell, gave me the same impression that the supreme moment had come. It seems monotonous, but I can assure you it wasn't for me.

I asked one of the soldiers where they were going to take me. He said they were going to take me to prison. It was an immense relief and at the same time a disappointment: I thought the sooner it would be over the better.

The soldiers handed me over to the prison authorities, together with a letter in which it was stated that I was a very dangerous person – I suppose that was the effect of the needle – that I should be thoroughly watched and kept *'incomunicado'* – that is to say, isolated: and that I was a *'cosa internacional'* – an 'international case'.

I stayed for three days in a cell of the Malaga prison. Being a *'cosa internacional'* I was treated correctly, being neither beaten nor held in chains. Of the general conditions in the prison I shall not speak.

After three days – on Saturday, February 13 – the cell door opened and two civil guards took me out. We went in a car to the railway station and took the train – the first regular train from Malaga to Seville.

We travelled in an overcrowded third-class compartment. The passengers – Andalusian peasants – behaved extremely nicely to me; they gave me sausage and cigarettes and Andalusian sweets. They tried to cheer me up. 'Eat, eat, poor devil,' they said to me, 'as long as you are still alive, eat sausage and cheese – afterwards it's too late.'

I shivered: one of them gave me his coat. It was almost a political demonstration.

The two civil guards after a time also melted a little: they untied my hands and shared their cigarettes and food with me. They showed me the letter which accompanied me, and I learned that I was being transferred to Seville to be put 'at the disposal of the chief of the armed forces of the Southern district – General Queipo de Llano'.

I knew General Queipo from before, as I knew Captain B – from my first visit to Seville in August, 1936. Unfortunately I had reasons to believe that it wouldn't be a mutual pleasure to meet again.

We arrived in Seville at night. The two civil guards took me to the prison where I was to live for the next three months and took leave of me like old friends with a nice handshake. The prison officials looked rather astonished.

For the first six days nothing happened. I walked up and down in my cell, and the arrival of my food at regular intervals was the only event of my days.

On Friday, February 19, the iron door of the cell swung open and three officers of the Falange stepped in. Two of them were men; the third was a young woman.

They greeted me very politely and I apologized for being unable to offer the young uniformed lady a better seat than the straw mattress of my bed. But she smiled – a rather charming smile as it seemed – and asked whether I was Mr Koestler, whether I spoke English. I replied in the affirmative to both questions. Then she asked me if I was a Communist. I had to reply in the negative to this.

'But you are a Red, aren't you?'

I said that I was in sympathy with the Valencia Government but didn't belong to any party.

The young lady asked whether I was aware what consequences my activity would have. I said I wasn't.

'Well,' she said, 'it means death.'

I asked why.

She said because I was supposed to be a spy.

I said that I wasn't, and that I had never heard of a spy who signed with his own name articles against one party in a war and afterwards went to the territory of that party with his passport in his pocket.

She said the authorities would investigate that point, but that in the meantime General Franco had been asked to spare my life by the *News Chronicle* and by Mr H in New York; that she was the correspondent of the newspapers of Mr H in Spain; and that General Franco had said he might reprieve me.

For me this was rather astonishing news.

V: Dialogue with Death

So the tenth day of my imprisonment – Friday, February 19 – I learn that I am condemned to death and that maybe Franco will grant commutation – that means, according to Spanish law, thirty years in prison.

The young lady who brought me this news, and who happened to be the correspondent of a chain of American newspapers, asked me whether I wanted to make a statement for her newspapers on my feelings towards General Franco.

Now, if you note that word 'maybe' in the first sentence of this article you will easily understand the logical implications of the young lady's question. It was something like a Biblical temptation, although Satan presented himself in the smiling mask of a young girl journalist; and at that moment – after the infernal days of waiting for torture and death – I had not the moral force to resist.

So I said that although I did not know Franco personally I had the feeling that he must be a man of humanitarian ideas whom I might entirely trust. The young lady wrote this down, seemed very pleased and asked me to sign it.

I took the pen, and then I realized I was going to sign my own moral death sentence; and that this sentence nobody could commute. So I crossed out what I had written and dictated another statement, which ran:

> I don't know General Franco personally, and he doesn't know me; so if he grants me commutation I must suppose that it would be mainly a political act.
>
> Nevertheless, I could not help being personally thankful

to him, as a man thanks another who has saved his life. But I believe in the Socialist conception of the human future, and shall never cease to believe in it.

This statement I signed.

There was no need to tell you about the previous moment of weakness. But I don't pretend to play a heroic role and prefer the human one.

The day after the visit I felt an immense relief. The second day I remembered the fatal 'maybe'; the third day it became an obsession.

Uncertainty is half of death, says Cervantes; and so it is. Everybody has his own philosophy of death. As for me, I am not afraid of death, but very afraid of the act of dying. During three months I remembered at least ten times a day the verse of Rilke:

'Lord, I do not ask Thee for a worthy life, but grant me the favour of a worthy death.'

Now, to be executed in a civil war is just one of the unpleasant manners of dying. And I had all the time to think it over and over. You think a tremendous lot if you are alone and have got nothing to do but to walk up and down and up and down, six and a half steps up and six and a half steps down, for at least eighteen hours a day; and that during ninety-seven days.

It was frightful, but not so frightful as the reader may imagine it. Human nature disposes of astonishing mental resources of which you do not know in normal circumstances. It is just a question of inner discipline and mental exercise to mobilize these forces and to obtain with their help a state of mind which enables you to regard your personal fate as unimportant, and life and death with relative indifference.

But, of course, you cannot live permanently on the top of a magic mountain, and there were hours, even entire days, of an almost absolute despair impossible to describe. But there were also events of great joy, of an almost absolute happiness, which I had never known since I was a child and maybe never shall know again.

Such events were: when I got a piece of soap and a comb (ninth day); two cigarettes (thirteenth day); a pencil and five sheets of paper (twenty-seventh day); five new sheets of paper (thirty-third day); the first book – John Stuart Mill's autobiography in a Spanish translation (thirty-fifth day); and so on.

One of the best achievements of the young Spanish Republic are the so-called 'model prisons', of Madrid, Barcelona, Seville. They are built on the most advanced principles and are the best in Europe. The cell windows are spacious and look on the big *'patio'* (courtyard). Every cell is furnished with an iron bed, a straw mattress; an iron table and chair; a wash-basin with flowing cold water, and a w.c.

Of course, the present abnormal conditions affect prison life too. The Seville prison is overcrowded; with a normal capacity of 800 it has 1,300 prisoners, and most of the single cells are occupied by four or even five prisoners.

The warders and lower ranks of the prison staff are still the men of the 'ancient regime'; that means that they still have some of the humanitarian traditions of the Republic. About 50 per cent of the warders belong now to the Falange (the Spanish Fascist Party), but with a few exceptions their attitude towards the prisoners, and especially towards the political prisoners, has not changed. They are indifferent, or kind; some of them even very kind and nice. As I said, I am speaking only of the lower staff. During my sojourn in the prison of Seville none of the prisoners was beaten or physically ill-treated.

The food was the regular prison food – rather bad coffee in the morning, soup at noon and more soup at night with sufficient white bread. After a certain time I became almost accustomed to it.

At 6.45 a.m. a trumpet sounded the hour to get up. At 7.30 the prisoners, except those who were kept isolated like me, were let out on the *patio*, where, according to the Spanish prison custom, they passed practically the whole day.

There are two *patios*, a smaller one with trees and flowers, almost a garden, originally designed for the political prisoners, and a bigger one, without trees and without flowers, for the criminals. But since the civil war began the roles have changed: now the political prisoners are in the 'bad *patio*' and the murderers, thieves and robbers enjoy the flowers in the garden.

At 8.30, breakfast; at 12.30, the first soup. At one o'clock the prisoners are taken from the *patio* back to their cells, where they pass the siesta hours until 3 p.m.

From 3 till 7 they promenade again in the *patio*; at 7 the night soup; at 9.30 the trumpet again, and to bed.

Yes, the day-life in prison is quite normal. But there are the nights.

Those who are condemned to death are shot between midnight and two in the morning.

I have a feeling of sickness remembering the night when I first heard these executions.

I woke up about midnight. In the silence of the prison, the black air charged with the nightmare dreams of 1,300 sleeping men, I heard the murmured prayer of the priest and the ringing of the mass bell.

Then a cell door, the third to the left of mine, was opened and a name was called. A sleepy voice asked '*Que*?' ('What?'), and the priest's voice immediately became stronger and the bell rang louder.

And now the sleepy man in his cell understood. At the beginning he only moaned, then with a suffocated voice he asked for help: '*Socorro! socorro!*'

'Man, there is no help,' said the warder accompanying the priest.

He said it neither in a hostile nor a friendly manner, just as stating a fact. For a moment the man who was going to die kept silent; the sober, quiet voice of the warder puzzled him. And then he began to laugh.

It was not the loud, shrill laughter of actors who play a man becoming mad; the man tapped his knees with his hands and his laughter was rather quiet and oppressed, gulping and hiccoughing. 'You are making fun,' he said to the priest. 'I knew at once that you were making fun.'

'Man, this is no fun,' said the warder in the same dry voice as before.

Then they took him out through the main entrance of the prison. I heard him shouting outside. But the detonation came only a few minutes later.

In the meantime the priest and the warder had opened the next cell, the second on my left. (We, the condemned to death, occupied a series of neighbouring cells.)

Again: '*Que*?' And again the prayer and the bell. This one was weeping and sobbed through his nose like a child. Then he asked for his mother: *'Madre; madre!'*

The warder said, 'Man, why did you not think about her before?'

They took him out.

They went to the next door. When my neighbour was called he did not say anything. Most probably he was already awake like me, and prepared. But when the priest ended his prayer he asked, as if of himself: 'Why must I die?' The priest answered with five words, pronounced with a solemn voice, but rather in a hurry: 'Faith, man. Death means liberty.'

They took him out.

They came to my cell, and the priest pushed the bolt back. I saw him through the spy-hole.

'No, not this one,' said the warder.

They went to the next door. He was prepared, too. He did not ask questions. While the priest prayed, he began in a low voice to sing the 'Marseillaise'. But after a few bars his voice broke and he, too, sobbed.

They took him out . . .

Until April 14 – exactly two months after my transfer to Seville – I was hermetically isolated from the outside world and was not allowed to get out of my cell.

On April 14 I was allowed for the first time to exercise for two hours in the courtyard. When I came out to the fresh air I collapsed.

It was at 1 p.m., during the siesta hours, when the 'normal', non-isolated prisoners were in their cells. But there were three others out in the courtyard with me; all three condemned to death, too.

One of them was Nicolas, a former militiaman. He gave me a piece of green salad which he had got from his wife.

The second day, when I came out at one o'clock we were only three. Nicolas had been shot the previous night.

The same day – April 14 – I was allowed for the first time to write a letter. I wrote to the British Consul at Seville, and a second time, three days later. On the 21st I received the Consul's reply, telling me that he had asked the authorities for permission to see me.

On the 28th I received the Consul's first visit and heard for the first time that the British Government and British public opinion took a friendly interest in my case.

On May 4 I got a companion in my cell. He was an Italian officer of Franco's army, arrested because of some insignificant dispute with the Spanish civil guards.

On the previous night he had heard executions and had an hysterical attack: both his legs became temporarily paralysed.

He told me that he was with the Italian troops who conquered Malaga – now I had to nurse him. To the astonishment of both of us we became good friends.

On May 8 the Military Judge of investigation came, and for the first time since my arrest I was interrogated.

I asked the judge what the charge against me was. He said, that according to military law, the charge was kept secret. But I happened to see the cover of my dossier and learned that the accusation was 'aiding military rebellion'.

So the charge of spying was dropped by the rebel authorities themselves. Nevertheless, 'aiding military rebellion' is a charge which involves capital punishment.

Four days later – it was Coronation Day, but I didn't know it – my cell door opened and I was taken out of prison. I had no idea where we were going or what would happen.

They took me to the aviation camp; there a little baby Douglas machine was waiting. It had only two seats – one for the pilot, one for me.

An hour later we landed at La Linea, the Spanish frontier station next to Gibraltar.

There I learned that I would be exchanged for a prisoner of the Valencia Government – Señora Hayja, wife of the pilot who had brought me there.

I could not believe it. I was absolutely dazed. It was all like a dream.

I had to wait two days in La Linea prison. But at last, on Friday, May 14, I stepped through the iron gate which separates the land of war from the land of peace – the entry to the blessed soil of Gibraltar.

It is still like a dream . . .

The Tourists

The tourists were on their own trip to Spain. Some of their illusions and passions are captured in Stephen Spender's *Port Bou*: 'And I am left alone on the bridge at the exact centre ... At the exact centre, solitary as a target ...' The current expression, ego-trip, could apply to much of their writing and Spender shows us some 'Pictures in Spain' of a tourist junket to an International Writers' Conference. However his article, 'Heroes in Spain', transcends the personal and makes a bold, pacifist statement: 'The dead in wars are not heroes: they are freezing or rotting lumps of isolated insanity.' And his other writing here, especially the piece on Picasso's *Guernica*, is aware and effective.

The most sensitive of the tourists admitted their visitors' status and in so doing qualified their writing on the war. W. H. Auden's unknown 'Impressions of Valencia' begins in this diffident mood but ends in political hyperbole. Louis MacNeice took the tourists' qualification a step further in his 'Today in Barcelona' by using the very limited genre of travel-literature-in-time-of-war. Laurie Lee, however, is all ego as he situates himself amidst the 'breathing dead'.

Roy Campbell, who claimed to have fought for Franco but who apparently only visited a trench and fired a rifle, excoriates the Leftist poets. A true believer in the Catholic Apocalypse, he condemns 'joint MacSpaunday' (Auden and Co.): 'The scrawny off-spring and the bloated sire / Sentenced by nature to the same hot fire.' Drieu la Rochelle was equally fervent for the Nationalists and the excerpt from his novel, *Gilles*, is a fantasy of his hero on a spy mission behind Red lines in Barcelona (in fact, Drieu visited Burgos for a few weeks). Walter/Gilles' adventure begins the Epilogue of his novel; the previous section is called 'Apocalypse'.

The worst tourists were pompous and crass and, like the worst tourists anywhere, they never really left their native mental landscape. Although Theodore Dreiser begins his 'August in Barcelona' with a controlled sympathy for the Republic, he soon departs on his world-sized ego-trip: meetings with leading politicians, international conferences, inside information, etc. (And as Orwell said of that arch-tourist to the war, the Duchess of Atholl, 'I hope they found some butter for [her].') Ernest Hemingway's travels were recorded in many American newspapers. They included trips to Spain, the filming of *The Spanish Earth*, and a visit to the White House. The film script (excerpted here) is essential Hemingway: lean, spare, visual, and with little of the sentimentality of his Spanish war fiction. Henry Hart, also an American, travelled unnoticed; by chance, he visited Guernica a year before it became famous and he wrote a published letter about it.

A few tourists understood the Spanish war and portrayed it in an atypical way. Although Ilya Ehrenburg later returned to Spain as a correspondent for *Izvestia*, his memories of his first visit in the spring of 1936 show best his biased but acute political perception. Herbert Read's experiences in World War I, his visit to Spain, and his sympathy for the Catalonian Anarchists came together in three remarkably fine poems. John Dos Passos, the American-raised son of a Portuguese father, had known Spain for years and he was able to see the ironic distance between the tourists and the natives. But he is always aware that unlike the Spaniards he meets, he is a visitor and can and will leave. This knowledge shapes his final note of pathos on the war.

Ilya Ehrenburg

From *Eve of War 1933–1941*

I find it difficult today to describe the Spain of that distant spring: I spent only a fortnight there though later, during two long years, I saw it spattered with blood and in torment; I saw nightmares of war such as Goya never dreamt of; the skies exploded into the strife on earth; the peasants still fired shotguns, but Picasso, in creating *Guernica*, already felt premonitions of the nuclear insanity.

I remember huge bullfight arenas filled with tens of thousands of people: workers in caps, peasants in broad-brimmed hats, women with head shawls, potters, cobblers, schoolboys.

Rafael Alberti was standing on the platform. He was quite unlike Mayakovsky: he looked like a frail dreamer. Until recently he had been writing lyrical poetry. Now he was reciting a modern *romancero*; the verses swept over the crowd like wind over a copse, and the people roused, rushed out into the street. The Young Socialists wore red shirts, the Young Communists blue ones with red ties. Priests turned away, old women crossed themselves in horror, respectable middle-class people looked over their shoulders, Fascists fired from windows. The brilliant sunshine alternated with heavy purple clouds.

It was an unusual spring for Spain: almost every day there were noisy showers and the red earth of Castile was dazzlingly green. Dear God, how many joyous cries I heard, how many wonderful plans, how many vows and curses! I remember at a workers' meeting in the Asturian coalfields of Mieres an old miner with a lean face raising his miner's lamp and saying: 'Three thousand comrades have died to rid us of the Fascists. They'll be wiped out. We shall go on. That's all, Spaniards!'

In Oviedo I saw the ruins of the University. The people said, like the old miner: 'No, this must never happen again.'

In the Zama district Fernando Rodríguez took me to the People's House where in 1934 the suppressors tortured and killed the miners. There were faded bloodstains on the walls, and the names of those who had been shot scratched with fingernails. Fernando Rodríguez told me: 'They hung me up by my arms and pulled at my feet. They called this the "aeroplane". They poured boiling water over my bare belly and then ice-cold water. But I didn't tell them where we had hidden our arms.'

Some boys came to me and handed me a painstakingly written letter: 'Oviedo, April 22 1936. Comrades, the Red Pioneers of Oviedo send May Day greetings to our comrades in the Soviet Union. Comrades, we are preparing for the second battle, it will come soon. We shall fight staunchly and bravely. *Salud y Revolución!*'

As I stood at the window I watched the boys skylarking about as they left the hotel; what was going on was little more than a game for them. I do not know what became of them but in the autumn of 1936 I read in a Fascist newspaper: 'In Oviedo, children, corrupted by Marxist teachers, attacked our officers.'

That spring I met the daughter of an Asturian miner, Dolores Ibárruri whom the workers called La Passionaria. She was an important political figure but remained a simple woman; she had all the traits of the Spanish character: gravity, kindness, dignity, courage and, most endearing of all, humaneness. I was told how in Austurias she had released the prisoners: she arrived with a crowd of workers, gave the soldiers the command 'Dismiss!', entered the prison and, when all the prisoners had come out, laughingly showed the crowd a large rusty key.

The directors of Ciudad Lineal, the company that owned the Madrid tramways, refused to reinstate the 'rebels' dismissed in the autumn of 1934. So the workers took over the running of the trams. They bore the letters UHP – Union of Proletarian Brothers – and under this banner the workers in 1934 fought the Fascists, the Foreign Legion, the Moroccans misled by the generals. Apart from the three magic letters the trams looked the same as before – shabby, with clusters of lively urchins hanging on to them. Number 8 said: 'To the Cuatro Caminos terminus.' Nevertheless no one knew where this tram would end up – at the depot or on a battlefield.

While I was in Madrid Fascists attacked the workers. A general strike was declared. I was living in a big hotel: bootboys, lift-boys, waiters, scullery-maids, all left. The proprietor mobilized the numerous members of his family, saying: 'We shall safeguard the interests of our clients against these lazy bastards. In the meantime we shall ask our clients to do what they can to help themselves.'

Later I witnessed a tremendous strike in Barcelona. The Spanish bourgeoisie, indolent and carefree, was dismayed. A lawyer said to me: 'I could never have believed that the workers had so much power. If Europe doesn't take a hand we shall be dependent on these semi-literate loafers.'

The government tried to pacify everyone. The peasants were told that the Institute of Agrarian Reform would very quickly change their conditions. But the Institute was in no hurry. In Spain there is a saying *mañana por la mañana* (roughly: tomorrow will do) or, as the Russians put it: 'on Thursday after the rain'. The peasants began to plough up the huge derelict estates of various absentee Counts and non-Counts. They drew up title deeds. In Castilian villages I saw many such documents. Count de Romanones, a deputy to the Cortes, owned 15,000 acres on one of his numerous estates; the peasants disarmed the Civil Guards and drew up a deed transferring the land to a co-operative. In the kitchen of the house they found a ham and some potatoes and wrote a clause into the document to the effect that these provisions were to be restored to the Count. The peasants in the village of Guadamez wrote: 'We have taken over the land, the guards can bear witness that we have harmed no one by either word or deed.' The peasants of another village, Polán, wrote: 'On the morning of 30th March representatives of the Municipal Council, together with representatives of the Federation of Land Workers, have, in the presence of the estate servants, taken over Ventilozia, viz. 6,920 acres of land.'

In Escalona, in Malpica, in the Toledo region, I heard peasants cry joyfully: 'Land!' Old men astride undersized donkeys raised their clenched fists, girls carried kids, young men stroked old battered rifles.

In April the Civil Guard (*gendarmerie*) rose against the government. An Assault Guard (*Asaltos*) was set up but it, too, regarded the Ministers of the Popular Front Government with suspicion. The Fascists shouted: 'Down with Azaña!' Azaña was the Prime Minister and later became President of the Republic. The workers opposed the Fascists. One might have expected the guards to disband the Fascists who were clamouring against the government, but they did not dare touch the well-dressed *caballeros* and took it out on the workers.

ABC, the monarchist newspaper, openly demanded intervention: 'Hitler has said that he will not let it happen . . . Europe will refuse to live in the grip of the Bolshevik pincers.' The paper was appealing for donations; at the time I copied out the following items: 'An admirer of Hitler – 1 peseta. For God and Spain – 10. Wake up Spain! – 5. A Nationalist Syndicalist – 10. A supporter of the Falange – 5.'

The Cortes passed a bill depriving retired generals who acted against the Republic of their pensions. The military sneered contemptuously: the Popular Front would not remain in power long. The generals Sanjurjo, Franco and Mola made no secret of their plans; I was told that Sanjurjo had said: 'Only a surgical operation can save Spain.' Priests and monks exhorted men to fight for God and Order. The walls were chalked with the words: 'Wake up Spain!' The former rulers strolled unperturbed in the streets of Madrid; I once caught sight of Gil Robles drinking white coffee on a café terrace. During his term of office 200,000 Fascists had been granted the right to carry arms; no one attempted to take these arms from them.

I talked to Socialists, to Companys, the Catalan Nationalist leader who had been in prison until the victory of the Popular Front. Everyone realized the danger of the situation but said that they had to observe the Constitution: liberty must not be infringed.

Nobody was frightened of the stocky, correct *caballero* called Gil Robles, or of the articles in the Fascist papers, or even of the sermons of the fanatical monks. What was frightening was that the peasants exultantly brought out their old shotguns, the unarmed workers raised their clenched fists. Meanwhile the supporters of the Falange took occasional potshots. Machine guns were accidentally discovered in churches. The police, the Civil Guard, the army regarded the articles of the Constitution with far less respect than did the newly appointed Minister of Internal Affairs, Casares Quiroga, the Socialist Prieto, or the fiery Companys.

I had to return to Paris: the French general election was to take place on 26th April and my newspaper wanted me to cover it. I regretted leaving; I was falling more and more deeply in love with Spain. In my articles I spoke of the Fascist danger. In an old issue of *L'Humanité* I have found a short note on the speech I made in the Paris House of Culture; I said that the Spanish Fascists were bound to rise. But in my heart I did not quite believe it – because I did not want to. (Too often not only rank-and-file participants in events, like myself, but even quite important politicians have taken and still take their own desires for a sober evaluation of the real situation; this seems to be inherent in human nature.)

From time immemorial the Pyrenees have seemed to the French a wall beyond which lies a different continent. When a grandson of Louis XIV ascended the Spanish throne the French king is alleged to have exclaimed: '*Il n'y a plus de Pyrénées!*' Nevertheless the Pyrenees are still there. But now, in April 1936, I did not notice them: people raised their clenched fists in just the same way; at railway stations one could see the same chalkings: 'Death to fascism!' and in the train frightened middle-class people carried on the familiar conversations about the need to 'curb the loafers'. *Frente Popular* and *Front Populaire* sounded alike. France was finding inspiration in the example of Spain . . .

Paris now was quite like Madrid: it did not have behind it the Asturian rising, the tortures, the prisons, the firing squads. Nor did it have the fanatical priesthood and the sabre-rattling generals; the French bourgeoisie was far more enlightened and shrewd: it counted on starving out the Popular Front. And the victors laughed and gave little thought to the future.

I was finishing my book of short stories *Beyond a Truce*. Irina had arrived from Moscow. It was unbearably hot in Paris; Lyuba and Irina went to Brittany; I told them that I had to send a report on the July 14 demonstration to my paper and finish the book, after which I would join them.

I remember a stifling summer evening in the rue du Cotentin. I was writing; then I laid my manuscript aside and turned on the radio: Léon Blum is consulting with the Minister of Education. In Madrid the crowd is storming the Montana barracks. Barcelona . . . The Columbus Hotel . . . Artillery . . . Colonel Aranda . . . Fighting in the region of Oviedo . . . killed, wounded . . .

I jumped up. I had to talk to someone. It was late – midnight – I would not find anyone. Yet I could not remain alone in the quiet room.

And the announcer was calmly saying that at the Rose Show in the Cours-la-Reine the first prize had been won by the rose Mme A. Meilland.

For some people life was split in two on June 22, 1941, for some on September 3, 1939, and for others on July 18, 1936. In what I have already written about my life there must be passages very dissimilar from the experiences of my contemporaries: there was a time when we all had different destinies, different themes. But from that evening, my life began to be very much like that of millions of other people: an individual variation on a general theme. Words familiar to all of us describe the cruel decade: announcements, *démentis*, songs, tears, war communiqués, air-raid alarms, retreat, advance, short leaves, brief meetings at wayside railway stations, talk about diplomatic Notes, tactics, and strategy, silence about the most important things, evacuation hospitals, a vast all-embracing blackout, and, as a memory of the past, the fleeting beam of a torchlight.

W. H. Auden

'Impressions of Valencia'

From *The New Statesman and Nation*, January 30, 1937

The pigeons fly about the square in brilliant sunshine, warm as a fine English May. In the centre of the square, surrounded all day long by crowds and surmounted by a rifle and fixed bayonet, fifteen feet high is an enormous map of the Civil War, rather prettily illustrated after the manner of railway posters urging one to visit Lovely Lakeland or Sunny Devon. Badajoz is depicted by a firing-party; a hanged man represents Huelva; a doll's train and lorry are heading for Madrid; at Seville Quiepo el [*sic*] Llano is frozen in an eternal broadcast. The General seems to be the Little Willie of the war; in a neighbouring shop window a strip of comic woodcuts shows his rake's progress from a perverse childhood to a miserable and well-merited end.

Altogether it is a great time for the poster artist and there are some very good ones. Cramped in a little grey boat the Burgos Junta, dapper Franco and his bald German adviser, a cardinal and two ferocious Moors are busy hanging Spain; a green Fascist centipede is caught in the fanged trap of Madrid; in photomontage a bombed baby lies couchant upon a field of aeroplanes.

Today a paragraph in the daily papers announces that since there have been incidents at the entrances to cabarets, these will in future be closed at 9 p.m. Long streamers on the public buildings appeal for unity, determination, and discipline. Three children, with large brown eyes like some kind of very rich sweet, are playing trains round the fountain. On one of the Ministries a huge black arrow draws attention to the fact that the front at Teruel is only 150 kilometres away. This is the Spain for which charming young English aviators have assured us that the best would be a military dictatorship backed by a foreign Power.

Since the Government moved here the hotels are crammed to bursting with officials, soldiers, and journalists. There are porters at the station and a few horse-cabs, but no taxis, in order to save petrol. Food is plentiful, indeed an hotel lunch is heavier than one could wish. There is a bullfight in aid of the hospitals; there is a variety show where an emaciated-looking tap-dancer does an extremely sinister dance of the machine guns. The foreign correspondents come in for their dinner, conspicuous as actresses.

And everywhere there are people. They are here in corduroy breeches with pistols on their hip, in uniform, in civilian suits and berets. They are here, sleeping in the hotels, eating in the restaurants, in the cafés drinking and having their shoes cleaned. They are here, driving fast cars on business, running the trains and the trams, keeping the streets clean, doing all those things that the gentry cannot believe will be properly done unless they are there to keep an eye on them. This is the blood-thirsty and unshaven Anarchy of the bourgeois cartoon, the end of civilization from which Hitler has sworn to deliver Europe.

For a revolution is really taking place, not an odd shuffle or two in cabinet appointments. In the last six months these people have been learning what it is to inherit their own country, and once a man has tasted freedom he will not lightly give it up; freedom to choose for himself and to organize his life, freedom not to depend for good fortune on a clever and outrageous piece of overcharging or a windfall of drunken charity. That is why, only eight hours away at the gates of Madrid where this wish to live has no possible alternative expression than the power to kill, General Franco has already lost two professional armies and is in the process of losing a third.

* *

W. H. Auden's response to *Authors Take Sides on the Spanish War*: I support the Valencia Government in Spain because its defeat by the forces of International Fascism would be a major disaster for Europe. It would make a European war more probable; and the spread of Fascist Ideology and practice to countries as yet comparatively free from them, which would inevitably follow upon a Fascist victory in Spain, would create an atmosphere in which the creative artist and all who care for justice, liberty, and culture would find it impossible to work or even exist.

Stephen Spender

'Pictures in Spain'

From *The Spectator*, July 30, 1937

Before we left Minganilla – a village between Valencia and Madrid, where we were banqueted and, after the banquet, danced to by the children whilst the women without their men stood round weeping – a woman took me to her house, showed me photographs of her two sons, both on the Madrid front, and insisted on giving me half a dozen sausages, about half of all she had, because she felt certain that I would be hungry before we reached Madrid. Then we of the International Writers' Congress got into our cars, and, as my car waited for the 'caravan' to start, one old beggar woman pressed forward from the crowd to ask me for some money. I was about to give her a few coppers when a boy leapt forward and exclaimed, with a passionate gesture, 'No, no, give her nothing. The Spanish people do not accept charity.'

This little incident lives in my mind with several others which go to impress on me what I can only call the seriousness of the people's movement in Spain. Another is my surprise when I saw for myself that the University City – with the Government buildings only separated from those taken by the rebels by yards – is still used as a place of learning, for in half-ruined class rooms, their walls perforated with bullets, the soldiers attend classes.

The welcome given to the International Writers' Congress by the people of small villages, by soldiers in the trenches, by a deputation of tramway workers in Madrid, by the common people in the streets, in cafés, in barber shops, in bars, if they happened to realize that one was a member of the Congress, were all signs that the Spanish people have acquired that passion for education and popular culture which goes with a fundamental revolutionary change in a nation's life. It was our good fortune to symbolize popular culture for them, and this explains the great welcome which we received.

To me, perhaps the strangest of my impressions of Madrid was that of the interior of a great and massively built church on the outskirts of the city – looking over, I think that part of the front which is called the Caso del Campo – where a vast collection of treasures from the palaces and churches of Madrid has been collected. The domed, gloomy, vast interior of the church, with its congregation of royal coaches, rood screens, crucifixes, candelabras, tapestries, ceramics, was like a meeting of all the centuries in a solemn fancy-dress ball, not of people but of objects. Our little party from the Congress walked round, feeling as out of place as a member of the audience on a stage set. We made M. Julien Benda sit on a royal coach, which suited him well, M. Egon Kisch looked handsome in an eighteenth-century wig, but apart from these courageous isolated attempts we did not succeed in adapting ourselves to our surroundings. Myself, I made no attempt to take the plunge back into the past. On the contrary, I thought in terms of making films of these stage properties, particularly one propaganda film, to show that the Republic cares for Spain's art treasures.

In this church all the lesser works of art from the palaces and churches of Madrid have been collected. Along the passages, in vaults and in chapels, there were placed thousands of canvases, a varied and unequal collection of ceramics, ivory crucifixes, antique watches, jewellery, fans, and in one vault so many images of saints that we could only make our way through them along the narrow gangway which they had discreetly left. Our guide explained that this vault had been the home of what Franco refers to as the 'Quinta Columna' of his allies in Madrid. But some of the French writers lifted their fists in vigorous response to one Saint Anthony, whose clenched hand was raised in an eternal '*Salud*'. There are traitors in both camps.

Everything in this collection was catalogued, giving the name of the palace or church from which it was taken, as well as its number in the depository. Among the pictures catalogued here and in the cellars of Madrid, taken from private collections, are 27 Grecos, 8 Rubens, 13 Zurbarans, 51 Goyas, 9 Titians, 6 Tintorettos, 6 Tiepolos, etc. Many pictures and many valuable first editions and manuscripts have now been brought to light for the first time.

Other pictures and treasures are in bomb-proof and damp-proof cellars of Madrid. The pictures from the Prado are in the vaults and cellars of Valencia, each of them packed so as to protect it from the damp. I was assured by members of the Government that nothing from these collections has been destroyed or (as has been said) given to the Russian Government in exchange for aeroplanes. The only pictures going abroad are those lent to Paris for the Exhibition of Spanish Art. I saw some of the pictures that are soon to be in Paris in the chapel of a seminary at Valencia. The chapel itself was strongly built, but the main arches under which the pictures lay in packing cases had been further strengthened by piles of sandbags placed above pillars or reinforced concrete.

It is true that at the beginning of the Civil War Anarchists burned churches and buildings in Spain which they saw not as things of beauty but as symbols of tyranny and superstition. Yet even in these early days, they removed and collected the treasures of art from the churches, which have been saved. Maria Theresa Leon, wife of the great poet Rafael Alberti, told me that when the Government made an appeal that art treasures should be saved, they were embarrassed by the quantity of stuff, some of it good, some trash, which was brought to them. Naïvely and eagerly the people look on the art treasures of Spain as their own heritage. The spirit in which, during a terrible siege, under bombardments, in a time of penury and hunger, the Junta del Tesoro Artistico in Madrid collected and arranged and catalogued meticulously the objects which we saw in that great church shows the same seriousness as that of the boy who passionately forbade me to give money to a beggar, as that of the women in Minganilla who received us with tears and asked one of us to speak to them in Spanish, just to show that we understood their fate (*suerte*). A people who speak in the language of war and armaments are looking ahead a month, perhaps a year, to victory. But a people who educate the soldiers in the trenches, who collect the art treasures of the nation because they have become the concern of the whole democracy, are looking forward not a month or a year, but to a future in which whole generations are liberated not by guns, but by the great tradition of Spanish painting and literature.

'Heroes in Spain'

From *The New Statesman and Nation*, May 1, 1937

G, a driver in the convoy of the Unit to which I managed to attach myself from Barcelona to Valencia, was formerly a 'cellist in a Corner House orchestra. Fat, frank, spectacled, and intelligent, he had learned to drive a lorry on the day of his arrival in Barcelona: he drove with too much concentration, leaning over the wheel to fix his attention shortsightedly on the road. In a moment of emotion, when we were driving along the moonlit coastal road between Tarragona and Tortosa, he told me that he had only wept three times in his life: once, at the Wembley Tattoo when the whole crowd was hysterical with imperialist fervour, and looking round he had a sudden vision of what it all meant and was leading to; once, when after playing musical trash for months in the restaurant, he went to Sadler's Wells, and hearing *Figaro* performed, realized what music might be and what the standards were by which he earned his living; once, that very morning in Barcelona, when he realized, as he put it, that 'the people in this town know they are free'.

All the time I was in Spain I remembered these three occasions on which G had wept; they seem to me a monument of personal honesty, of the spirit in which the best men have joined the International Brigade. I believe that at certain moments in history a few people – usually unknown ones – are able to live not for themselves but for a principle. One man goes out to Spain because his dislike of the Corner House orchestra and his love of Mozart suddenly becomes a rule of action with which his own life is identified. A young girl, who happens to be an Anglo-Catholic, and who is politically ignorant, goes out to nurse the wounded because she wishes to alleviate human suffering. Her patients, as soon as they are convalescent, bully her for her lack of 'ideology', and she suffers far more than they are able to imagine.

The unity which exists today in Governmental Spain is the unity of a people whose lives are identified with a principle. This unity is real, though it is something far more difficult to put one's finger on than the obvious differences of the political parties. Talk to people and they are best able to express their differences of opinion, and these differences soon produce various degrees of feeling. Read the editorials of the newspapers in Valencia and the differences which are labelled under such initials as UGT, FAI, CNT, POUM, soon appear very alarming indeed, especially when 'unity' is being discussed. As one newspaper correspondent said: 'The more they speak of unity, the more they seem to quarrel.'

Yet the unity which was G's and my own first impressions of Barcelona is a reality which is probably moulding Spanish democracy more quickly than those who deal in journalism and political controversy realize. The attitude of the Spanish people to members of the International Brigade is a good test of their fundamental agreement. In the first place, propaganda about the Brigade has perhaps not been handled as tactfully as it might have been. For example, the battle of Morata was a turning point in the war because the Spanish troops rallied instead of fleeing at a critical moment. When I went along the lines at Morata, in March, I found that the Spanish Lister battalion was entrenched in positions nearer the enemy lines than any trenches of the Brigade. Yet almost all the credit for Morata has gone to the Brigade. Again, quite apart from the decisive action of the Republican Air Force, which is now 90 per cent Spanish, Spanish troops fought courageously at Guadalajara, yet all the glory went to the Italian Garibaldi battalion.

Tactless propaganda about the International Brigade might appear humiliating to the Spanish people, so it is sometimes suggested that the Brigade is rather resented in Spain. Yet during my six weeks of travelling in Spain I was almost invariably mistaken for a member of the Brigade and treated with extraordinary generosity on that account. Again, it is suggested that the Anarchists are afraid of what the Brigade may do after the war is won. But in practice, Anarchists and members of the Brigade work and fight side by side and the boundaries between political movements are broken down at the front.

I went to Barcelona, Valencia, Madrid, Morata, Albacete, and

Tortosa (where the entire population had camped out on the hills at night for fear of an air raid); and I travelled a good deal between these places, going in trains, lorries, and private cars. My first and last impressions were not the struggle for power amongst the heads of committees in the large towns, nor inefficiency and bureaucracy, common as they are during a revolution which is also a war; but the courage of the people in Madrid, the enthusiasm of 80 per cent of the people everywhere for the social revolution, the generosity of the workers wherever I met them, in the streets, in trains, in lorries; the marked difference between the awakening younger generation of Spanish workers and the stupefied older ones. Every observer who stays in Republican Spain comes back again and again to a realization that it is the people of Spain who count.

At first the war strengthened and unified the social revolution, but in the long run war demands its own measures which threaten to engulf the whole social system. I set beside the story of G, the lorry driver, the story of H, a member of the International Brigade, who first came out as correspondent for one of the most reactionary English newspapers. H fought in the battle of Morata, where there were four hundred casualties in three days out of a battalion of six hundred men. The worst part of this battle was fought without trenches or other protection, except olive trees, in hilly country amongst the fields and olive groves. On the first day of the battle a friend of H died of a stomach wound, bleeding to death. H stayed by him, under fire, until he died. That night H disturbed his comrades, who were trying to sleep, by walking along the lines shouting out that he was thirsty and must have water . . . The next morning he happened to be fighting next to a friend of mine in the olive grove. He said repeatedly to my friend: 'You see that wall over there? How far do you think it is?' My friend answered, 'One hundred yards.' 'Well, you take a range of 120 and I'll try one of 100,' etc. . . . That evening he appeared in the lines holding a bundle of telegraph wires which he waved above his head. He said, 'Look, I've cut Franco's communications.' He had gone mad.

I tell this story in order to counteract the propaganda about heroes in war. The final horror of war is the complete isolation of a man dying alone in a world whose reality is violence. The dead in wars are not heroes: they are freezing or rotting lumps of isolated insanity.

People try to escape from a realization of the violence to which abstract ideas and high ideals have led them by saying either that individuals do not matter or else that the dead are heroes. It may be true that at certain times the lives of individuals are unimportant in relation to the whole of future history – although the violent death of many individuals may modify the consciousness of a whole generation as much as a work of art or a philosophical treatise. But to say that those who happen to be killed are heroes is a wicked attempt to identify the dead with the abstract ideas which have brought them to the front, thus adding prestige to those ideas, which are used to lead the living on to similar 'heroic' deaths.

Perhaps soldiers suspect this, for they do not like heroic propaganda. When I was at the Morata Front several men complained of the heroics in Left-wing papers. Some praised very highly the report of the battle of Morata, written by Philip Jordan, which appeared in the *News Chronicle*: but they complained that even that, restrained as it was, was too heroic. I had the impression that soldiers in a war have an almost pathetic longing to know the truth.

I returned from Spain feeling more strongly than I have ever felt before that I support the Spanish social revolution. Since the war must be won if the revolution is to be retained, there is nothing to do but accept it as a terrible necessity. Shortly before he died, the poet Garcia Lorca is reported to have said that he would write in time of war the poetry of those who hate war; and when the Indian writer Mulk Raj Anand asked the soldiers fighting in the trenches at Madrid what message they would send to the Indian peasants and workers, they answered: 'Tell our Indian comrades that we hope that when the time comes, they will not have to fight for their freedom as we are doing.' I like the Spanish people because it seems to me that they are emotionally honester than any other people. There are few heroics, no White Feathers, and genuine hatred for the necessity of the war, in Spain. A war such as the present one may be necessary: but it seems to me that the Left-wing movement in this country can never afford to forget how terrible war is; and that not the least of its crimes is the propaganda which turns men into heroes.

Poems from Spain

Ultima Ratio Regum

The guns spell money's ultimate reason
In letters of lead on the spring hillside.
But the boy lying dead under the olive trees
Was too young and too silly
To have been notable to their important eye.
He was a better target for a kiss.

When he lived, tall factory hooters never summoned him.
Nor did restaurant plate-glass doors revolve to wave him in.
His name never appeared in the papers.
The world maintained its traditional wall
Round the dead with their gold sunk deep as a well,
Whilst his life, intangible as a Stock Exchange
    rumour, drifted outside.

O too lightly he threw down his cap
One day when the breeze threw petals from the trees.
The unflowering wall sprouted with guns,
Machine-gun anger quickly scythed the grasses;
Flags and leaves fell from hands and branches;
The tweed cap rotted in the nettles.

Consider his life which was valueless
In terms of employment, hotel ledgers, new files.
Consider. One bullet in ten thousand kills a man.
Ask. Was so much expenditure justified
On the death of one so young and so silly
Lying under the olive trees, O world, O death?

Port Bou

As a child holds a pet
Arms clutching but with hands that do not join
And the coiled animal watches the gap
To outer freedom in animal air,
So the earth-and-rock flesh arms of this harbour
Embrace but do not enclose the sea
Which, through a gap, vibrates to the open sea
Where ships and dolphins swim and above is the sun.
In the bright winter sunlight I sit on the stone parapet
Of a bridge; my circling arms rest on a newspaper
Empty in my mind as the glittering stone
Because I search for an image
And seeing an image I count out the coined words
To remember the childish headlands of this harbour.
A lorry halts beside me with creaking brakes
And I look up at warm waving flag-like faces
Of militiamen staring down at my French newspaper.
'How do they speak of our struggle, over the frontier?'
I hold out the paper, but they refuse,
They did not ask for anything so precious
But only for friendly words and to offer me cigarettes.
In their smiling faces the war finds peace, the famished
    mouths
Of the rusty carbines brush against their trousers
Almost as fragilely as reeds;
And wrapped in a cloth – old mother in a shawl –
The terrible machine-gun rests.
They shout, salute back as the truck jerks forward
Over the vigorous hill, beyond the headland.
An old man passes, his running mouth,
With three teeth like bullets, spits out 'pom-pom-pom'.
The children run after; and, more slowly, the women
Clutching their clothes, follow over the hill;
Till the village is empty, for the firing practice,
And I am left alone on the bridge at the exact centre
Where the cleaving river trickles like saliva.
At the exact centre, solitary as a target,

Where nothing moves against a background of cardboard houses
Except the disgraceful skirring dogs; and the firing begins,
Across the harbour mouth from headland to headland
White flecks of foam gashed by lead in the sea;
And the echo trails over its iron lash
Whipping the flanks of the surrounding hills.
My circling arms rest on the newspaper,
My mind seems paper where dust and ink fall,
I tell myself the shooting is only for practice,
And my body seems a cloth which the machine-gun stitches
Like a sewing machine, neatly, with cotton from a reel;
And the solitary, irregular, thin 'paffs' from the carbines
Draw on long needles white threads through my navel.

Fall of a City

All the posters on the walls
All the leaflets in the streets
Are mutilated, destroyed or run in rain,
Their words blotted out with tears,
Skins peeling from their bodies
In the victorious hurricane.

All the names of heroes in the hall
Where the feet thundered and the bronze throats roared,
FOX and LORCA claimed as history on the walls,
Are now angrily deleted
Or to dust surrender their dust,
From golden praise excluded.

All the badges and salutes
Torn from lapels and from hands
Are thrown away with human sacks they wore
Or in the deepest bed of mind
They are washed over with a smile
Which launches the victors when they win.

All the lessons learned, unlearnt;
The young, who learned to read, now blind
Their eyes with an archaic film;
The peasant relapses to a stumbling tune
Following the donkey's bray;
These only remember to forget.

But somewhere some word presses
On the high door of a skull, and in some corner
Of an irrefrangible eye
Some old man's memory jumps to a child
– Spark from the days of energy.
And the child hoards it like a bitter toy.

'Guernica'

From *The New Statesman and Nation*, October 15, 1938

Picasso's *Guernica*, at the New Burlington Gallery

André Gide writes in *Verve* that *Guernica* fails because it is *excentric*, it breaks away from its centre, or has no centre. Other critics complain that it is neither expressionist nor abstract, but falls between two stools; that it is terrifying without producing any sensation of pity; and so on. All these criticisms are attempts to answer the question whether or not this picture is a great masterpiece. Otherwise, they would not be criticisms at all, but just descriptions, which so far from being *against* it, might well be an account of its merits.

Guernica affects one as an explosion, partly no doubt because it is a picture of an explosion. If one attempts to criticize it, one attempts to relate it to the past. So long as a work of art has this explosive quality of newness it is impossible to relate it to the past. People who say that it is *excentric*, or that it falls between two stools, or that it is too horrible, and so on, are only making the gasping noises they might make if they were blown off their feet by a high-explosive bomb. All I can try to do is to report as faithfully as possible the effect that this very large and very dynamic picture makes on me.

In the first place, it is certainly not realistic in the sense that Goya's etchings of another tragedy in Spain are realistic. *Guernica* is in no sense reportage; it is not a picture of some horror which Picasso has seen and been through himself. It is the picture of a horror reported in the newspapers, of which he has read accounts and perhaps seen photographs.

This kind of second-hand experience, from the newspapers, the news-reel, the wireless, is one of the dominating realities of our time. The many people who are not in direct contact with the disasters falling on civilization live in a waking nightmare of second-hand experiences which in a way are more terrible than real experiences because the person overtaken by a disaster has at least a more limited vision than the camera's wide, cold, recording eye, and at least has no opportunity to imagine horrors worse than what he is seeing and experiencing. The flickering black, white, and grey lights of Picasso's picture suggest a moving picture stretched across an elongated screen; the flatness of the shapes again suggests the photographic image, even the reported paper words. The centre of this picture is like a painting of a *collage* in which strips of newspaper have been pasted across the canvas.

The actual figures on the canvas, the balloon-like floating head of a screaming woman; the figure throwing arms up in despair; the woman running forwards, and leaving behind one reluctant, painful, enormous, clumsy leg; the terror of a horse with open mouth and skin drawn back over the teeth; the hand clutching a lamp and the electric lamp glowing so that it shows the wires, as though at any moment the precious light may go out; the groaning bull, the woman clutching her child, a complex of clustered fingers like over-ripe fruit; all this builds up a picture of horror, but to me there is grandeur in the severed arm of a hero lying in the foreground, clutching the noble, broken, ineffective sword with which he has tried to ward off the horrors of mechanical destruction; and there is pity in the leaves of the little plant growing just above this hand.

Picasso uses every device of expressionism, abstractionism, and effects learnt from *collage*, to build up the horror of Guernica. Diagonal lines of light and shade in the background suggest searchlights and confusion, and the violent contrasts of the faces revealed in a very white light suggest the despair of light and darkness in air raids; despair of the darkness because it is too complete and you are lost; despair of the light because it is too complete and you are revealed to the enemy raiders.

The impression made on me by this picture is one that I might equally get from a great masterpiece, or some very vivid experience. That, of course, does not mean that it is a masterpiece.

I shall be content to wait some years before knowing that. But it is certainly worth seeing. And if you don't like, or resist, or are overwhelmed by explosions, there are the sixty-seven studies for *Guernica*, some of them quite unlike anything in the picture itself, which are certainly amongst the most beautiful and profound drawings Picasso has ever made.

(Ed. note: Picasso's *Guernica* is now exhibited at the Museum of Modern Art New York.)

Roy Campbell

From *Flowering Rifle*

Against the Bogus prophets of the Day
Chained to Corruption, Failure, and Decay,
What can I do but take the trampled sand,
Diestro by the Rightness of my hand,
Whose opening Palm, of Victory the Sign,
Branched from the mesa with the Bread and Wine
By the same toil engendered as the grain
With many million more, the Might of Spain,
With palms of triumph foresting the day
To wave the golden harvest on its way,
Of which strong millions, strictly contraband,
I introduce this sample to a Land
Where all the sweet emoluments are thrown
To that smug, sinister, and bungling drone,
The first-shut Left, so dextrous with the dirk,
The striker, less in battle than from work:
The weed of Life that grows where air is hot
With 'Meetings' for its aspidistral pot:
That leaves its labour to the hammering tongue
And grows, a cactus, out of hot-house dung;
A manual head-ache, fastened in a fist,
And fed with fumes of foul carbonic mist:
A vegetable cramp: a bolted clam
Whose grudging doors on life and daylight slam:
The 'No' to life translated as 'I Am',
A Life-constricting tetanus of fingers
Under whose sign an outworn Age malingers,
While from its back the nails eat slowly through
For communists out-fakir the Hindu,
And hanker for stagnation thrice as vast
Where all must starve beneath the lowest Caste;

The fungus that by still decaying grows:
Sleep's Aegis, save when dealing dirty blows:
Like the raised claw-bunch of an ancient stork:
With cork-screwed fingers, like a crumpled fork,
In a rheumatic ecstasy of hate
Clenched at the world, for being born too late;
This weary fist infects the world entire
As common in the palace as the byre,
As limply fungoid in the idle rich
As when it grimly toadstools from a ditch,
Or, friend to every cause that rots or fails,
Presides in Bloomsbury with tinted nails;
As doomed anachronisms, Sire and Son,
Capitalist and communist make one,
The scrawny offspring and the bloated sire
Sentenced by nature to the same hot fire;
So in red Bloomsbury the two are tied
Like gangsters to be taken for a ride –
Smug rebels to Society, the tame
Charaders in a dreary parlour game,
Where breaking crockery gives a lawless thrill
And Buffaloes each smug suburban Bill,
Where the Left Fist will pelt you from the fence,
But when you lift a hand in self-defence,
Although it scorns the bourgeois law and state,
Off to the lawyers takes the broken pate,
And at the first sign of a lifted quirt
Will cling its Mother Grundy by the skirt –
From every communist you can unsheath
The snug fat 'bourgeois' creeping underneath,
And every Babbitt is a foxes' hole
From which a scrawny 'comrade' snarls for dole!
So in Red Spain they're fighting side by side
By common desperation both allied,
Both indispensable and no more strange
Than the unhealthy hide is to the Mange –

Since my existence has been lived and fought
As theirs at Oxford ready-made was bought

And in my teens I'd shed like threadbare trousers
Every experience possible to Wowsers;
I know what wrings their withers night and morn
To wish (quite rightly) they had not been born
Since of the English poets on your shelf
The only sort of 'Worker' is myself,
Grown wiser in the company of mules
Than they with learned pedantries of fools,
And, since I was not sent with foreign cash,
Like some, to spread the bolshevistic rash,
Able both to explain the 'Spanish Worker'
From the inside, as to expound the Shirker,
The Communist, whose bungling Left we fight
With this Right hand – in every sense the Right!
So that when I approach that Red Left Lug
And honourably would discharge my plug
Of truth, the buckshot of my deadly mug,
To pepper with reality its dream –
Like an anemone, with folding seam,
Into its neck it tries to disappear,
And where it wagged the Man, he wags the ear, –
Who every time contrives to swing the lead
When I would raise my trumpet to his head,
Though in this cud of victory that I chew
There's balsam for the spittle of the Jew:
Since in a land where everything's called New
That's ready to dilapidate in two –
With '*New Verse*' and '*New Statesman*' to be new with
Alas, it's a New Newness they could do with!
All things that date the most, this label means,
Today's boneshakers, last night's crinolines,
That with the latest fashion and the mode
Still to the scrap-heap point the shortest road –
So I must strive its meaning to re-New,
And stir the fossils in their rancid stew,
By showing them a thing they've seldom seen –
A writer who is not a dead machine
Turned out like Ford cars in a time of crisis
From Charlie-factories of Cam or Isis

And only guaranteed to run down-hill
Where failure can be headed for a spill.
For naught have they espoused in prose or rhyme
But perished through incompetence or crime:
What they uphold of its own self will fall
And out the Blums and Beneshes will crawl;
Though Lenin triumphed, into fullness blowing,
Ere these lugubrious Mascots could get going,
That was his luck, for Luck where they appear,
As from a Bunyip, howling flies in fear –
As now poor Lenin's cherished dream of Spain,
Through their support, has gurgled down the drain:
When from his eminence Azana fell,
It was upon the day they wished him well;
A letter came, from Woolfs and Huxleys sent
Support and sympathy to represent,
And straightway all his energies expired,
Something collapsed in him, he went all tired
And from the State executive was fired:
And flawlessly this axiom has been kept
What Auden chants by Spender shall be wept –
Go ask the poor old Negus if I lie
And Largo Caballero by and by!
For they're signposts that always point the path
First to Geneva, afterwards to Bath,
When, crunched by the Right-handedness they lack,
Each Thug or slaver takes the scrap-yard track,
With these funeral croakers at his back;
Vultures and crows so rally to the field
And where they 'group' you know the doom is sealed,
Before it hits our nostrils ripe and hot
They've long ago divined the inward rot,
And as by sympathy I sense the rose
Of Victory before its buds unclose,
So they (before it trumpets to the nose)
Anticipate the maggot on its way
With it co-operate in swift decay.
And so with one more carcass strew the way:
Which you may spoor, by no exception crossed –

One trail of causes villainously lost!
See, how they come Democracy to save
The moment it begins to dig its grave,
While jutting bonework corrugates the scurf,
With murderous paws to shovel its own turf
A starved hyena at whose sapless dugs
The Russian Romulus in frenzy tugs,
While Spanish Remus has the brighter wheeze
To polish off its last remaining fleas –
Till even such a chump as Herbert Read
Woke up to it that things had gone to seed,
And chose the next most mouldy thing he could
That promised nits and jiggers in the wood,
Who now in Anarchism's foetid cell
The elixir of life pretends to smell.
Decrepitude for them's the only Right,
Though as 'humanitarians' they write
With greasy Tartuffades to slime the cause
That has more victims in its murderous jaws
Than ever were destroyed in mortal fight,
Blasted with bombs, or heaved with dynamite,
Or executed here, to serve them right:
Not only that, but if we well examine,
Invariably they side with filth and famine,
Morality for them has never mattered,
Except when crime or failure must be flattered:
For all their talk of what is Right or Wrong,
What matters most to them is – 'Does it Pong?'
For they'll have nothing but what's stale or late
And to be 'modern' must be out of date.
They bury facts as crocodiles their meat
Returning later to 'debunk' the treat
Which most they live for: like their friends, the Reds
Who pulled the mouldering corpses from their beds,
Who in Huesca's graveyard raised a Bar,
And drummed with thighbones to the shrill guitar,
Doomed by the same sub-realistic curse
In living bodies to forestall their hearse,
A doomed and dying species, with their cause

Condemned by the inexorable laws,
Who only by inversion can exist
As perverts, in a charnel-breathing mist,
From Death and Sin their scrawny themes to twist –
And with such bards to trumpet them to battle
No wonder British Reds stampede like cattle!

Theodore Dreiser

'Barcelona in August'

From *Direction I*, November–December, 1938

We felt war immediately as we crossed the border of Spain in an old car, and sped towards Barcelona. A sense of impending catastrophe difficult to define at first. Spain is beautiful. The air, the colour, the little farms, many unchanged in appearance, have great charm. But everything is infected by fear. A flight of birds may startle you as if it were an air raid. In all the little villages, the central squares or market-places are cut across by deep trenches into which people may throw themselves at the sound of the siren announcing aeroplanes. As we near Barcelona, shell-shattered homes and villages grow more frequent. I saw one village cut literally in half by a shell. One part standing and with people going about their business. The other smashed, wiped out, dead. Then several villages I saw were completely shattered, annihilated. Little villages, without any possible military significance. In these, most of the people were gone. But there were usually a few old ones, sitting in the ruins of their homes, cooking, even, between broken walls. In a certain village I saw only one old woman, sitting in a dream of misery.

Barcelona is a beautiful city. It is one of the fine cities of the world. I wish I could describe its charm beside the sea. It has great modern buildings, great powerful docks. Many have been destroyed, but it is still a magnificent city.

But five miles of serpentine subways cut under the city. They have built them irregularly, with openings at all sorts of unexpected spots, with several entrances at all central places. They have built them like rabbits' burrows, so that if one entrance or exit is blocked, they can escape by another. The passages are very clever and very deep. There is room for benches, in some places. In others real shelters, with running water, lights, have been prepared. Some people spend half the day in these places, when an air raid has been announced. Big sirens have usually time to announce a raid five minutes before the bombs can drop. Sometimes they keep screeching off and on for a whole day. There have been several three-day raids, when planes kept coming over the city again and again, not always to drop bombs, but to terrorize.

The hotel at which I stayed was a big handsome structure, in the most luxurious European style. Its kitchen had been carried partly away by a bomb. But business went on as usual. In the dining-room, waiters served on silver platters – one bun and the black juice they call coffee. There is no meat, no sugar, no butter, no milk. They serve a sort of pap, made out of vegetable matter. It is nourishing, to some extent, and fried with sauce, vaguely resembles meat. The heavy furniture and hangings are still there. But there are no sheets on the beds. All available linen or fine cloth has been taken for bandages for the wounded. There is no soap. In the whole of Barcelona, you cannot buy a piece of soap. When I had been there a few days, I developed an itch on my neck and cheek. I could get no soap nor ointment. At the drugstore, I was given a sort of herb, which had no effect on my neck whatsoever. I was told that all ointments or antiseptics were needed for the wounded. And over a third of the inhabitants of Barcelona are suffering from the 'itch' without any way of treating it. (It was only two weeks after I got back to Paris that I got rid of mine!)

The clothes of the people show what they endure. The clothes of the middle-class people are now as miserable as those of the poor. Their shoes are worn out, broken open, tied with strings. They go about on foot. Since one of the big power plants was destroyed, there are no street lights and no street-cars. A few official cars are the only means of getting about. Most horses and donkeys have disappeared. In the morning, you see little groups of people setting out on foot with sacks. They go out to forage in the country around Barcelona. They come back in the evening with a few sticks of fire wood, a cabbage, or a few turnips, etc., or with nothing at all. There are 12 million Loyalists in territory which before held about two million. They are slowly starving.

Suffering has brought out a marvellous spirit in the people which is stronger than anything you can imagine. I spoke to Del Vayo and Negrin. Del Vayo is a stocky, honest man in civilian clothes. Negrin, too, wears civilian clothes. They impress you as intellectuals rather than politicians. They said they had, in certain black moments, considered giving in, to save the people more suffering. But they were convinced that the people themselves would not give in. They would rather get new leaders and go on. Del Vayo said they can go on fighting for a year, a year and a half.

Such spirit as there is in Spain seems to me – well – beautiful.

Of course Hitler and Mussolini are backing Franco, but not to the extent he had hoped. On the other hand, France and Russia have not been helping the Loyalists nearly as much as has been thought. When I first arrived in Paris to attend a conference called by Bonnet of France and Lord Cecil of England, against the bombing of Open Cities, I was greatly surprised to find that the conference was a sort of diplomatic manoeuvre to reconcile other nations to England's attitude of Hands-off – the making of humanitarian phrases without humanitarian aims. In some measure, this prepared me for the attitude of Chamberlain and Daladier in the Czechoslovakian crisis. This indifference of certain powerful individuals representing England and France, to the fate of the Spanish Government. A protest was voiced against Hitler's treatment of Catholics, but no protest against Franco or Mussolini's bombing of Open Cities was allowed. The *Apasionara*, famous Loyalist woman envoy, was not allowed to speak. When they learned of my views on Spain at a luncheon just before I was to speak, they did everything to put my speech off, and only at the end of the session, as I still sat on the platform, were they obliged to call on me. (This speech was printed in *Direction* last month.) The next day I spoke at a French Writers' Congress which showed the true spirit of the French people towards Spain. But this spirit of sympathy and would-be co-operation, is everywhere blocked by those in authority. The Loyalists have large sums in the banks of Paris, which belong to the Government of Spain. But since Franco also claims these funds, financial powers have been able to keep them tied up 'till the end of the war'. The Loyalists need them desperately now, but are not even allowed credit against them. When I left Barcelona, I told Del Vayo I would telephone the French minister Bonnet to ask if he could send a few automobiles, urgently needed for transportation across the border. In Paris, Bonnet said he would see what could be done. But nothing was done, at least during the remaining two weeks of my stay in Europe.

*   *

Theodore Dreiser's response to *Writers Take Sides*:
I am against Franco and Fascism generally. My reasons are that I believe that Fascism means a lack of intellectual freedom, a strongly militaristic and repressive social control joined seemingly with the continuance and strengthening of false religious, racial and economic ideologies, and generally speaking, the antithesis of any hope for equitable treatment which other forms of government at least pretend to offer the individual.

As regards Franco specifically, I believe he stands for the continuance of the Dark Age in Spain, where the Church and the soldiers control the wealth and welfare of the country, to the enslavement of the great mass of the people. I don't believe that Franco or the Fascists would ever let the Church itself regain the enormous economic power which the Church in Spain had, but I do believe that the Church under Franco would be the same as it is under Mussolini, an instrument through which the great mass of the people may be kept ignorant and subservient to a system which promises nothing for them.

From *The Spanish Earth*

Reel One

This Spanish earth is dry and hard and the faces of the men who work on that earth are hard and dry from the sun.

'This worthless land with water will yield much.

'For fifty years we've wanted to irrigate, but they held us back.

'Now we will bring water to it to raise food for the defence of Madrid.'

The village of Fuenteduena where 1,500 people live and work the land for the common good.

It is good bread, stamped with the union label. But there is only enough for the village. Irrigating the wasteland of the village will give ten times as much grain, as well as potatoes, wine, and onions for Madrid.

The village is on the Tago River and the main highroad that is the lifeline between Valencia and Madrid. To win the war, the rebel troops must cut this road.

They [the villagers] plan to irrigate the dry fields.

They go to trace the ditches.

Reel Two

This is the true face of men going into action. It is a little different from any other face you will ever see.

Men cannot act before the camera in the presence of death.

The villagers of Fuenteduena hear this voice and say: 'Our guns.'

The front-line curves North to Madrid.

These were the doors of houses that are empty now. Those

who survived the bombardment bring them to reinforce the new trenches.

When you are fighting to defend your country, war, as it is, becomes an almost normal life. You eat and drink and sleep and read the papers.

The loudspeaker of the people's army has a range of two kilometres.

When these men started for the lines three months ago, many of them held a rifle for the first time. Some did not even know how to reload. Now they are instructing the new recruits how to take down and reassemble a rifle.

This is the salient driven into Madrid itself when the enemy took University City. After repeated counterattacks, they are still in the Casa de Velasquez, the palace on the left with the two pointed towers, and in the ruined clinical hospital.

The bearded man is Commander Martínez de Aragon. Before the war he was a lawyer. He was a brave and skilful commander and he died in the attack on the Casa del Campo on the day we filmed the battle there.

The Rebels try to relieve the Clinic.

Julian, a boy from the village, writes home. 'Papa, I will be there in three days. Tell our mother.'

Reel Four

Madrid, by its position, is a natural fortress and each day the people make its defence more and more impregnable.

You stand in line all day to buy food for supper. Sometimes the foods run out before you reach the door. Sometimes a shell falls near the line and at home they wait and wait and nobody brings back anything for supper.

Unable to enter the town, the enemy try to destroy it.

This [body] is a man who has nothing to do with war. A book-keeper on his way to his office at eight o'clock in the morning. So now they take the book-keeper away, but not to his office or to his home.

The Government urges all civilians to evacuate Madrid.

But where will we go? – Where can we live? – What can we do for a living?

I won't go. I am too old. – But we must keep the children off the street except when there is need to stand in line.

Recruiting is speeded up by the bombardment. Every useless killing angers the people. Men from all businesses, professions, and trades enlist in the Republican Army.

Meanwhile, in Valencia the President —

Julian catches a ride on an empty truck and comes home sooner than he expected.

Reel Five

Julian drills the village boys in the evening when they come home from the fields.

In Madrid, a future shock-battalion of bullfighters, football players, and athletes is drilling.

They say the old good-byes that sound the same in any language. She says she'll wait. He says that he'll come back. He knows she'll wait. Who knows for what, the way the shelling is. Nobody knows if he'll come back. Take care of the kid, he says. I will – she says, but knows she can't. They both know that when they move you out in trucks, it's to a battle.

Death comes each morning to these people of the town, sent by the Rebels from the hills, two miles away.

The smell of death is acrid high explosive smoke and blasted granite.

Why do they stay? – They stay because this is their city, these are their homes, here is their work, this is their fight – the fight to be allowed to live as human beings.

Boys look for bits of shell fragments as they once gathered hailstones. So the next shell finds them. The German artillery has increased its allowance per battery today.

Before, death came when you were old and sick, but now it comes to all this village. High in the sky in shining silver it comes to all who have no place to run, no place to hide.

Three Junkers' planes did this.

The Government pursuit planes shot one of the Junkers down.

I can't read German either.

These dead came from another country. They signed to work in Ethiopia, the prisoners said. We took no statements from the dead but all the letters we read were sad. The Italians lost more killed, wounded, and missing in this single battle of Brihuega than in all the Ethiopian war.

Reel Six

The Rebels attack the Madrid–Valencia road again. They have crossed the Jarama River and try to take the Arganda bridge.

Troops are rushed from the North for the counterattack.

The village works to bring the water.

They arrive at the Valencia road.

The infantry in the assault where cameras need much luck to go. The slow, heavy-laden undramatic movement forwards. The men in echelon in columns of six. In the ultimate loneliness of what is known as contact. Where each man knows there is only himself and five other men, and before him all the great unknown.

This is the moment that all the rest of war prepares for, when six men go forward into death to walk across a stretch of land and by their presence on it prove – this earth is ours. Six men were five. Then four were three, but these three stayed, dug in and held the ground. Along with all the other fours and threes and twos that started out as sixes. The bridge is ours.

The road is saved.

The water comes to bring more food. The road can carry it.

The men who never fought before, who were not trained in arms, who only wanted work and food, fight on.

Two Dispatches on Hemingway

From *The New York Times*, May 19, 1937

Hemingway Sees Defeat of Franco

'Returns from Spain Certain Rebels Will Be Unable to Capture Madrid

LIMITS WAR TO TWO YEARS

Says Rebel Failure at Bilbao Would Shorten Strife – Finds World Conflict Deferred'

Ernest Hemingway, novelist and war correspondent, returned from Spain yesterday on the French liner *Normandie* after spending several weeks with the Loyalist forces on the Madrid front.

Mr Hemingway said it was his conviction that the Insurgents were doomed to defeat, because he considered Madrid an impregnable city favoured with natural defence possibilities which General Franco could never overcome. He pictured the Loyalists as growing stronger every day in forces and morale, and the Insurgents growing weaker.

'If General Franco takes Bilbao the war will probably continue for another two years, and if he doesn't the war could possibly end late this Fall or in the Spring,' he said. 'The war has changed greatly. It is no longer a war of militia, but a serious war of trained troops, and the forces of the defenders of Madrid increase their strength every week, and time is definitely on their side. Franco has been hammering away at Madrid since last November, and he lost his chance to take the city in that first month.'

He said General Franco's Moorish troops had been largely

'killed off' and that there were no more to be had. Another arm of the insurgent force from which much was expected, the Italian division, suffered complete rout before the Loyalists, and the Italians have demonstrated their complete inability to fight on foreign soil, 'at least not in Spain', Mr Hemingway declared.

He said the Italians lost more men at Brihuega than in the entire Ethiopian campaign.

As to the German factor in the war, the author said that as far as he could find out there was no German infantry serving with General Franco, all the German soldiers being in the artillery, the air force, transport, signal corps, anti-aircraft and tank corps, or serving as technicians.

'The reason why Franco is out of luck,' Mr Hemingway said, 'is that Madrid lies in this big plateau, with all the defensive forces grouped together and fighting from the inside, like a boxer; they can make Franco lead every time anywhere along his tremendous front. To do so he has to move many times as far as the defenders. And each time there they are, waiting for him.'

He said the Spanish Civil War had undoubtedly delayed 'the coming European war' for years, because it has served as a proving ground for European war machinery. For one thing it had demonstrated that the German equipment is not up to what it should be for continental warfare, he declared.

The author said that Spain revisited was a revelation to him. He expected to encounter great difficulty getting to Madrid, but had none. In sections of the country where fighting is not being waged he found the people living normally, going ahead with their farming as though the rest of the country were not inflamed by war. He said he expected to find most of his old Madrid friends killed, but he found all but two or three still living in Madrid, unharmed.

From *The New York Times*, *July 9, 1937*

PRESIDENT SEES WAR FILM

Hemingway Picture of the Spanish Revolt Shown at White House

Special to THE NEW YORK TIMES

WASHINGTON, July 8 – President and Mrs Roosevelt saw a preview, at the White House tonight, of the film on the Spanish Civil War made by Ernest Hemingway. They invited a few guests to come in after dinner to see the film.

Mr Hemingway and Joris Ivens, Dutch director of the picture, were guests at the White House at dinner.

*　　　　*

Hemingway's response to *Writers Take Sides*:
Just like any honest man I am against Franco and Fascism in Spain.

Henry Hart

Letter to the editor of *From Spanish Trenches*, Marcel Acier

Guernica, Spain, February 20, 1937

Dear Marcel:

You asked me to write at least once and tell you what it is actually like here in the Basque country now that all Spain is in the turmoil of war. How often on the boat coming over I wondered what it would be like. In the United States there are only a few people, all over eighty, who remember what civil war is like.

In Bilbao, where we are staying, the war is a reality every minute of the day. The population has doubled and the streets are swollen with refugees. Sandbags are piled against the windows and everywhere there are signs – '*refugio*' – telling the people where to seek shelter when next the German planes are overhead.

But here in this lovely little village of Guernica – we could call it a village at home although it has five or six thousand people – I have no awareness of war. I cannot believe, as I sit in the window of this little hotel, that only twenty miles away is the battle line I visited yesterday, or that shells are falling in Madrid, or that Malaga is in ruins and seven thousand men, women, and children, fleeing from that unhappy city, have just been massacred from the air.

No, I have difficulty, here in this little country town, lying amid these grey and green Basque mountains, in believing there is a war. It is true that my eye cannot find any young men, but save for this, there is no sign of war. The señora who keeps this hotel talked at lunch about spring, whether it is really here, whether it is safe to plant, or whether a frost will come and destroy what was planted too soon. Yes, now that I recall a certain strain in her voice, I can see that her's is no ordinary concern. There is not much food, and an early spring will help. So perhaps I am shutting my eyes, as one does when one has been too long amid pain.

And yet this morning, when I visited the building which, a hundred years ago, housed the Basque parliament; when I saw the carefully preserved trunk of the great oak under which, many hundreds of years ago, the Basque parliament met and under which the Spanish kings swore to respect the *feuros* (the separate and democratic laws of the Basques); and when the librarian unlocked the vault and showed me the book of the Basque constitution, hand-illumined in 1342, and told me one of the sentences of our constitution is from the ancient code – it was as though the scholarly librarian and I were immersed in the remote past before Columbus set out on his voyage.

But I see now that once again there was an undertone, for when the librarian asked me to write a few words in the guest book, as he hospitably asks all who visit here to do, I wrote without thinking, and as a matter of course, 'May Euskadi (the Basque race) always fight Fascism.' And when I translated this, the librarian nodded and accepted it as a matter of course. And so you can see that though the serenity of this little town seems untroubled, there is underneath, in all of the people, the recognition that a modern scourge is abroad and that it must be vanquished . . .

Poems about Spain

Words Asleep

Now I am still and spent
and lie in a whited sepulchre
breathing dead

but there will be
no lifting of the damp swathes
no return of blood
no rolling away the stone

till the cocks carve sharp
gild scars in the morning
and carry the stirring sun
and the early dust to my ears.

Andalucia, 1936

A Moment of War

It is night like a red rag
drawn across the eyes,

the flesh is bitterly pinned
to desperate vigilance,

the blood is stuttering with fear.

O praise the security of worms
and cool crumbs of soil,
flatter the hidden sap
and the lost unfertilized spawn of fish!

The hands melt with weakness
into the gun's hot iron,

the body melts with pity,

the face is braced for wounds,
the odour and the kiss of final pain.

O envy the peace of women
giving birth and love like toys
into the hands of men!

the mouth festers with pale curses,
the bowels struggle like a nest of rats,
the feet wish they were grass
spaced quietly.

O Christ and Mother!

But darkness opens like a knife for you
and you are marked down by your pulsing brain

and isolated,

and your breathing,

your breathing is the blast, the bullet,
and the final sky.

Montpellier,
October 1937

Louis MacNeice

'Today in Barcelona'

From *The Spectator*, July 20, 1939

I was in Barcelona from 29 December till 9 January. The most surprising things I saw were on 9 January – in Toulouse, where I landed by plane from Spain: food in the shops and on stalls in the streets, drink in the cafés, well-clad people, the street-lamps lit. It only takes one ten days to find these things surprising.

I had arrived in Barcelona after dark, the streets like limbo but crowded. A feeling of thousands of people circulating round one in the night. That is one thing there is plenty of here – human beings; two and a half million now against one million before. These people's lives have become very much simplified and as-similated to one another; the topics of conversation are few and universal, money has lost its diversifying force, and everyone, one feels, is by necessity in the same boat. For this reason one feels very much at home in the dark streets of Barcelona. There may be bitter dissensions among the politicians, but the people in the streets, one feels, have become a family party – or, if you prefer it, are in on the same racket – united by material necessities, by hunger, by the fear of sudden death which enhances the values of life. I have never been anywhere where these values were so patent. It would be difficult to be a Hamlet in Barcelona.

The shops are ghosts of shops, only open in the morning, the counters and shelves bare, one object every two yards. The cafés are ghosts of cafés – no coffee, beer, spirits, or wine, people making do with coloured water which is called lemonade or with terribly degraded vermouth (yet in one café there was a string quartet). They close at nine and the chairs are piled on the tables. But the people, though thin and often ill, are far from being ghosts of people. Facts in a city at war are necessarily uncertain; how can one know the truth about the Front or unravel the paradoxical knots of Spanish party politics or sort out truth from propaganda? One fact, however, is as clear – and as refreshing – as daylight: the extraordinary morale of these people – their courage, good-humour, and generosity.

Their strength, of course, can also be their weakness. Optimism on the Government side has already meant several gains for Franco. Again, while a people must obviously adapt themselves to war conditions, it does not seem altogether desirable that war should become quite so much a habit as it has in Barcelona; one feels the people have almost forgotten about peace and might not know what to do with it if it came. Yet without this confidence and this adaptation to circumstances, Barcelona no doubt would have already given way to Goliath. Her people are essentially non-defeatist; no one this New Year admitted for a moment that Franco's present offensive might succeed. I saw a new *comedor* [dining-hall] for children in an industrial district, which is being converted from a theatre and adjacent cinema.

In this, once the great city of cafés and taxis, you now have to get about by walking. And instead of cocktails and seven-course meals there are food queues, rationing of acorns, a ladleful of lentils for dinner. By ordinary people food cannot be bought though it can be obtained by barter: soap, flints, and tobacco are among the best currencies. (I am told that Arabs come into the port and sell soap at 250 pesetas a kilo.) In my hotel (where the bombing commissions stay) we had a privileged access to food – at fancy prices: a dish of chickpeas at 30 to 40 pesetas, horse and chopped swedes at 45, fried sprats (a very rare delicacy) at 60. (A superintendent of a *comedor* gets 400 pesetas a month salary.) People's rations at the moment (they are always decreasing) are as follows: Bread: 150 grammes per day except on Sundays; chickpeas (100 gr.) and peas (50) on one ticket, but you only get these once a week or maybe once a month; Oil: 1 litre, but they have had none now for three months and then it was like machine oil. They have had no fish on ration tickets for two months, no meat for one month. Those who, instead of having ration-cards go to the *comedores*, seem to me to be better off, because at any rate they know what they will get. And the children are considered first; for all that their diet is causing a vast increase in rickets and in skin diseases such as scabies. I should add that the people who work in the *comedores* seem invariably good-humoured, kindly, and strictly conscientious.

In these extremities statistics are more important than impressions, but here are some snippets from my visit. The crowing of cocks: most characteristic sound in Barcelona (as if you were to hear cocks in Piccadilly). Lots of people keep hens or rabbits on their window balconies. Lack of tobacco: to give a man a cigarette is to give him the Kingdom of Heaven; I gave a Spaniard three cigarettes one night, and next day he sent me in return a hunk of dry bread wrapped in paper. Refugee colonies: often in converted convents, beds in the gloom under towering Gothic arches, old women with eye diseases making jokes about Mr Chamberlain, the children doing eurhythmics. Schools: shortage of teachers, but the children clean (though washed in cold water) and happy. The walls often decorated with figures from Walt Disney – the Big Bad Wolf representing Fascism – or with Popeye the Sailor knocking Mussolini for a loop. All the children seem to be natural artists; in some schools they still print their own poems on lino-cuts.

Air raids: The siren is like the voice of a lost soul, but the anti-aircraft defence is beautiful both to hear and to see – balls of cottonwool floating high in the blue day, or white flashes at night. The searchlights also are beautiful, and the red tracer bullets floating in chains gently, almost ineptly, upwards like decorations at a fair. After the raid on the centre on New Year's Eve the streets were heaped with powdered glass, and crowds collected to look at a spatter of black blood-spots 15 feet high on a wall. During an alarm in Tarragona four girls romped down the square with their arms round each other's necks. Ruins: near the cathedral a house six storeys high, its face and floors torn away; on the top storey a plate-rack fixed to the wall with all its plates unbroken and a shelf with two unbroken bottles. The district to the side of the port, Barceloneta, has been evacuated; all the streets are rubble, and all the houses like skulls. Irony: the Banco de Vizcaya still announces stock market prices for July 17, 1936, and the chemists sell cures for obesity. Recreation: every Friday afternoon a crack orchestral concert, well attended, in the enormous Teatro di Liceo; the theatres and cinemas all running; a newsreel showing a fashionable dog show in Moscow. And people still playing *pelota*. But the

Zoo is macabre – a polar bear 99 per cent dead, a kangaroo eating dead leaves.

In the Barcelona airport I met an American seaman, an ex-member of the International Brigade, short, square, and tough, with a face like a gangster. On his lapel he wore the insignia of all the Government parties – to create good feeling, he said. He expressed the greatest admiration for the Spaniards – even, in spite of what some people say, as soldiers. I shared his admiration and, as I flew down from the Pyrenees to a country where money still goes, I felt that my descent into this respectable landscape was not only a descent in metres but also a step down in the world.

*   *

Louis MacNeice's response to *Authors Take Sides on the Spanish War*: I support the Valencia Government in Spain. Normally I would only support a cause because I hoped to get something out of it. Here the reason is stronger; if this cause is lost, nobody with civilized values may be able to get anything out of anything.

Drieu la Rochelle

From *Gilles*

Between his closed suitcase lying on a folding stand next to a narrow washbasin, and the bed upon which he had earlier stretched out, a man was walking, doing an about-face after every two steps. He smoked cigarette after cigarette. Now and then, even though it was August, he coughed and spat. The man was in his shirt-sleeves and sweated continuously. Was it only because of the heat?

Nervously, he kept looking at his watch. Once he saw himself in the mirror but turned away.

He was waiting for a certain hour to come, and at the same time he feared what that moment might bring. He forced himself not to look too often at his watch, each time he raised his wrist he began smoking again deeply, pleasurably.

Finally, since night had long ago fallen in the narrow street where his hotel stood, his time came and he suddenly left the room.

At the bottom of the staircase, in the entry-way, a fat man seemed to be waiting for him. He called out in broken and heavily accented English:

'Well, here you are Mr Walter. I was going to leave without you.'

'You would be mistaken if you had,' the man answered, in the same language but with a different accent.

The porter looked at both of them suspiciously.

The two men went out. Walter addressed his huge companion:

'Mr Van der Brook, we shouldn't go into that quarter. Contrary to what you think, it has to be much more dangerous than before.'

'Walter, you saw last night that life went on there just as before.'

'Yes, but yesterday evening we didn't go anywhere; whereas

tonight you want to go in places. People are going to notice us.'

'Ah! women always need money, and no civil war is going to stop them.'

'Men need money too. You're too well dressed . . . And don't talk so loud.'

'Ah! tomorrow I'll be gone. I've got my reservation on the plane. You can always work around the situation, wherever you are.'

Walter looked at him coldly.

The other man added:

'You too will soon have your reservation to leave, on a ship.'

Walter was quite embarrassed to cross the Ramblas with this fat Dutchman who looked exactly like the caricature of a bourgeois in a Communist newspaper. He was huge, with a ruddy complexion and had a smugly cunning air. He probably understood nothing of what was going on around him and, in spite of a certain cowardice which possessed him, he seemed oblivious to the ever-present dangers. It was true that he drank constantly, and before leaving the hotel he must have lifted quite a few. Walter had met him the previous evening in the lobby of the hotel. When the Dutchman said he was leaving by aeroplane, Walter hadn't left his side.

Walter looked at no one and walked as though in a dream. Was the danger he was running more deadly in the streets than in his hotel? In any event, it wasn't in his room that he would find a way to leave Barcelona.

They had crossed the Ramblas diagonally and came into the Barrio Chino. The crowd wasn't quite as thick there and it seemed to Walter that every pair of eyes was fastened on them. How far would they be able to go? To the corner? To the next?

Were they followed? For a time it seemed as if they were.

Van der Brook demanded that they first have a drink in a bar, in order to feel the pulse of the area. No one appeared to pay much attention to them there, but was it real? They finally went to the night-club that was Van der Brook's goal. Walter knew it well. He had been there in quite different circumstances. Everything had changed: himself and the world. In previous times he could have said that he certainly fitted in well in this world which moved slowly but surely to its horrible conclusion. But for the time being at least, his consciousness was reduced to the narrow reflexes of fear. He was tempted by death, but each time he found himself in death's grip he trembled ceaselessly.

The presence of danger weakens the very depths of being, and brings about wondrously quick changes and mimicry. Walter didn't ask himself, upon entering the cabaret–brothel, how the people there were going to act, he knew immediately that he would adapt to their style. He was totally 'within the context of facts' as teachers say in their quiet little classrooms.

There were many people in the *Lune* cabaret: show-girl whores and spectators mingling as usual, these latter being of quite varied yet undetermined social origins. And not everyone in the place looked shifty.

Their presence went unnoticed. However Walter wasn't very reassured and wondered why he had given in so easily to the other man. Couldn't he have taken him elsewhere right away? But for that the Dutchman would have to have been drunker, and he was too used to liquor so he was just a little high. What is more, if he drank too much he would make them conspicuous.

From what Walter knew, this Van der Brook was simply a business man of the worst sort, and a drunkard, and yet there was in his attitude, in the midst of these events, something which transcended this description, a kind of incomprehensible calm or absurd defiance. The Dutchman invited first two, then three women over to their table, among whom his preference seemed equally divided. These women, almost naked, appeared immediately to Walter to be the most familiar monsters of his nightmare of fear, as distant or as close to him as the men who would perhaps kill him. Nothing could surprise him, everything confirmed in his mind the ghastly certainty of the world's unrelenting movement.

The women, who had been among the first of the mob that had set upon them soon after their arrival, looked at them with a hateful yet fearful curiosity. Each of them wondered what they were. Were they the masters of the day? But which masters? Anarchists? Communists? Of course there were still many foreigners in Barcelona, but they scarcely ever showed themselves. Considering their quite clean appearance and their Nordic looks, they were doubtlessly taken for Communists more or less Russian or Russi-fied. Yet the club and the quarter were under the control of the Anarchists and the POUM.

From the first words spoken to his companion and himself, it was obvious that the women thought themselves under observa-tion from the neighbouring tables. There were several members of the Anarchist militia. He began to study the manner of certain looks while he pretended to drink, smoke, and flirt with a sad, scared brunette whose glances around the room he watched care-fully to better direct his own.

In any case they asked questions:

'What country are you from? What are you doing in Barcelona?'

Van der Brook, while answering that he was a Dutchman, made the cajoling gestures of a shop-keeper on a spree. He also said that he was a salesman, a Socialist, and that he was in good stead with the current leaders. As for Walter, he was Belgian, a chemist on a holiday and also a Socialist.

Van der Brook seemed relaxed but Walter none the less noticed that he too was secretly studying the room. From time to time he looked towards the door and didn't miss a single entrance. He was loud, drank a great deal, and stood rounds for everyone. That was bad. Stares riveted on them; Walter realized that they were coming from only one table. At that table there were four or five men. Their undivided attention was on them; less for Walter, poorly dressed and quite retiring, than for Van der Brook. They were un-doubtedly dreaming about his money. They were going to give him a rough time. They were talking about it, or so it seemed, among themselves. There was going to be a fight. He weighed the possibilities for a moment, then decided on a course of action:

'We're being watched,' he said to his companion, as though telling him a good joke. 'There are some men who want your wallet. For God's sake don't show it, don't look at anyone. And keep laughing.'

He guffawed, while the other man, not at all troubled, looked at him with a strangely disdainful expression. None the less he also burst out laughing, and with more ease than Walter. Walter ex-changed a few words with the sad brunette, then said to Van der Brook in English:

'I would advise you to go to the lavatory. While you're there try to find a way out. I'll join you later in the main street we left before coming into this little one.'

The other man turned a little too quickly to see who was coming in. Each time that he looked at the people entering he seemed somewhat disappointed. Was he waiting for someone? Didn't he really come here just to have a good time?

'You're getting rid of me,' said the Dutchman with a frown.

'Don't be ridiculous. I told you not to come here. I'm giving you your only chance to get out. If we get up together they'll jump us.'

Still the Dutchman slyly studied the room.

'OK.'

The Dutchman's blotchy skin clouded somewhat and he sweated twice as much as before, but he didn't tremble. Why didn't he tremble? That old Holland phlegm?

Walter and Van der Brook talked leisurely with the women. Then the Dutchman said:

'If I leave without paying and you stay . . .'

'I'll pay. I'll take care of it.'

Walter didn't quite know how he would take care of it. For the time being he hoped that the others wouldn't think that Van der Brook was trying to run out. Then, if Van der Brook found a way out, that they wouldn't come after him because he looked like only a chance drinking acquaintance. Ever since his entrance he had forced himself to speak to the Dutchman in the obsequious and envious manner of a tourist guide.

They kept on talking, laughed, tried to joke. The Anarchists seemed less interested in them than in two men who had just come in and sat down not far from Van der Brook. He too had noticed them and suddenly seemed to relax. He got up and with an obscene gesture showed he had an urgent need. One of the women laughed, patted him on the belly, and started off with him to the toilet. That was all right. Walter went back to his conversation with the sad brunette. But everything was becoming silent around him. Out of the corner of his eye he saw the trouble about to start.

Two men at the dangerous table got up, laughing derisively. Each of them had a huge Colt on his hip. The silence at that table spread to two or three nearby groups. Oh! of course the majority of people in the room continued their chatter, yelling and laughing.

But just as the two Anarchists were about to catch up with the Dutchman, the two other men, whom Walter had scarcely noticed and who had entered a short time before, also got up and blocked their way. They spoke in muffled, conciliatory tones, yet there was a real hardness in their stance. What did it mean? Walter looked around for the Dutchman; he had disappeared.

The two Anarchists had been joined by their table partners: all of them were outraged, screaming and pulling out their revolvers. Walter got up and easily made his way to the street door. No one stopped him nor talked to him: he probably went unnoticed, all attention was concentrated on the fight. As he left a shot rang out. He turned around – a distant scuffle, then he was outside.

On an obscure impulse he plunged into the first doorway to his left. It was a sort of open-air passageway where he bumped into a heavily breathing body – Van der Brook. Walter had a hunch: 'He's not the man I thought. Those two were blocking his escape and were protecting him personally. They came in after us, we were followed.' Van der Brook moved towards the street but Walter said:

'No.'

They huddled together under a porch overhanging the passageway. Not much protection, but what could they do? Walter was breathing nearly as heavily as the other man.

Van der Brook tried the door against which they had crouched.

'It's opening,' he rasped.

They found themselves in a rather dark room, poorly lighted from the street by only a faint ray; it seemed to be a store, more or less abandoned. Van der Brook snapped on his lighter, his fat hand no longer shook; Walter, still trembling, examined Van der Brook's determined face, before checking out the room – it was in fact an empty store with another door opposite the one they had just closed.

He asked:

'Who are those guys that intervened?'

The other man put out his lighter and answered in a harsh voice unknown to Walter:

'I don't know.'

Walter, however, thought quickly to himself: 'Who does he work for? For us? No. My instinct tells me otherwise. In any case I must do what I have to, it's my only chance to leave Barcelona.'

The other man put his lighter on again. Walter looked at him intently. 'I can't believe he's one of ours. Shit! who cares anyway. I'm not going to take any chances by asking questions.' The other man also looked at him in a shrewd way, as he had never done before. (He's a tough one. Me too, maybe.) The Dutchman said:

'Stay next to this door, I'll go to the other.'

'OK.'

He moved away, turning his back on Walter who felt around in his pocket. He took his revolver by the barrel and struck the other man, with all his strength, savagely, on the back of the neck. Van der Brook gasped, then reeled forward. The lighter had fallen. Walter threw himself forward also, groped and swung. His blows met only air. The other man had fallen, grunting like an animal.

Walter was on him, finding his head and pounding again and again with short, swift blows. The head fell back on the floor. Gilles felt for it again and hammered away about the temple. He stopped ... The other man only moaned. Then he stuffed the revolver into his pocket, and with both hands squeezed the Dutchman's neck for a long time.

He struck a match. The man was lying on his shoulder, his nose flattened against the wooden floor. Walter knew where he kept his wallet, took it out and went to the second door. It was locked. He went back to the door through which they had entered. He opened it and, losing his head, ran towards the street without closing it. In the street he turned left, the opposite direction from the night-club, not even glancing that way. After a few steps, taking hold of himself again, he made a painful attempt to slow down, to act normal. Oh my God! no street to the right or the left. Yes, over there, far away, on the left. Run? No. Slow down, slow, more.

'I'm going to live, I'll make it. No one will call out, no one will see me. I'm invisible.'

Everything always happens: he came to the corner, turned, it was a dead-end. He walked back. Far away there was a crowd in front of the night-club. He turned away from it and walked like a drunk trying desperately to go in a straight line. No one called out or ran after him. He was starting to like this street, it was friendly to him.

Later after several detours and several mistakes, he found himself on the Ramblas. Why the Ramblas which had seemed to him earlier such a dangerous place? Still, after all that had happened, he needed to mix with the crowd. He felt Van der Brook's wallet in his pocket and little by little regained confidence and boldness. He even discovered that this was the best place to look through the contents of the wallet. While walking among the hurrying groups he opened it. Yes, the Air France airline ticket was there. And in another compartment there was money, a lot of money. This sudden discovery of money astonished him, he hadn't thought about it. He remembered Van der Brook for the first time. Was he dead? Oh God! was he really dead? Yes, he had choked him long enough. What if they found him right away? He hadn't closed the door. What madness! Exactly the kind of stupidity that does one in. What about those fellows who had stopped the militiamen? They knew Van der Brook; they must know that he was going to take the plane the next morning. There were other papers in the wallet. He took out two or three and put the wallet back in his pocket. Throw them away? Not yet. Suddenly he wanted to smoke and he realized that he had not thought about smoking since leaving the dark store. He slipped the papers into his pocket and took out the pack of cigarettes that he had almost finished off at the hotel two hours earlier. What time was it? Eleven. That first cigarette was delicious. Oh! to smoke, smoke all his life. But he was thirsty. A horrible thirst. Funny, he was never thirsty, but he was now. Amazing what a man must do to be thirsty. Go and drink. But first let's look at those papers. Maybe he was going to learn who Van der Brook really was. Passport? Yes, Dutch. Maybe false like his own. Credentials. Some more ... Jesus Christ! International Red Relief Fund ... Comrade Van der Brook ... He was a Communist. Oh well, so much the better, at least he hadn't knocked off a neutral or a pal. But then that was bad for the plane trip ... In the middle of the Ramblas he began sweating again. Even without this business the undertaking was already dangerous enough: pretend that he had purchased this ticket at the last minute from Mr Van der Brook who was on the passenger list.

But that was impossible. He was sweating. His cigarette was almost finished but he didn't light another. All of this, for nothing. An idea. Arrive at the last moment and, without mentioning Van der Brook, ask if by chance there might be an empty seat. They would give him the seat of the missing passenger. But they would rather give it to someone known to them. There must be plenty of candidates. Even so, it might be worth a try. The plane was leaving at six. What could he do until then? Not go back to his hotel. Although he was convinced that he wasn't at all suspected, he could be the victim of a police raid. Go over to the port and find a place to sleep? Or go immediately to the airfield? How? One important thing: don't arrive at the airfield looking too dirty or too much like a fugitive. It would be bad not to have any luggage. The most dangerous thing was walking about alone. 'I've been in the streets alone so often, how suspicious I must have looked.'

He glanced at the other papers. A short, handwritten message greatly interested him. Damn. That was a find. He read and re-read it several times. Then put it back in the wallet with the other papers. He placed the ticket to one side with the money. The money would come in handy from now on until his return to normal life. If I don't use it I know to whom I can give it.

He went into a bar, went directly to the toilet, threw the wallet on top of a cabinet, returned, asked for a beer, and right off the bat started a conversation in gibberish with the first person to come in. He was a hard to understand idiot who looked at Walter with those surprised yet wary and stupid eyes that he had so often seen across from his own. Annoyed, he turned towards three barroom philosophers who, in infinite detail, were commenting upon a short fascinating discussion that one of them had had two hours earlier in a garage, it seemed, with a fellow upon whom he now heaped all the sins of Israel. 'So I said to him . . .' As soon as Walter had let out three words of his rotten Spanish the three irate citizens forgot, in an instant, the highly interesting subject of their conversation and began looking him over.

Walter said he was going to join the militia: ordinary men, of the free-floating type, in all countries and in all circumstances, dislike volunteers. Going over and above the call to war seems to them a spoiling of man's principal task – which is to do exactly that for which they criticize the bourgeois: to enjoy life not without some complaining. Walter was sorry he had spoken.

'You got any family?'

'No. Or rather, I'm divorced.'

'Oh! then that's different. You haven't got anything to lose.'

'If you had kids like we do . . .'

All of a sudden he thought of his departure again. Was he going to do something stupid just because he wanted to get it over with, to get out of Barcelona fast? Nah! It was his life style and his luck to hurry things . . . But sometimes it was a good idea to know when to change habits. Oh, to hell with it.

Walter explained his situation to the men: his wife had left him. The three men had admiration for a cuckold going off to war. Overcome with compassion they drank with him. Walter dragged it out until two o'clock in the morning. As he pretended to be a little drunk and to have forgotten the name of his hotel, one of his new-found friends took him home and gave him a bed. In his exhaustion and nervous unwinding he let himself drift off to sleep, trusting to his instinct. And in fact at five o'clock he jumped out of his chance bed, was greeted by an unconscious grunt, and took off.

Shortly thereafter he decided to go past his hotel and pick up his valise. It would be too suspicious to arrive at the airfield with no luggage. And he would shave. It wasn't far. At the street corner near his hotel he looked around. Nothing out of the ordinary. He paused before ringing the bell: the hotel didn't appear to hide any trap for him. He decided not to shave and kept a watchful eye on the night clerk in case he should try and ring up the police concerning his early morning departure. In the mirror he didn't look too unkempt. He paid the bill, took his suitcase, and left.

(Translation by Michael Berkvam.)

Poems for Spain

The Heart Conscripted

The shock of silver tassels
the sledded breath . . .
I who have fought my battles
keep these in a sheath.

The ulcer of poetic pride
from which the Lake Poet perished
the owl's indifferent hood –
these have vanished.

I only hear the sobbing fall
of various water-clocks
and the swift inveterate wail
of the destructive axe.

Lorca was killed, singing,
and Fox who was my friend.
the rhythm returns: the song
which has no end.

A Song for the Spanish Anarchists

The golden lemon is not made
     but grows on a green tree:
A strong man and his crystal eyes
     is a man born free.

The oxen pass under the yoke
  and the blind are led at will:
But a man born free has a path of his own
  and a house on the hill.

And men are men who till the land
  and women are women who weave:
Fifty men own the lemon grove
  and no man is a slave.

Bombing Casualties in Spain

Dolls' faces are rosier but these were children
their eyes not glass but gleaming gristle
dark lenses in whose quicksilvery glances
the sunlight quivered. These blenched lips
were warm once and bright with blood
but blood
held in a moist bleb of flesh
not split and spattered in tousled hair.

In these shadowy tresses
red petals did not always
thus clot and blacken to a scar.
These are dead faces
Wasps' nests are not more wanly waxen
wood embers not so greyly ashen.

They are laid out in ranks
like paper lanterns that have fallen
after a night of riot
extinct in the dry morning air.

John Dos Passos

From *Journeys Between Wars*

The House of the Wise

Valencia still centres around the Plaza Castelar with its underground flower market and its yellow trolley-cars and its Coney Island buildings now hung with bunting and Republican flags and plastered with posters, but instead of the old afternoon quiet every inch of the city is packed with a rambling crowd in which young men enormously predominate. There's the feeling that the town's been turned inside out like an old coat and that all the linings show.

At the office of the censor of the foreign press it's cosy and a little embarrassing, like a club. You meet old friends, you read the mimeographed sheets telling you what the government wants you to know. You snap at rumours. Inside, beyond a roomful of typewriters, the censor himself sits owl-like in his big glasses at a little desk under a blue light.

The newspapermen are tendered a lunch by the Minister for Foreign Affairs at the restaurant at the Grao, the big old restaurant on the beach where years ago . . . the rice was just as good. Through the windows of the glassed-in porch you could see a warship hull down on the blue horizon. Non-intervention. The Minister with his curious whistling diction makes an excellent speech, a heart to heart talk in two languages. There's no question about our feeling that he has the right on his side. The wine is good. It's the old famous *paella* and the shrimps and the little clams. But the food at official luncheons does not digest. It stays in a hard lump in your throat. You think of those who are being led. It all depends whether your heart is with the hounds, or the hares. Official luncheons are hunt breakfasts.

Afterwards two Frenchmen and an American stroll round the port. A sentry politely shoos us off the wharves. The port is crowded with freighters. As we turn away from the port to walk up the long dusty road full of carts and trucks to Valencia, we see a dark-grey bow nosing past the breakwater, a big dark-grey steamship is slipping silent into the harbour: a Mexican.

We walk back to Valencia talking about the mysteries of the Mediterranean these days, the unannounced blockades, the unreported sinkings, the freighters with their names painted out that run without lights slipping through the blockades, the Mexicans as they are called; some of them are Russians but they can't all be Russian. One of the Frenchmen tells of a contract through a Czechoslovakian intermediary, between the Loyalist government and Krupp. Europe is a tangle these days that nobody has yet unravelled. There's rarely been a time when the wise guys knew so little.

Back in the town I meet an old friend who takes me to see the place where the paintings from the Prado are stored. Double cement vaults have been built under the already strong stone vaulting in a chapel of a High Renaissance church. That's where the paintings are. A huge collection of tapestries from the royal palace in Madrid has just arrived. They are being unpacked before being put away by an old man and two young men. A couple of experts, museum directors in black suits, hover around. It's quiet under the frescoed dome. They unfold the tapestries for us on the clean marble steps of the chancel, the magnificent Crucifixion that Charles V always took with him on his campaigns, a Marriage at Cana, some enormous Apocalypses. We spell out the ornate symbolic figures, the horsemen of war, pestilence, famine, and death. 'It's like that now,' the old man says. 'These are the days we are living.' The young men look at the tapestries and at us and shrug their shoulders.

Casa de los Sabios is what people call the converted hotel where the Government has put up some college professors and literary people who have lost their homes and have nowhere else to go. Its real name is the House of Culture. It's dreary in the parlour there, dinner is a gloomy function there. It's like being in quarantine. We feel like old trunks in somebody's attic. There in every mouthful in every low-voiced conversation in every gesture you feel the choking strands of the tangle that nobody dares unravel It seems hours before the oranges come that signify the end of dinner.

It's a relief to get out on the pitch-black streets where there are unstrained voices, footsteps, giggling, the feeling of men and women walking through the dark with blood in their veins. We turn into a narrow street and walk towards a dim blue light. In the narrow stone street the smell of orange blossoms from the groves outside the city is intolerably sweet. We duck into a narrow door and through a dank stone passage enter a little lit-up bar. There are militiamen, a couple of sailors, a sprinkling of civilians. It smells of coffee and brandy. As we settle at a small table a frog-faced soldier comes up and introduces himself. He's a Serb serving in the International Brigade. He wants to tell his story. We piece it out with a little English, a little French, a little Spanish. He's a political exile living in Brussels. He was living with a Belgian girl who had a little boy by a former divorced husband. It's not his child but he loves it as his own, such a smart little boy. He couldn't help it, he had to leave them to come to Spain to join the International Brigade to help save Madrid from the Fascists. And now the former husband is trying to take the child away from the girl because they are Reds. The court has granted the child to the husband. What can he do? He's heart-broken. It's all in a letter. He shows us the letter. What can he do? What can he do? We tell him he's a good guy and he goes away.

Thoughts in the Dark

It's quiet at night in the Casa de los Sabios. Lying in bed it's hard not to think of what one has heard during the day of the lives caught in the tangle, the prisoners huddled in stuffy rooms waiting to be questioned, the woman with her children barely able to pay for the cheap airless apartment while she waits for her husband. It's nothing they have told her, he was just taken away for questioning, certain little matters to be cleared up, wartime, no need for alarm. But the days have gone by, months, no news. The standing in line at the police station, the calling up of influential friends, the slow-growing terror tearing the woman to pieces.

And the hostages penned in the tar-paper barrack eating the cold rice with a piece of stale meat in it, playing cards on gritty blankets in corners of the floor, and the sudden hush when the door opens and the officer steps in, behind him two soldiers with guns. He tries to keep his voice steady when he reads the names. Eyes stare out of pale faces. Feet scuffle on the dirty floor of the office. 'I am obliged to inform you that you have been ordered to be shot . . . at once.'

And the man stepping out to be court-martialled by his own side. The conversational tone of the proceedings. A joke or a smile that lets the blood flow easy again, but the gradual freezing recognition of the hundred ways a man may be guilty, the remark you dropped in a café that somebody wrote down, the letter you wrote last year, the sentence you scribbled on a scratch-pad, the fact that your cousin is in the ranks of the enemy, and the strange sound your own words make in your ears when they are quoted in the indictment. They shove a cigarette in your hand and you walk out into the courtyard to face six men you have never seen before. They take aim. They wait for the order. They fire.

Valencia, April, 1937

Valencia–Madrid

The big Hispano which the Generalitat furnished for the famous French journalist in Barcelona was standing outside the Hotel Victoria. That nest of newspaper correspondents, governmental agents, spies, munition salesmen, and mystery women is empty and quiet now. A pale boy in a green baize apron is sweeping the stairs down. It is seven in the morning. We pile in with our packages of food and our bags and our boxes of chocolate and extra cigarettes and spin out of town over the bridge. As the road climbs up out of the green plains of the *huerta* of Valencia into the dry mountains of the province of Cuenca we tell each other our surprise at the lack of military traffic on the road and at the fact that it is in such excellent condition. With the railway cut this road is the main feeder of Madrid in munitions and food. We pass the map from hand to hand. We talk knowingly about a number of things we know very little about.

Towards noon the famous French journalist began to call for an aperitif. We stopped in a dry dilapidated village where we found home-made vermouth in the café run by the UGT and with the help of some little boys tried to rustle up some ham to go with it. There was nothing to eat in any of the little stores or at the *posada*, but we eventually fell on a completely equipped pastry shop. We bought the woman out and the famous journalist photographed the little boys and everybody exclaimed about the excellence of Castilian sponge cake. When we asked the little boys what the sores on their faces came from the woman said it was because they'd been scared by the Fascist bombers flying over the village.

Thirty miles farther along the road in another grey-stone town clustered round a towering grey-stone church we stopped for lunch. In a small inn an old man and two girls were most cheerfully and seemingly tirelessly serving a meal of fried eggs with tomatoes and little steaks with fried potatoes, accompanied by good bread, washed down by a fine dense wine, to roomful after roomful of officers, soldiers, truck drivers, political party officials. This was far from the famine we had been warned to expect.

Then we were off chugging up over bare huge faintly green slopes of ranked hills that rose against indigo distances under continuously changing clouds, and down into the broad canyon of the Tagus; then up again over continually bolder hills until the road crossed a ridge with two towns with square towers on it. From the winding downward slope beyond we could look down into the valley of the Jarama and the red brick walls and the pointed slate spires of Alcala de Henares and beyond over the straw-coloured plain with cloud shadows moving across it at the great white barrier of the Sierra.

In the outskirts of Alcala we begin to see troops, field kitchens, youngsters in ill fitting tin hats, some in the mushroom German shape and others in the more elegant French shape with a keel down the middle. There were many trucks and men marching in formation on the broad road into Madrid, but nothing like what memories of the Western Front had led us to associate with a road leading up to an army. Then suddenly the outskirts have closed in on us and we are in Madrid, passing the big terracotta-coloured bull-ring, honking our way through a broad crowded asphalt street under an enormous steely twilight sky.

As we drive into the great stone city with its broad streets and squares and avenues where the skimpy trees are just coming into leaf the twilight deepens fast on the queues of women in shawls and men with mufflers standing in line for bread and oil and beans outside the half-shuttered food stores, the young men and girls strolling, the crowds coming out of moving-picture theatres. The unlighted houses are dark. Their windows stare blankly in the last light. A raw wind blows dust and newspapers among the crowds and flutters the edges of hastily-put-up posters. The city has a grim look as if stamped out of iron. In spite of the cries of newsboys and sellers of lottery tickets and the clang of street-cars and the roaring motors of trucks and automobiles all lettered with names of brigades or political parties, there's a grim silence about the city. For some reason we have an idea we ought to report to an official. We go to a public building and rub our behinds on red plush in a chilly ante-room for a while. Everything in there is delay, red tape, and obstruction, just like old times. The official wouldn't think of seeing anybody till next week. We head for the Hotel Florida. It's too dark to see anything on the Gran Via. The driver is getting nervous. He wants to get his car in a garage. It's quiet and black in the Plaza de Callao. While we are piling our bags on the pavement we stop suddenly. The noise that went on when the motor stopped was machine guns. We listen. Not very near but getting nearer; up the street from the front night, shattered and dented with gunfire, pours into the city.

Madrid, April, 1937

Metropolitan Stroll

The mid-morning sunlight was hot on the Gran Via in spite of the frigid dry wind of Castilian springtime. Stepping out of doors into the bustling jangle of the city I couldn't help thinking of other Madrids I'd known, twenty years ago, eighteen years ago, four years ago. The street-cars are the same, the long-nosed sallow madrileño faces are the same, with the same mixture of brown bullet-headed countrymen, the women in the dark-coloured shawls don't look very different. Of course you don't see the Best People any more. They are in Portugal and Seville or in their graves. Never did see the Best People at this time of the morning. The shell holes and the scars made by flying fragments and shrapnel have not changed the general look of the street, nor have the political posters pasted up on every bare piece of wall, or the fact that people are so scrappily dressed and that there's a predominance of uniforms in khaki and blue denim. It's the usualness of it that gives it this feeling of nightmare. I happen to look up at the hotel my wife and I stayed in the last time we were here. The entrance on the street looks normal and so does the department store next door, but the top floor with the balconies where our room was is shot as full of holes as a Swiss cheese.

Nobody hurries so fast along the street, and hardly anybody passes along the Gran Via these days without speeding his pace a little because it's the street where most shells fall, without pausing to glance up at the tall New-Yorkish telephone building to look for new shell holes. It's funny how the least Spanish building in Madrid, the proud New York baroque tower of Wall Street's International Tel and Tel, the symbol of the colonizing power of the dollar, has become in the minds of the madrileños the symbol of defence of the city. Five months of intermittent shellfire have done remarkably little damage. There are a few holes and dents but nothing that couldn't be repaired in two weeks' work. On the side the shelling comes from the windows of several stories have been bricked up. The historically exact ornamentation has hardly been clipped.

Inside you feel remarkably safe. The whole apparatus of the telephone service still goes on in the darkened offices. The elevators run. It feels like Sunday in a New York downtown building. In the big quiet office you find the press censors, a cadaverous Spaniard, and a plump little pleasant-voiced Austrian woman. They say they are going to move their office to another building. It's too much to ask the newspapermen on the regular services to duck through a barrage every time they have to file a story, and the censors are beginning to feel that Franco's gunners are out after them personally. Only yesterday the Austrian woman came back to find that a shell fragment had set her room on fire and burned up all her shoes, and the censor had seen a woman made mincemeat of beside him when he stepped out to get a bite of lunch. It's not surprising that the censor is a nervous man; he looks underslept and underfed. He talks as if he understood without taking too much personal pleasure in it the importance of his position of guardian of those telephones that are the link with countries technically at peace, where the war is still carried on with gold credits on bank ledgers and munitions contracts and conversations on red plush sofas in diplomatic ante-rooms instead of with six-inch shells and firing squads. He doesn't give the impression of being complacent about his job. But it's hard for one who is more or less of a free agent from a country at peace to talk about many things with men who are chained to the galley benches of war.

The Nights are Long

The correspondents take their meals in the basement of the Hotel Gran Via almost opposite the Telephone building. You go in through the unlit lobby and through a sort of pantry and down some back stairs past the kitchen into a cavelike place that still has an air of pink lights and night-club jippery about it. There at a long table sit the professional foreign correspondents and the young world saviours and the members of foreign radical delegations. At the small tables in the alcoves there tend to be militiamen and internationals on sprees and a sprinkling of young ladies of the between the sheets brigade. This particular night there's at a special table a group of British parliamentary bigwigs, including a duchess. It's been a big day for them, because General Franco's gunners have bagged more civilians than usual. Right outside of the hotel, in fact under the eyes of the duchess, two peaceful madrileños were reduced to a sudden bloody mess. A splatter of brains had to be wiped off the glassless revolving doors of the hotel. But stuffed with horrors as they were, the British bigwigs had eaten supper. In fact they'd eaten up everything there was, so that when the American correspondents began to trickle in with nothing in their stomachs but whisky and were fed each a sliver of rancid ham, there was a sudden explosion of the spirit of Seventy-Six. Why should a goddam lousy etcetera duchess eat three courses when a hard-working American newspaperman has to go hungry. A lightly punch-drunk little ex-bantamweight prize-fighter, who was often in the joint wearing a militiaman's uniform and who had tended in the past to be chummy with the *gringo* contingent who were generous with their liquor, became our champion and muttered dark threats about closing the place up and having the cooks and waiters sent to the front, lousy profiteers hiding under the skirts of the CNT who were all sons of loose women and saboteurs of the war and worse than Fascists, *mierda*. In the end the management produced a couple of long-dead whitings and a plate of spinach which they'd probably been planning to eat themselves, and the fires of revolt died down.

Still in Madrid the easiest and most sustaining thing to get, though it's high in price, is whisky; so it's on that great national food-drink that the boys at the other end of the wires tend to subsist. One of the boys who'd been there longest leaned across the table and said plaintively, 'Now you won't go home and write about the drunken correspondents, will you?'

Outside the black stone city was grimly flooded with moonlight that cut each street into two oblique sections. Down the Gran Via I could see the flashlight of a patrol and hear them demanding in low voices the password for the night of whoever they met on the sidewalk. From the west came a scattered hollow popping lightly perforating the horizon of quiet. Somewhere not very far away men with every nerve tense were crawling along the dark sides of walls, keeping their heads down in trenches, yanking their right arms back to sling a hand grenade at some creeping shadow opposite. And in all the black houses the children we'd seen playing in the streets were asleep, and the grown-ups were lying there thinking of lost friends and family and ruins and people they'd loved and hating the enemy and hunger and how to get a little more food tomorrow, feeling in the numbness of their blood, in spite of whatever scorn in the face of death, the low unending smoulder of apprehension of a city under siege. And I couldn't help feeling a certain awe, as I took off my clothes in my quiet clean room with electric light and running water and a bathtub and lay down on the bed to read a book, but instead stared at the ceiling and thought of the pleasant-faced middle-aged chambermaid who'd cleaned it that morning and made the bed and put everything in order and who'd been coming regularly every day, doing the job ever since the siege began just as she'd done it in the days of Don Alfonso, and wondered where she slept and what about her family and her kids and her man, and how perhaps tomorrow coming to work there'd be that hasty loudening shriek and the street full of dust and splintered stone and instead of coming to work the woman would be just a mashed-out mess of blood and guts to be scooped into a new pine coffin and hurried away. And they'd slosh some water over the cobbles and the death of Madrid would go on.

Madrid, April, 1937

The Literary Homefront

Those writers farthest from the war understood it least and shouted the loudest. Whether in London, New York, or Paris, they formed a kind of Literary Home Front. Their motives were often unstable combinations of conscience and trendiness and they were almost never mediated by reality. Most of what was written by these partisans is embarrassingly bad and the best is either ironic comment on war (Yeats), satire on the dictators and the Spanish war (Shaw), satire on the Abyssinian and Spanish wars as well as the Literary Home Front (Evelyn Waugh and Wyndham Lewis), present or later reminiscence (J. Leslie Brewer and Sam Atyeo), or theoretical statement (Santayana and Maritain).

In London and New York, two remarkable pamphlets were published: *Authors Take Sides on the Spanish War*, which contained the opinions of writers as diverse as Samuel Beckett, C. Day Lewis, Geoffrey Grigson, Hugh MacDiarmid, T. S. Eliot, and Ezra Pound: and *Writers Take Sides* with the best of American prejudice: Sherwood Anderson, William Faulkner, John Steinbeck, I. F. Stone, and Robinson Jeffers. Only in France, with its proximity to the war and its direct parallels to the Spanish political situation, did the level of discourse break through to the *sérieuse*. Sam Atyeo, an Australian painter and ex-diplomat living in Paris at the time, tells of Franco's propaganda campaign. Jacques Maritain, in his brilliant essay, 'The Idea of Holy War', rejects the Catholic call of a Crusade for Christ. In so doing, he adds an almost singular note of reason and sanity to the shouts on the Literary Home Front.

Authors Take Sides

The Question

To the Writers and Poets of England, Scotland, Ireland, and Wales
It is clear to many of us throughout the whole world that now, as
certainly never before, we are determined or compelled, to take
sides. The equivocal attitude, the Ivory Tower, the paradoxical,
the ironic detachment, will no longer do.

We have seen murder and destruction by Fascism in Italy, in
Germany – the organization there of social injustice and cultural
death – and now revived, imperial Rome, abetted by international
treachery, has conquered her place in the Abyssinian sun. The
dark millions in the colonies are unavenged.

Today, the struggle is in Spain. Tomorrow it may be in other
countries – our own. But there are some who, despite the martyrdom of Durango and Guernica, the enduring agony of Madrid,
of Bilbao, and Germany's shelling of Almeria, are still in doubt,
or who aver that it is possible that Fascism may be what it proclaims it is: 'the saviour of civilization'.

This is the question we are asking you: Are you for, or against,
the legal Government and the People of Republican Spain? Are
you for, or against, Franco and Fascism? For it is impossible for
any longer to take no side.

Writers and Poets, we wish to print your answers. We wish the
world to know what you, writers and poets, who are amongst the
most sensitive instruments of a nation, feel.

Signed: *Paris – June 1937*
 Aragon   *Nancy Cunard* *Pablo Neruda*
 W. H. Auden *Brian Howard* *Ramon Sender*
 José Bergamín *Heinrich Mann* *Stephen Spender*
 Jean Richard Bloch *Ivor Montagu* *Tristan Tzara*

The Answers

FOR THE GOVERNMENT

Samuel Beckett

¡UPTHEREPUBLIC!

C. Day Lewis

The struggle in Spain is part of a conflict going on now all over the world. I look upon it quite simply as a battle between light and darkness, of which only a blind man could be unaware. Both as a writer and as a member of the Communist Party I am bound to help in the fight against Fascism, which means certain destruction or living death for humanity.

Douglas Goldring

I was perhaps the first English writer to see Fascism in action, in Ireland, 1919–21. The Black and Tans invented 'Shot while trying to escape', and many other familiar horrors subsequently copied by Hitler and Mussolini. I have spent nearly twenty years of my life, as a writer, trying to warn the younger generation against what is in store for them if they persist in pursuing the 'good time' or trying to live in (with apologies to my old friend the late Mary Butts) 'Crystal Cabinets' or 'Ivory Towers'.

 As my convictions have remained unchanged since, in 1919, I was the English secretary of Henri Barbusse's 'Clarté' movement, you can be certain that I am against Fascism wherever it appears, against Franco and for the legal Government and the people of Republican Spain. Fourteen years ago I spent a spring in a Mallorcan 'Anarchist' or co-operative fishing village. It was a paradise; without crime, distress, repression, or 'Loranorder'. Spain will, no doubt, be crushed by the dead weight of Fascist bombs. But in the end Spain is unconquerable, superb, humanity's chief hope. *No pasaran.*

Geoffrey Grigson, Editor, *New Verse*
For potted shrimps in the club, for reading the *Manchester Guardian*, for holding hands in the cinema, we are paying willingly with the lies, the insolence and the cynicism hung between us and intervention in Spain.

I am equivocal enough to be *against* politically, and not *for*, to fear and distrust any mass in its own control . . .

Jack Lindsay
I believe Fascism to be utterly evil and destructive. I stand with every fibre of my being for the People of Spain against the murderous attack of the feudalist remnants backed by Hitler and Mussolini for their imperialist world-war purposes; I believe this is an epic conflict in which ideas like Freedom and Culture leap out with a new tremendous urgency, an irresistible demand on our loyalty. To be above the battle, when such a cause is concerned, is to be sub-human.

Hugh MacDiarmid
I am a member of the Communist Party and wholly on the side of the legal Government and the People of Republican Spain – as are the vast majority of the people of Scotland, where at successive General Elections a majority of the total poll has been cast for Socialism, and where – if we had had national independence – we too would have had a Socialist Republican Government long ago. Practically all the Scottish writers of any distinction today are of the same way of thinking. But for the connection with England, Fascism would never be able to raise its head in Scotland itself. If we are subjected to a Fascist terror in Scotland, the London Government will be to blame, as it is mainly to blame for the horrible tragedy inflicted on our Spanish comrades – a tragedy which must, and will, be turned yet into a glorious victory over the Principalities and Powers of Darkness, and end with the liquidation of Franco and all his fellow-murderers.

Raymond Postgate

I am wholly against Franco and in favour of the Spanish workers; but not for the reasons suggested in your manifesto, such as the horrors of Durango, Guernica, Madrid, or Bilbao. War means such atrocities, and whoever begins the conflict they are soon committed on both sides. Judgements given under the influence of such stories are unstable and emotional decisions; I wish that every supporter of the Spanish Government who relies on them would look into his mind and find a surer basis for his opinion.

The fight between Franco and the Spanish workers is a fight between the capitalist, clerical, and feudal owners and the exploited workers. It is the class struggle between the rich and the poor, the exploiters and the exploited, which has surely been sufficiently explained to everybody by now. For that reason, even if all the atrocities were disproved, I would still be on the side of Socialism.

NEUTRAL

T. S. Eliot

While I am naturally sympathetic, I still feel convinced that it is best that at least a few men of letters should remain isolated, and take no part in these collective activities.

Ezra Pound

Questionnaire an escape mechanism for young fools who are too cowardly to think; too lazy to investigate the nature of money, its mode of issue, the control of such issue by the Banque de France and the stank of England. You are all had. Spain is an emotional luxury to a gang of sap-headed dilettantes.

AGAINST THE GOVERNMENT

Edmund Blunden

I know too little about affairs in Spain to make a confident answer. To my mind (subject to that first reservation), it was necessary that somebody like Franco should arise – and although England may not profit by his victory I think Spain will. The ideas of

Germany, Italy, etc., in your document do not square with those I have formed *upon the whole* of the recent history of those countries. Memories of 1914–18 perhaps do not allow me to see some incidents you mention in the isolated and flamboyant way the manifesto has them.

Arthur Machen

Mr Arthur Machen presents his compliments and begs to inform that he is, and always has been, entirely for General Franco.

Evelyn Waugh

I know Spain only as a Tourist and a reader of the newspapers. I am no more impressed by the 'legality' of the Valencia Government than are English Communists by the legality of the Crown, Lords, and Commons. I believe it was a bad Government, rapidly deteriorating. If I were a Spaniard I should be fighting for General Franco. As an Englishman I am not in the predicament of choosing between two evils. I am not a Fascist nor shall I become one unless it were the only alternative to Marxism. It is mischievous to suggest that such a choice is imminent.

*   *

Evelyn Waugh from *Scoop*

Ishmaelia, that hitherto happy commonwealth, cannot conveniently be approached from any part of the world. It lies in the north-easterly quarter of Africa, giving colour by its position and shape to the metaphor often used of it: 'the Heart of the Dark Continent'. Desert, forest, and swamp, frequented by furious nomads, protect its approaches from those more favoured regions which the statesmen of Berlin and Geneva have put to school under European masters. An inhospitable race of squireens cultivate the highlands and pass their days in the perfect leisure which those peoples alone enjoy who are untroubled by the speculative or artistic itch.

Various courageous Europeans, in the seventies of the last century, came to Ishmaelia, or near it, furnished with suitable equipment of cuckoo clocks, phonographs, opera hats, draft-treaties, and flags of the nations which they had been obliged to leave. They came as missionaries, ambassadors, tradesmen, prospectors, natural scientists. None returned. They were eaten, every one of them; some raw, others stewed and seasoned – according to local usage and the calendar (for the better sort of Ishmaelites have been Christian for many centuries and will not publicly eat human flesh, uncooked, in Lent, without special and costly dispensation from their bishop). Punitive expeditions suffered more harm than they inflicted and in the nineties humane counsels prevailed. The European powers independently decided that they did not want that profitless piece of territory; that the one thing less desirable than seeing a neighbour established there, was the trouble of taking it themselves. Accordingly, by general consent, it was ruled off the maps and its immunity guaranteed. As there was no form of government common to the peoples thus segregated, nor tie of language, history, habit, or belief, they were called a Republic. A committee of jurists, drawn from the Universities, composed a constitution, providing a bicameral legislature, proportional representation by means of the single transferable vote, an executive removable by the President on the recommendation of both houses, an independent judicature, religious liberty, secular education, *habeas corpus*, free trade, joint stock banking, chartered corporations, and numerous other agreeable features. A pious old darky named Mr Samuel Smiles Jackson from Alabama was put in as the first President – a choice whose wisdom seemed to be confirmed by history, for, forty years later, a Mr Rathbone Jackson held his grandfather's office in succession to his father Pankhurst, while the chief posts of the state were held by Messrs Garnett Jackson, Mander Jackson, Huxley Jackson, his uncle and brothers, and by Mrs 'Teeny' Athol (née Jackson), his aunt. So strong was the love which the Republic bore the family that General Elections were known as 'Jackson Ngomas' wherever and whenever they were held. These, by the constitution, should have been quinquennial, but since it was found in practice that difficulty of communication rendered it impossible for the constituencies to vote simultaneously, the custom had grown up for the receiving officer and the Jackson candidate to visit in turn such parts of the Republic as were open to travel, and entertain the neighbouring chiefs at a six days' banquet at their camp, after which the stupefied aborigines recorded their votes in the secret and solemn manner prescribed by the constitution.

It had been found expedient to merge the functions of national defence and inland revenue in an office then held in the capable hands of General Gollancz Jackson; his forces were in two main companies, the Ishmaelite Mule Tax-gathering Force and the Rifle Excisemen, with a small Artillery Death Duties Corps for use against the heirs of powerful noblemen; it was their job to raise the funds whose enlightened expenditure did so much to enhance President Jackson's prestige among the rare foreign visitors to his capital. Towards the end of each financial year the General's flying columns would lumber out into the surrounding country on the heels of the fugitive population and return in time for budget day laden with the spoils of the less nimble: coffee and hides, silver coinage, slaves, livestock, and firearms would be assembled and assessed in the Government warehouses; salaries would be paid, covering in kind those deposited at the bank for the national over-draft, and donations made, in the presence of the diplomatic corps, to the Jackson Non-sectarian Co-education Technical Schools and other humane institutions. On the foundation of the League of Nations, Ishmaelia became a member.

Under this liberal and progressive regime, the Republic may be said, in some ways, to have prospered. It is true that the capital city, Jacksonburg, became unduly large, its alleys and cabins thronged with landless men of native and alien blood, while the country immediately surrounding it became depopulated, so that General Gollancz Jackson was obliged to start earlier and march farther in search of the taxes; but on the main street there were agencies for many leading American and European firms; there was, moreover, a railway to the Red Sea coast, bringing a steady stream of manufactured imports which relieved the Ishmaelites of the need to practise their few clumsy crafts, while the adverse trade balance was rectified by an elastic system of bankruptcy law. In the remote provinces, beyond the reach of General Gollancz, the Ishmaelites followed their traditional callings of bandit slave or gentlemen of leisure, happily ignorant of their connection with the town of which a few of them, perhaps, had vaguely and incredulously heard.

Occasional travelling politicians came to Jacksonburg, were

entertained and conducted round the town, and returned with friendly reports. Big-game hunters on safari from the neighbouring dominions sometimes strayed into the hinterland and if they returned at all dined out for years to come on the experience. Until a few months before William Boot's departure, no one in Europe knew of the deep currents that were flowing in Ishmaelite politics; nor did many people know of them in Ishmaelia.

It began during Christmas week with a domestic row in the Jackson family. By Easter the city, so lately a model of internal amity, was threatened by civil war.

A Mr Smiles Soum was reputed to lead the Fascists. He was only one-quarter Jackson (being grandson in the female line of President Samuel Smiles Jackson), and three-quarters pure Ishmaelite. He was thus, by right of cousinship, admitted to the public pay-roll; but he ranked low in the family and had been given no more lucrative post than that of Assistant-Director of Public Morals.

Quarrels among the ruling family were not unusual, particularly in the aftermath of weddings, funerals, and other occasions of corporate festivity, and were normally settled by a readjustment of public offices. It was common knowledge in the bazaars and drink-shops that Mr Smiles was not satisfied with his post at the Ministry of Public Morals, but it was a breach of precedent and, some thought, the portent of a new era in Ishmaelite politics when he followed up his tiff by disappearing from Jacksonburg and issuing a manifesto, which, it was thought by those who knew him best, he could not conceivably have composed himself.

The White Shirt movement which he called into being had little in common with the best traditions of Ishmaelite politics. Briefly his thesis was this: the Jacksons were effete, tyrannical, and alien; the Ishmaelites were a white race who, led by Smiles, must purge themselves of the Negro taint; the Jacksons had kept Ishmaelia out of the Great War and had thus deprived her of the fruits of victory; the Jacksons had committed Ishmaelia to the control of international Negro finance and secret subversive Negro Bolshevism, by joining the League of Nations; they were responsible for the various endemic and epidemic diseases that ravaged crops, livestock, and human beings; all Ishmaelites who were suffering the consequences of imprudence or ill-fortune in their financial or matrimonial affairs were the victims of international Jackson-sm; Smiles was their Leader.

The Jacksons rose above it. Life in Ishmaelia went on as before and the Armenian merchant in Main Street who had laid in a big consignment of white cotton shirtings found himself with the stuff on his hands. In Moscow, Harlem, Bloomsbury, and Liberia, however, keener passions were aroused. In a hundred progressive weeklies and Left Study Circles the matter was taken up and the cause of the Jacksons restated in ideological form.

Smiles represented international finance, the subjugation of the worker, sacerdotalism; Ishmaelia was black, the Jacksons were black, collective security and democracy and the dictatorship of the proletariat were black. Most of this was unfamiliar stuff to the Jacksons, but tangible advantages followed. A subscription list was opened in London and received support in chapels and universities; wide publicity was given to the receipt in Ishmaelia of three unused penny stamps addressed to the President by 'A little worker's daughter in Bedford Square'.

In the chief cities of Europe a crop of 'patriot consulates' sprang up devoted to counter-propaganda.

Newspapermen flocked to Jacksonburg. It was the wet season when business was usually at a standstill; everything boomed this year. At the end of August the rains would stop. Then, everybody outside Ishmaelia agreed, there would be a war. But, with the happy disposition of their race, the Ishmaelites settled down to exploit and enjoy their temporary good fortune.

(*Ed. Note:* The following replies were sent to *Authors Take Sides* by 'General Gollancz Jackson', and 'Messrs Garnett Jackson and Huxley Jackson': nés Victor Gollancz, David Garnett, and Aldous Huxley.)

Victor Gollancz

Of course I am for the legal Government and the people of Republican Spain.

Of course I am against Franco and Fascism.

Fascism is culturally and intellectually a species of *dementia praecox* – a refusal any longer to carry the burden of being human, and a slipping back, happy sometimes but always disgusting, into the primeval slime. The writer, poet, or artist who says the whole thing is no concern of his is either a knave or a fool, or more probably both.

David Garnett

The question whether I am for or against a military adventurer who calls in the weapons of foreign despots against his own people appears to me to have been settled a century or two before I was born. I am an Englishman and a liberal who has always enjoyed personal liberty and been free to think and speak as he likes. I cannot conceive a tolerable world without such freedom.

The question for Englishmen and Frenchmen today is not whether they are for or against Fascism, but when they will have to fight in defence of their liberty against the German and Italian dictatorships and with what weapons. What we have to consider is the strategy necessary to defeat the disciplined but rather top-heavy enemies of liberty.

Aldous Huxley

My sympathies are, of course, with the Government side, especially the Anarchists; for Anarchism seems to me much more likely to lead to desirable social change than highly centralized, dictatorial Communism. As for 'taking sides' – the choice, it seems to me, is no longer between two users of violence, two systems of dictatorship. Violence and dictatorship cannot produce peace and liberty; they can only produce the results of violence and dictatorship, results with which history has made us only too sickeningly familiar.

The choice now is between militarism and pacifism. To me, the necessity of pacifism seems absolutely clear.

George Bernard Shaw's response to *Authors Take Sides*

In Spain both the Right and the Left so thoroughly disgraced themselves in the turns they took in trying to govern their country before the Right revolted, that it is impossible to say which of them is the more incompetent. Spain must choose for itself: it is really not our business, though of course our Capitalist Government has done everything it possibly could to help General Franco. I as a Communist am generally on the Left; but that does not commit me to support the British Party Parliament system, and its continental imitations, of which I have the lowest opinion.

At present the Capitalist powers seem to have secured a victory over the General by what they call their non-interference, meaning their very active interference on his side; but it is unlikely that the last word will be with him. Meanwhile I shall not shout about it.

From Shaw's play *Geneva*

General Flanco de Fortinbras enters at the door. He is a middle-aged officer, very smart, and quite conventional.

FLANCO: Pardon. Is this the International Court?

JUDGE: It is.

FLANCO: My name is Flanco de Fortinbras – General Flanco de Fortinbras. I have received a summons.

JUDGE: Quite so, General. We were expecting you. You are very welcome. Pray be seated.

The secretary places a chair between the judge and Bombardone. Flanco crosses to it.

JUDGE [*before Flanco sits down*]: You know these gentlemen, I think.

FLANCO [*sitting down carelessly*]: No. But I have seen many caricatures of them. No introduction is necessary.

JUDGE: You recognize also the British Foreign Secretary, Sir Orpheus Midlander.

Flanco immediately rises; clicks his heels; and salutes Sir Orpheus with a distinguished consideration that contrasts very significantly with his contemptuous indifference to the two leaders. Sir Orpheus, as before, waves a gracious acknowledgement of the salute. Flanco resumes his seat.

FLANCO: I have come here because it seemed the correct thing to do. I am relieved to find that His Excellency the British Foreign Secretary agrees with me.

BOMBARDONE: In what capacity are you here, may I ask?

FLANCO: Do I seem out of place between you and your fellow-talker opposite? A man of action always is out of place among talkers.

BOMBARDONE: Inconceivable nothingness that you are, do you dare to class me as a talker and not a man of action?

FLANCO: Have you done anything?

BOMBARDONE: I have created an empire.

FLANCO: You mean that you have policed a place infested by savages. A child could have done it with a modern mechanized army.

BOMBARDONE: Your little military successes have gone to your head. Do not forget that they were won with my troops.

FLANCO: Your troops do fairly well under my command. We have yet to see them doing anything under yours.

BOMBARDONE: Ernest: our valet has gone stark mad.

FLANCO: Mr Battler may be a useful civilian. I am informed that he is popular with the lower middle class. But the fate of Europe will not be decided by your scraps of Socialism.

JUDGE: May I recall you to the business of the court, gentlemen. General: you are charged with an extraordinary devastation of your own country and an indiscriminate massacre of its inhabitants.

FLANCO: That is my profession. I am a soldier; and my business is to devastate the strongholds of the enemies of my country, and slaughter their inhabitants.

NEWCOMER: Do you call the lawfully constituted democratic government of your country its enemies?

FLANCO: I do, sir. That government is a government of cads. I stand for a great cause; and I have not talked about it, as these two adventurers talk: I have fought for it: fought and won.

JUDGE: And what, may we ask, is the great cause?

FLANCO: I stand simply for government by gentlemen against government by cads. I stand for the religion of gentlemen against the irreligion of cads. For me there are only two classes: gentlemen and cads; only two faiths: Catholics and heretics. The horrible vulgarity called democracy has given political power to the cads and the heretics. I am determined that the world shall not be ruled by cads nor its children brought up as heretics. I maintain that all spare money should be devoted to the breeding of gentlemen. In that I have the great body of public opinion behind me. Take a plebiscite of the whole civilized world; and not a vote will be cast against me. The natural men, the farmers and peasants, will support me to a man, and to a woman. Even the peasants whom you have crowded into your towns and demoralized by street life and trade unionism, will know in their souls that I am the salvation of the world.

BOMBARDONE: A Saviour, no less! Eh?

FLANCO: Do not be profane. I am a Catholic officer and gentleman, with the beliefs, traditions, and duties of my class and my faith. I could not sit idly reading and talking whilst the civilization established by that faith and that order was being destroyed by the mob. Nobody else would do anything but read seditious pamphlets and talk, talk, talk. It was necessary to fight, fight, fight to restore order in the world. I undertook that responsibility and here I am. Everybody understands my position: nobody understands the pamphlets, the three volumes of Karl Marx, the theories of the idealists, the ranting of the demagogues: in short, the caddishness of the cads. Do I make myself clear?

BOMBARDONE: Am I a cad? Is Ernest here a cad?

FLANCO: You had better not force me to be personal.

BOMBARDONE: Come! Face the question. Are we cads or gentlemen? Out with it.

FLANCO: You are certainly not gentlemen. You are freaks.

BATTLER: Freaks!

BOMBARDONE: What is a freak?

JUDGE: An organism so extraordinary as to defy classification.

BOMBARDONE: Good. I accept that.

BATTLER: So do I. I claim it.

JUDGE: Then, as time is getting on, gentlemen, had we not better come to judgment?

BATTLER: Judgment!

BOMBARDONE: Judgment!

BATTLER: What do you mean? Do you presume to judge me?

BOMBARDONE: Judge me if you dare.

FLANCO: Give judgment against me and you pass out of history as a cad.

BATTLER: You have already passed out of history as a Catholic: that is, nine tenths a Jew.

BOMBARDONE: The bee in your bonnet buzzes too much, Ernest. [*To the Judge*] What is the law?

JUDGE: Unfortunately there is no law as between nations. I shall have to create it as I go along, by judicial precedents.

J. Leslie Brewer

'Too Late?'

From *Time and Tide*, October 24, 1936

Spain. *A Protest Meeting against the Attack upon Democracy in Spain.* I feel we should go. Ring up Evelyn and George, dear. Ask them to meet us outside. Inside, if you like. Ask them to try and keep seats.

We shut the drawing-room door to keep the cat off the chairs. Leave a note for the girl saying we shall only want hot milk when we get in. Through the rain, then down Nassington Avenue to the Tube.

Because Calvo Sotelo, on the morning of July 14th lay on a slab, dead, in bloodstained vest and pants, because lorries are now, in the early evening, rumbling along the road to Saragossa, because Madrid workmen are lying, cold, unburied, on the hot rocks of the Guadarrama we are, at this moment, my wife and I, walking to the Tube station. Or, if you like, because an assault has been made upon Democracy in Spain we are going to a Protest Meeting. We are not staying in, we are not playing Bridge, we have not asked Evelyn and George to come out here. Something is taking us into town, to protest.

We know Spain. We have had several delightful holidays there, usually with George and Evelyn. We have seen, and photographed, the geese in the Cathedral cloister in Barcelona. Two years ago we were in Tossa. I read somewhere that the parish priest in Tossa kept a stock of penny whistles to give to good children. When the troubles came his stock was seized. All day (so the paper said) the cork woods above the town echoed with the noise of children, good and bad alike, piping triumphantly on penny whistles. If I close my eyes, here in this tube train full of English clerks in mackintoshes, a hundred feet below Hampstead High Street. I can walk about again in Toledo. Last April, in this suit, I stood to have my photograph taken in the Alcazar with two of the cadets. One told me that his name was Enrique and his mother English, 'from by Bristol'.

'Civil War in Spain' ... 'Insurgent planes have bombarded several small towns in the Province of Toledo' ... 'Alcazar mined'. What does it all mean to most people? To me it means that Enrique, those cadets, the officer who politely insisted on walking with us to show us the way to El Greco's house, are, for some reason, fighting the big, cropped-haired men who carried our cases from the station, the workmen we saw, sitting in the sun, watching the big, gleaming cars go by, themselves shod in shoes made from old tyres.

What are we, my wife and I, going to protest against?

Not against people, individuals, or at least not against Spanish people we know. Our officer, Enrique, the workmen sitting by the roadside, cannot be praised or blamed for what they are doing. You cannot praise or blame any individual *pigeon* when, at a shot, the whole flight divide and sweep suddenly and with precision to the right and to the left. A general protest, if you like against all fighting. That most certainly, but not against any individuals.

Franco? Goded and Burriel? Sanjurjo, who crashed in Portugal because he took a suitcase too many? They fired the shot, obviously, which scattered the pigeons. Against them I am protesting, but only as the instruments of something else. They are the gun, not the fowler.

And the fowler? I fear him but I can neither name nor place him. This I do know, whenever I open my morning paper, even sit in my little garden, a great shadow falls across me. 'Shall Abyssinia be excluded from the League?' ... The Nuremburg speeches, Palestine (... '13th Brigade, based on Nazareth') ... 'Would fifty tons of bombs paralyse London?' Great fighting planes from Hendon roar over our house on Sunday mornings ... My boy whistles, blancoing his khaki belt in the kitchen. My neighbours are neither mad nor wicked. Yet here, it seems, is the vile, inexorable, collective outcome of individual wills, the world over.

It is against that I am going to protest this evening. But how can I make my voice heard?

I know we shall join George and Evelyn, in a few minutes, in a comfortable hall, full of people just like ourselves, folding mackintoshes carefully away under the chairs, pretending to look for friends, avoiding the sellers of little, well-printed pamphlets. Speakers, honest, rational men, will prove conclusively to us that the Government of Spain was a democratically-elected government, a true expression of the will of the people. We shall clap, and as we clap bombs from German and Italian planes will almost certainly be falling on our counter-parts in some Spanish village or town. How can we make our voices heard before it is too late? Can our voices ever be louder than the bombs or our wills more compelling than loaded rifles?

Barcelona workers, unarmed, advanced upon machine guns until someone reached the gunner and called him 'comrade' and held out a hand. A will more compelling than loaded rifles?

These people in this crowded carriage, the people I shall see at the meeting, my neighbours and fellow-clerks, none of us desires the evils which are coming to pass. Yet somewhere, around us, among us, is a force we fear, driving the world, and us, forward to horror, sometimes making us its weapons or accomplices. This force is no person: no person could be so evil. It is an aggregate of wills, desiring this or that advantage and the desires are incompatible. It is a vile ectoplasm, rising from offices, counting houses, embassies the world over, blanketing us from the sun.

I am going to this meeting, as I have to twenty drab, earnest meetings in the last year, in the desperate hope that I shall see, before it is too late, the mass of people, my neighbours, transformed and all our scattered elements fused at last into a single, answering will. We, too, have our desires and they are not incompatible. Unfortunately, we, the Last International, scarcely know that we exist. But from the suburbs of Europe can arise a will, a reply to the challenge of the bombers over our back gardens. I wonder sometimes, nursing my hat at a meeting, how words, compassion, thought, can ever answer cruelty. What answer is this to Franco, Hitler, Mussolini – my wife and I going, arm in arm, through the rain, along Euston Road to the Friends' Meeting House?

It is a portent, a fragment of a will which, if united with similar, existing (though dormant) wills throughout the world could dismiss these men, their systems, storm-troopers, prison camps, with the ease of a sleeper, waking from an evil dream.

It is a gesture of kinship to Spanish people like ourselves. That sense of kinship can meet rifles and silence them, go deep under the skin and smash the wires by which ordinary men and women are made to dance like puppets, shoot, sell, slave, salute.

I wonder, as I look round the hall, is it too late?

'Politics'

'In our time the destiny of man presents its meaning in political terms.' – *Thomas Mann*

> How can I, that girl standing there,
> My attention fix
> On Roman or on Russian
> Or on Spanish politics?
> Yet here's a travelled man that knows
> What he talks about,
> And there's a politician
> That has read and thought,
> And maybe what they say is true
> Of war and war's alarms,
> But O that I were young again
> And held her in my arms!

Wyndham Lewis

From *Revenge for Love*

A red patriarch, Percy Hardcaster reclined, propped by a plethora of red cushions, upon a wide reddish settee, in Red invalid magnificence. A red punkah should have been there to complete the picture. He was surrounded by men and women – by the Red men and Red women. There were four women beside him upon the settee; in the place of honour Gillian Phipps pressed up against his sick leg, which stuck straight out pointing at the assembly with all the declamatory force of Lord Kitchener's forefinger ('I want *you*') terminating in an ironshod stump, provided by the Lerroux administration.

In the place of lesser honour, because leg to leg with his more ordinary and less dramatic limb, was Ellen Mulliner. It was further very marked indeed, the manner in which Percy Hardcaster displayed his preference for his new acquaintance, and was at no pains to conceal his desire to confirm his more recent success – rather than to advertise his triumph of long standing, which was already dating. It would have been impossible to find a more flagrant case of omission to be *off with the old* before being *on with the new*.

Before Percy Hardcaster, both upon the floor and upon chairs, was an impressive grouping of salon-Reds – of Oxford and Cambridge 'pinks'; a subdued socialist-leaguer; the usual marxist don; the pimpled son of a Privy Councillor (who had *tovarish* painted all over him); a refugee (an equinal head-piece, flanked by two monstrous red wings, which were the sails flung out by his eardrums, and which moved back against his head, as if he had been subjected to a hundred-mile-an-hour wind, in moments of agitation). And there were three sturdy 'independents' ('friends of Soviet Russia') from the headquarter-staff of the Book Racket. The roster contained other fish and fowl and more or less good red herrings. And Percy's protruding artificial limb pointed pointedly at one and all, and his eyes looked over the top of it steadily but not unkindly at the lot of them. But it was a cowed group round Percy – this man-of-action almost frightened them. A veteran of the *Ten Days that Shook the World* would have had less effect than this *grand blessé* of a month's standing. He was a *workman* – that, too, was calculated to provoke almost a panic, in the uninitiated; to whom a communist *workman* was distinctly an alarming notion. They soon got used to this, however. After all he had written pamphlets (and a Red playlet) which Collett's Bomb-Shop carried as a stock-in-trade: this made him much more human – almost a 'Leftie' PEN man. And it was not long before they became aware that he possessed a Juan Gris (so a *possessive* man with a disarming 'culture') and was able to discuss Bracque as well as Trotsky.

Of course all the men thought constantly how exceedingly unpleasant it would be to have a wooden leg. An advertisement it was not, from that standpoint, of unsalonesque class-warfare. It made their own legs feel quite uncomfortable to look at it – and they couldn't help looking at it, Percy saw to that! But of course such things only happened to workmen – no one but a workman would ever go where things of that order were likely to occur to his legs (just look how they fall off scaffoldings, or lose their arms in printing-presses or Lancashire looms, and think nothing of it). But one and all in their hearts determined that it was more necessary than ever to see to it that they should remain *the brains* of the Revolution. Never must they allow themselves to be inveigled into situations where such a drastic disfigurement awaited them, now or at any future time. So Percy's pointing had the opposite effect to Lord Kitchener's pointing. But all were anxious to hear how it happened.

'So what it boils down to, Percy,' said one who had known him before he went to Spain on this particular ill-fated job of work, 'was a rivalry between the two prison guards, wasn't it?'

'That's what it amounted to,' said Percy.

'And the head guard revenged himself true to fascist principles, when you turned down his blackmailing proposition?'

At the word 'fascist' a most ferocious growling grew in volume and was at once seen to be proceeding from a small and spectacled, pinkfaced and pinkminded, pugdog-like client of the Left from Brasenose – whose little father often shook his bald and toothy little head in his big London Club when the 'young generation' was mentioned (as it often was, especially after a study of Mr Haselden's morning cartoon), and allowed it to be understood that *his* ill-sprung little offspring was as proper a sample of really flaming-youth as could be met with between Half Moon Street and World's End, though there was no harm in the young devil (damn it, sir, he's too stupid!) and he could quite see that the young man should desire to kill his father – he had always wanted to kill *his* – and once his wild oats were sown like his father before him he would be sitting in that self-same club and writing a letter to *The Times* – insisting testily that our government should hand back at once Australia to the Blackboys, whom we had against every Christian principle dispossessed, but whom we had now quite sufficiently educated in the gentle ways of true democracy to enable them to take their place beside Mr Litvinov in the Council Chamber of the League of Nations (without any undue embarrassment to Mr Litvinov – on the score of their imperfect understanding of Freedom) and that the White Australians should gracefully withdraw from the Island Continent (just as the Anglo-Indians had left India – as they would have by that time, bag and baggage, and have left it to the Baboos to whom it belonged) and return to the Mother Country and settle down on the dole – unless, indeed, this influx should be found to bring down wages still further by the new threat of unemployment and so ultimately 'benefit the country'.

Having stared steadily at the growler for a moment or two, Percy inflated his chest and started dotting a few i's, and crossing a few t's.

'No, Geoffrey, you haven't quite got that right,' he said frowning. 'Alvaro Morato was undoubtedly acting for the governor of the prison. He was his factor, in the prison – for all the matters of graft.'

'Ah!' breathed out deeply Geoffrey to indicate that the key to the whole business was now in his hands, and there was a murmur of understanding everywhere.

'Yes. The Governor worked through Alvaro – who naturally had his rake-off. Alvaro named his figure to me – a stiff one he said, but it was worth it.'

'Oh, he got as far as that, did he?'

'Yes. He wanted five thousand pesetas.'

'A king's ransom!'

'You're right – not a Communist's anyway! I told him so. I asked him what he thought we were – bloody capitalists? – and he said, *no*. But England was very rich, he said, and Spain was poor. To which I replied that England wouldn't be rich long if she paid dirty dogs like him five thousand pesetas for a job that wasn't worth as many hundreds. He properly flew off the handle at that, and said I ought to go back to England where I came from – provided I could get out of the prison, of course, which he would make it his business to see that I didn't: and that they didn't want a lot of lousy Reds like me in the land of Ferdinand and Isabella. Further I had quoted something from the Epistle to the Corinthians at him (I'd been reading up about St Paul) – he said I was insulting a Catholic saint and was an atheist. I said I *was* – but it was a great man I had quoted and nothing so silly as a saint! When I was taken to the hospital he told the sisters there I was an atheist. They refused to give me bed-pans all the time I was there except once in the morning – because, they said, I was anti-Christ. My mosquito curtain was taken away and I was left at the mercy of a colony of malarial mosquitoes, which sent my temperature up once or twice round a hundred and seven – so much that I heard afterwards they were expecting me to die and that a priest was standing by to offer me the sacrament!'

Don Percy paused, out of breath, and a babble of indignant remarks churned up the smoky air all round him, while he mopped his brow with a red-spotted handkerchief, very *proletariado* and proud-of-it.

Ellen Mulliner, upon his left hand, ran her fingers over his perspiring thatch of khaki-blond, with a possessive anxiety – whispering to him in some caution, evidently, not to overtax his strength by holding forth at too great a length, or by reviving these painful memories in too great detail. But Percy ducked and with a touch of crossness reassured her shortly; then silenced the officious young woman with a roguish push.

Upon the other side of him Gillian pressed his hand and a tear stood in her eye, as she gazed sternly at this man who had been broken upon the Spanish rack in the interests of *étatisme* and Dictatorship. Others would be broken after him – even the State

Triumphant, even Dictatorship itself might break men too – but he had been broken, and he *was* for something else, which had not *yet* broken as many men as the present system (at least only in other quarters of the Globe).

'How perfectly beastly!' exclaimed the girl next to Gillian, whom the old bed-pan yarn, heard for the first time, had impressed very deeply, as she suffered greatly from constipation. 'It's like hearing about the Inquisition, isn't it? They still live in the age of Torquemada in that awful country. Spain is terrible. I think it is worse than Germany.'

A 'Leftie' reporter had out his notebook, and he had noted that Hardcaster, the English syndicalist, had been put in a cell the window of which looked out upon a swamp, and there had been left practically to his own devices for three days and three nights, to be eaten up by malarial mosquitoes, so that to his wound (undressed) was superadded a pestilential fever, and that the nursing sisters – wrongly supposing him to be unconscious – had rubbed salt into his sores.

'It reminds me of Oranienburg,' said the refugee, his ears sinking back against his head, and his hair withdrawing from the front of his scalp – which involuntary muscular operation caused his eyes to assume a Chinese obliquity, in the blushing mask of a beaten hound.

'But did not the doctors do anything?' thundered Geoffrey sternly, self-appointed precentor.

'The *doctors*? They stood beside my bed with the *bonnes sœurs*, and laughed themselves sick at the sight of my face!'

Sensation. The reporter's pencil galloped in the suspense of utterance following upon these revelations.

'I was unrecognizable! They showed me my face in a glass. It was scarcely human. I don't mind owning that it frightened me when I saw it. In fact I went off in a faint.'

There was now a tense silence for some moments. Then the same girl, who sat beside Gillian, exclaimed:

'The brutes! The perfectly fiendish brutes!'

Gillian was dumb with a lofty horror of proud indignation, that made her bird-like beauty pass into a hawk's profile of almost malevolent passion of destruction directed towards the rank and file of the aviarium around it.

At that moment Jack – his trajectory made tortuous by the gossiping groups intervening – came over from the *buffet froid*. He stood upon the outskirts of the immediate audience of Hardcaster, grinning. Attempting to attract her attention by a cough or two, his irrepressible animal eyes were fixed upon Gillian, and were especially busy with her bust, which was thrust out at the saturnalian angle of a young *tricoteuse*. At length she became aware of him. But she immediately flashed over at him such an Oh-*you*-there! For-god's-sake-take-your-grin-away! sort of look out of her dry eye, that seeing himself so unmistakably *de trop*, the grin departing from his face, he hurriedly left the circle gathered about Hardcaster.

'But a report should be drawn up at once and sent to the Foreign Office!' exclaimed a Public School Boy.

'Haven't we got an ambassador in Madrid?' said the third girl upon the settee upon Gillian's side of Hardcaster.

'Or a consul in Barcelona!' called out the Public School boy, very red in the face.

Gillian turned upon the young woman, one place removed from herself, who had opened her mouth for the first time (and who was not quite out of the top drawer by a long way) and remarked, with a laugh of unpleasantly playful scorn:

'If you had been born in a legation, my dear, you wouldn't ask *that*!'

At this Percy Hardcaster turned his head, with a definite access of admiration in his eyes and laughed in hearty approval over this sally of hers, which had afforded a glimpse of Gillian Communist in a highly-placed cradle, enjoying infantile extra-territoriality, and her first lispings enshrined in affairs of state: while the young woman definitely not of top-drawer status looked suitably crushed, but certainly gave Gillian rather a spiteful look.

'You said that the other guard, Percy,' Geoffrey said, 'was, if anything, a dirtier piece of work than the – than who is he —?'

'Alvaro Morato,' said Percy. 'Did I give you that impression, Geoffrey? No, that's not quite right.'

Percy frowned gravely – it was obvious that in a matter of such international moment he was anxious that nothing should be said to distort, or to weigh unduly, upon one side or the other, the evidence (direct or indirect, substantive or contingent, intrinsic or extrinsic, parole or under seal) – seeing that he was the principal, and indeed the sole, witness: no *plena probatio* existed. It was Percy first, and Percy last, and Percy all the time who would testify. Or if Percy was to be a party to the action, then Percy was prepared to march forward through Rejoinder, Surrejoinder, Rebutter, and Surrebutter, holding aloft, with steady hand, the exact image of the truth, and nothing but the truth, so help me Lenin!

'Serafín – that is what he was called,' said Percy, when he had sufficiently paused and collected himself and focused his mind on the facts, 'and I can assure you he was some seraph and all! – he was not a bad type in his way. That he got behind me when the firing began is true, and that I shouldn't be in the mess I'm in if he'd acted like a man, that is true too. He was shot on the ground where he was shamming he'd been hit. Though of course *I* had got what was meant for *him* and he was never hit at all. He just fell down and shammed dead. But old Alvaro had it in for him, because he'd taken the job on at a tenth the figure fixed by the governor, so he plugged the poor devil for muscling in on his racket!'

'These police gangsters are unthinkably awful,' said one of the men from the headquarters of Propaganda Limited, or Red Dope for Leftie Schoolteachers.

'The police-terror gets worse in Spain every day,' said Geoffrey: 'it is really a bit too much over the odds at present. The Germans have nothing on them in the matter of sheer beastliness.'

'And the Jesuits are behind it!' hissed the girl-neighbour of Gillian, still thinking of nuns and torture by bed-pan.

Letter on Spain

To Robert Shaw Barlow

Hotel Bristol, Rome
November 3, 1936

Dear Bob,
I am glad to know that you are well again and going your
usual rounds . . .

Yes, of course I am concerned about the war in Spain, and some
of my connections there may be actually fighting – of course on
the nationalistic side. I have no inside knowledge of the affair: but
reflecting on it from a distance, I have a notion that it may be very
important: a sort of turning-point in history, which in my
thoughts I call *The Revolt of the Nations*. Since the triumph of
Christianity, and again after the Reformation and the English,
American, and French revolutions, our part of the world has been
governed by ideas, by theories, by universalistic sects like the
Church, the Free Masons, the Free Trade Industrial Liberals, and
last of all the Bolshies. Such influences are non-natural, non-
biological; whereas the agricultural, military, and artistic life of
nations is spontaneous, with ambitions that impose morality, but
are not imposed by morality of any sort. Now isn't that perhaps
what the world is returning to after two thousand years of hypno-
tization by medicine-men and prophets?

Spain has always been the most unfortunate of countries, and is
now having a hard struggle to throw the Bolshies off, that had got
hold of her always execrable government. But my friends write
that the young people are unrecognizable in their energy and
discipline, and that we shall soon see a new Spain as vigorous as
in the Middle Ages. And of course Spain would not be alone in
the transformation.

Yours ever

Writers Take Sides

Letters about the war in Spain from 418 American authors published by the League of American Writers, 318 Fourth Avenue, New York City.

February 1, 1938

Donald Ogden Stewart

'To the Writers of America':

Fascism has appeared in the Western Hemisphere, not in the lurid imagination of alarmist prophets, but in the actual and openly acknowledged event. On Armistice Day the papers carried the news of the establishment in Brazil of a corporate state under dictatorial authority, and the abolition of parliamentary bodies elected by the people.

We know how German Fascism has murdered and destroyed, how Italian Fascism has conquered her place in the Abyssinian sun, how Japanese militarism fights in China her undeclared wars. We know how Fascist countries everywhere destroy civil liberties within their borders and ignore international law beyond them. Today the struggle rages east of us and west of us. Tomorrow it may be in our midst. It is constantly drawing nearer.

But there are some who, despite the martyrdom of Durango and Guernica, the enduring agony of Madrid, of Bilbao, the shelling of Almeria and Lerida, of Barcelona, and Valencia, are still in doubt, or who aver that it is possible that Fascism may be what it proclaims it is: the saviour of civilization.

We urge you to dispel the least shadow of that doubt. This is the question we would have you answer: 'Are you for, or are you against Franco and Fascism? Are you for, or are you against the legal government and the people of Republican Spain?' We desire to print your answers. We wish the whole country to know what is felt by the most sensitive instruments of the national life, you American writers. Your verdict has world importance.

Yours sincerely,
Donald Ogden Stewart
President, League of American Writers

AGAINST FASCISM

Sherwood Anderson
Sure I am against all the damn Fascists or any other kind of dictator.

William Faulkner
I most sincerely wish to go on record as being unalterably opposed to Franco and Fascism, to all violations of the legal government and outrages against the people of Republican Spain.

John Steinbeck
Just returned from a little tour in the agricultural fields of California. We have our own Fascist groups out here. They haven't bombed open towns yet but in Salinas last year tear gas was thrown in a Union Hall and through the windows of workingmen's houses. That's rather close, isn't it?

Your question as to whether I am for Franco is rather insulting. Have you seen anyone not actuated by greed who was for Franco? No, I'm not for Franco and his Moors and Italians and Germans. But some Americans are. Some Americans were for the Hessians England sent against our own revolutionary army. They were for the Hessians because they were selling things to them. The descendants of some of these Americans are still very rich and still touchy concerning the American Way, and our 'ancient liberties'. I am treasonable enough not to believe in the liberty of a man or a group to exploit, torment, or slaughter other men or groups. I believe in the despotism of human life and happiness against the liberty of money and possessions.

I. F. Stone
Only the writer who draws his sustenance from the caved-in teat of a decayed past can be a Fascist. Fascism is capitalism seeking by brutality to evade the logic that moves mankind inexorably towards the common-sense solution of the paradox that puts want amid plenty, idle men beside idle factories, underfed children in a land of rotting crops. Fascism, by its very nature, must be anti-rational and anti-humane.

Criminal disunity among liberals and the Left helped Fascism to victory in Italy and Germany. The Popular Front has made it possible for the people of Spain to fight the greatest battle against Fascism the world has yet seen. It is not strange that the allies of Spanish Fascism are to be found in brown shirt and in black shirt in the most backward section of the Catholic Church, among ignorant Moors and in those refined upper circles of the British aristocracy so delicately bred that they prefer the murder of children in Barcelona to the loss of a penny on their profits from Rio Tinto.

If the Spanish people win, the forces of Fascism will be set back the world over. Should the Loyalists lose, we may expect a tidal wave of reaction, obscurantism, race hatred, and thuggery, menacing our own lives and our own homes. We must never forget that the barricades in Madrid are barricades everywhere – in defence of freedom, of culture, and of humanity.

Dorothy Thompson
I have your letter asking me if I am for or against Franco. I think it is rather a laughable question to ask me.

I have expressed myself on this subject in my column time and again. I have also been permanently expelled from Germany. I wrote a piece on the bombing of Guernica which I believe has been translated into most European languages, and used as propaganda by the Loyalists.

I am not, however, a Communist, and I dislike having my anti-Fascist opinions used as Communist propaganda.

Samuel Yellen
It appears to me obvious that every writer as a writer must be against the spread of Fascism, whether in Italy, Germany, Japan, Brazil, or Spain. No further reason would be necessary than the burning of the books in Germany ...

But the writer has another duty as a citizen, a duty which should intensify his opposition to Fascism. For Fascism has meant the oppression of workers and farmers in Italy in the interest of the employing and land-owning classes, the development of a horrible and ignorant 'race' hatred in Germany, the loosing of imperialism and militarism in Japan, the suppression of civil liberties in Brazil, and the effort to stamp out the legally chosen government of the people of Republican Spain ...

NEUTRAL

Robinson Jeffers
You ask what I am for and what against in Spain. I would give
my right hand, of course, to prevent the agony; I would not give
a flick of my finger to help either side win.

Sam Atyeo

From *Up and Down Under: Being the Author's Adventures in Art and Diplomacy*

Something I think of importance is the propaganda in France during the early part of the Spanish war and of course the fact that Blum had stirred up almost everybody who wasn't a workman.

The Spanish Republican government was considered Comm by the Right exactly as was Blum's government, a smack at the Republicans was a smack at Blum and vice versa. As for being Comm, in the 1936 elections in Spain there were 474 members elected to the Cortes of which only 16 were Comms, and Spain had no diplomatic relations with the Soviet Union – but with the Vatican! Negrin (whom I knew after he was booted out) was not nearly as left as Attlee. As for the anti-Church contention, they've been attacking churches in Spain for over a hundred years. The very quality of the Church in Spain provokes opposition. Their record of brutality must put them in the big league with Stalin, Hitler, Musso, etc., etc. (And after the war a man couldn't get work unless he had a good conduct certificate from the local priest.)

As far back as December 1935, the Spanish Government made a contract with France for the supply of most of its military material. France's Government (M. Blum's Popular Front) was at the time making important social reforms against a powerful opposition from the Right. When the Spanish war broke, a highly organized propaganda machine started to function in France. Its first act was to give great publicity to the resignation of some members of the Spanish Embassy in Paris, resignations prompted, it was said, by the fact that the Republican Government had fallen into the hands of Communists and that the Communists were persecuting the Church (nuns being raped, holy sepulchres being defouled, etc., etc.). This was to become the classic line, it wasn't subtle, but it became very effective when the large and vociferous French Comm party claimed that the war in Spain was a Capitalistic war being fought against International Communism and that the only people resisting this Capitalistic aggression were the Communists. *Tiens! Merde!*

There were a few groups of students and artists who worked doing publicity for the Republican Government, they were not organized, and finally they were either taken over by the Comms or ground to bits between the Fascist and Communist machines.

Franco's propaganda was minutely organized and had seemingly unlimited helpers. I'll give you a personal illustration of this. One night when I was having a drink with Alexander Werth in a 'bistrot' near *la Place d'Italie*, there came up to the bar a little nondescript man and he got into a loud conversation with two tall young workmen. He produced a letter he said he had received from his Spanish brother-in-law. He read bits of the letter, loud enough to be heard by all: his brother-in-law, he said, was an ardent Republican, but had become so disgusted with the atrocities committed by the Communists, who had taken over the Government, that he was joining Franco. Franco was an old Spanish General and had come out of retirement (he was neither old nor retired) to defend the homeland. He added that some French newspapers had swallowed the anti-Franco propaganda, but that was because their correspondents were living in luxury Palaces in Madrid, paid for by the Government. The little *type* eventually left, followed a few minutes later by the workmen. Alex Werth said, 'This casual little encounter is altogether too pat, let's follow them.'

They put on the same scene in three 'bistrots', at the entrance of the fourth, they were waiting for us, and wanted to know why we were following them. We said we were in total admiration of their act and naturally we were for the good cause. They were quite pleased, like actors taking a bow. One of the 'workmen' turned out to be an Irish priest, and the other a Jesuit seminarist, the little guy was editor of a Catholic action broad-sheet. They worked for a large organization, spreading the word round in public places, while the female members wrote piles of letters to members of Parliament.

Eventually, all this propaganda – and it was coming from everywhere: Maurras in the *Académie Française*, lots of writers and artists (who should have known better), and the thieving politicians (some of them to emerge again with Pétain and Charlie le Roi) as well as the ordinary *mec* in the street – all this pro-Franco stuff got to the public, split France down the middle and forced Blum into accepting a non-intervention policy. After solemn assurances from Germany and Italy, he finally announced and applied a total embargo on all arms to Spain and he closed the French–Spanish frontier. This was the death of the Spanish Republican Government, Spain's second Republic.

P.S. How successfully the Franco propaganda functioned and still functions is easily put to the test. Ask almost anybody, anywhere in France today, what they think of Franco? You'll be surprised how many will tell you, 'Franco saved Spain from Communism.'

From 'The Idea of Holy War'

There is a kind of thinking that makes much of the possibility of
a holy war. This notion of a holy war is worth examining. The
fact that civil war – social war, political war, class war, a war of
international interests and of international interventions – should
take on in Spain an added characteristic: that of a war of religion,
is a fact to be explained by infinitely deplorable historical circumstances past and present. If this fact adds to the gravity of such a
war, it does not suffice to transform it into a holy war, that is to
say (for here one must speak in rigorously defined terms) in a war
theoretically elevated to the level of the sacred, and consecrated
by God. We are sorry, in saying this, to run counter to the convictions of many Spanish Catholics. The question at stake, since
it concerns essential points in the philosophy of culture and in
theology and is extremely important for all modern civilization,
demands a purely objective treatment, and we feel obliged in
conscience to set forth what we believe to be the truth on this
point.

It has been said that 'the Spanish national war is a holy war, and
the holiest that history has known'.[1] To judge by prevalent psychological attitudes and states of mind, one may well ask whether
in a general way, and apart from certain restricted groups, there
is in fact any correspondence between the alleged idea of holy war

---

[1] 'La guerra nacional española es guerra santa, y la mas santa que registra la his-
toria.' Reverend Ignacio G. Menendez-Reigada, O. P., *La guerra nacional espanola ante
la moral y el derecho* (*La Ciencia Tomista*, Salamanca, 1937, fasc. I y 2). The Reverend
Menendez-Reigada justifies this assertion by saying that what is at stake in the present
war is the very existence of all religion, natural or positive, as well as of the natural
foundation of society. One may be allowed a doubt whether Providence has no
other means to save those primordial foundations of human life except by the victory
of the Spanish nationalists and their allies. At any rate the argument under discussion
would tend in itself to prove that what we have is really a just war, not a *holy war* in
the strict sense that the philosophy of history and culture must accord to this word
and which is the object of the present observations.

and the feelings actually manifested. All the relevant evidence suggests that a cold resignation to a sanguinary fatality and to all that man does on the grounds that war is war actually plays a larger role in affairs than does religious fervour.

But our present study is not meant to dwell on this plane. Whatever may be true of the effective sincerity and authenticity on the psychological level of the idea of a holy war in a given set of circumstances, it is the intrinsic value of that idea that we wish to consider, and in its relation to historical reality.

In the case of forms of civilization 'sacral' in their nature, like the civilization of the ancient Hebrews, or Islamic civilization, or the Christian civilization of the Middle Ages, the notion of a holy war, however difficult to explain, might have had a meaning. (For this reason holy war was directed against strangers threatening these 'sacral' if temporal communities; it had no place within them as between brothers and fellow-citizens.)

In its essence war is of the things that belong to Caesar and pertains essentially to temporal concerns, since it shakes to the very foundations – to the point of the sacrifice of individuals – the temporal community; every war includes political and economic interests, the lusts of flesh and blood. Nevertheless, in a civilization of a sacral type, this increment of the terrestrial could itself play an *instrumental* role in relation to spiritual ends really having – I do not mean solely in intention, I mean in the objective evolution of history – the primacy. When the Crusaders in all their greed and ambition set out to deliver the tomb of Christ, this religious aim really served as magnet for the rest and really characterized it. (Even then, considering the way it was actually conducted and all the impurities it carried with it, did such a war really please God as much as people thought? That is another question. The Crusades in the end failed in their principal purpose.)

But with respect to forms of civilization like ours, in which (according to the teachings of Leo XIII on this subject) the temporal is more sharply distinguished from the spiritual and, having become quite autonomous, no longer serves as an instrument for the sacred, in civilizations of a secular type,[2] the notion of holy

[2] Cf. *Humanisme integral*, pp. 156 ff. We should remember that according to the views set forth in this work, the superordination of the Church with respect to civil society is maintained as against all liberal theology, but it is held that in the historical

war loses all significance.[3] Just or unjust, a war against a foreign power or a civil war remains, then, necessarily what it is in itself and essentially, something profane and secular, and not sacred; moreover, not only something profane, but of easy access from the world of darkness and sin. And if, defended by one side, attacked by the other, sacred values happen to be involved, they do not of themselves render either holy or sacred a complex that is profane in nature; in fact, it is these values which are secularized by history in its objective movement and borne along by its temporal ends. The war in question does not become holy, it only runs the risk of blaspheming the holy. And the abominable means employed today make such a result inevitable. It runs the risk also of raising anti-religious hatred to the heights of a paroxysm without remedy. If some rash individuals fire upon the people from a few church buildings, the people will want to raze all churches to

---

perspective of modern times this superordination functions as a principal cause of higher status with reference to a *principal cause* of lower status, and not with reference to an *instrumental cause* or ministering agency as was often the case in the Middle Ages. When in the encyclical *Divini Redemptoris* the Pope exhorts the nations to curb the propaganda of atheism, he asks them to do this as principal causes, not as ministering cause or instrument in the service of the Church. Likewise under modern conditions the aid that the civil authority must tender to the Church takes the form of a free collaboration and not of ministering agency (and therefore it is exercised in actuality through the support given to the liberties of the Church rather than by putting at her service the temporal instruments of external power). Finally, when the Church exercises its spiritual power in matters that are at the same time spiritual and temporal, what is being exercised is its direct power *in spiritualibus*, not its indirect power *in temporalibus*; and, similarly, when the ecclesiastical authority makes it a matter of duty for Catholic citizens of a country (for instance in fulfilling their function as voters) to defend the religious liberties and those goods appertaining to spiritual interests which are involved in the temporal, she is not using the temporal as agency but is illuminating and guiding, by an act with a direct bearing upon the spiritual (and valid only in this context), the conscience of those citizens with respect to the act to be accomplished.

We should observe furthermore that the passage from one historical perspective to another – for instance, from an age of sacral to an age of secular civilization –

---

[3] Or shall one call sacred, though not in a strict sense of the word, any war where religious interests are concerned, and more generally interests involving those forms of good that man considers supreme? Then anyone, the moment he is convinced that his war is just, can also say that he is waging a holy war: for in any just war supreme forms of good are involved. And in every civil war there are, alas, and on each side, enough human values at stake, and partial truths set up one against the other, so that any man, aided and abetted by passion, can *under the influence of his passions*, be persuaded that he lives and dies for justice.

the ground and blot out all marks of religion. A few priests encourage a recourse to violence, and all priests will be held as public
enemies.

We do not condemn in and for itself the use of force. We have
sought to show elsewhere that in the hierarchy of means such a
means is far from the highest, and that by reason of the axiom:
the order of means corresponds to the order of ends, temporal history
justifies a Christian in setting above this means a world of other
means;[4] nevertheless it is not evil in itself and intrinsically. Nor
do we think that the recourse to this means is excluded in itself
and in principle from the defence of religion (although, of the
means to defend it, it is surely the least good).[5] But if, in certain
extreme cases, citizens turn to force to defend religious liberties,
it will be – I mean in the climate of history in which our modern
civilizations exist – because these liberties concern, as higher
values, the common welfare of the earthly city and of civilization,
and not because the latter would be functioning as ministering

---

occurs only gradually, and with a different rate of development in different regions.
(In this respect France seems to have been in advance of other nations.) We are of the
opinion that Don John of Austria at the battle of Lepanto and John Sobieski at the
gates of Vienna were the last representatives in history of the medieval holy war. But
social memory and imagination naturally lead the intelligence into an anachronistic
view. There is no easier error for those who neglect the philosophy of history.

Even Spain bears witness to the passage of modern history, since the French
Revolution, into an age of secular civilization. The evidence is the fact that in order
to combat one side aided by Soviet Russia and open to its ideology, the other side is
not only aided by National-Socialist Germany, which also persecuted Catholicism,
as well as Italian Fascism, but is also open to ideologies and historical currents whose
aim is anything but the spread of the Kingdom of God and whose inspiration is
entirely political and imperialistic. Let us quote a few articles from the programme
of the Spanish Falange: '3. We demand an Empire. We affirm that the historic

---

[4] Cf. *Humanisme intégral*, pp. 261–99.

[5] Apropos of war the Reverend Gerald Vann recently wrote: 'Christianity will
not flourish through the suicide of Christians, even if one could suppose that it
profits from the murder of non-Christians. And what is the situation in the case of
a civil war, where the support of religion would be the aim on one side? Shall we,
in the presence of contemporary facts which impose themselves upon our attention,
be blind to the impossibility of maintaining such a cause pure and unalloyed by less
worthy aims, to the inevitable danger of a world war with stakes quite different from
those at first envisaged, to the inevitable conclusion: chaos and anarchy?' Rev.
Gerald Vann, O.P., *The Colosseum*, March 1937: 'The union of Christians is based, in
the twentieth century as in the first, not on the triumph of the "good" sides in political struggles or in civil wars, but upon the secret solidarity of our divine life nour-
ished by the same Eucharist.' Rev. M.-D. Chenu, O.P., *Sept*, May 28, 1937.

agencies for the holy, and would be set in motion as its instruments. Thus the principle of the primacy of the spiritual could, in civilizations of a sacral type, express itself in the idea of a holy war, of which the Middle Ages made so great a use. In our civilizations of secular type it excludes this idea by virtue of the very principle of the transcendence of the sacral order: for, since it is no longer the instrument of the earthly city (as was possible only where the earthly city was sacrally constituted), a holy war, if one wished at all costs to preserve the idea of it as an idea-force, would then pass for the instrumentality of the sacral order itself acting through its own means, which is absurd: the proper means of the kingdom of God not being the force of arms nor bloodshed. Let us invoke then, if we believe it just, the justice of the war we wage, but let us not invoke its sanctity. Let us kill, if we think killing our duty, in the name of the social order or of the nation; that is already horrible enough; let us not kill in the name of Christ the King, who is not a war-chief but a King of grace and charity, who died for all men, and whose kingdom is not of this world. 'If my kingdom were of this world, my servants would certainly strive that I should not be delivered to the Jews . . .'[6] When the inhabitants of a village refused to receive Jesus, James and John said, 'Lord, wilt thou that we command fire to come down from heaven, and consume them?' And turning, he rebuked them, saying: 'You know not of what spirit you are. The Son of Man came not to destroy souls, but to save.'[7]

'God knows, war is always, even under the least sorry of auspices, something so terrible and inhuman! Man seeking out man

---

achievement of Spain is the Empire . . . Spain insists on its status as the spiritual axis of the Spanish world in order to assert its pre-eminence in universal enterprises. 4. . . . We shall give back to the army on land, sea, and in the air, in the public consideration, all the dignity it so well deserves and will work towards a Spain whose whole existence is informed by a military spirit, in accordance with the image of its army. 23. The essential mission of the state is, by means of a rigorous discipline of education, to create a strong and unified national spirit, and to establish in future generations patriotic pride and joy . . . 25. Our movement incorporates Catholic feeling – traditionally glorious and predominant in Spain – for the sake of national reconstruction. The Church and the State will reconcile their respective instrumentalities without recognition of any encroachment or any activity which might infringe upon the dignity of the state or upon national integrity.'

---

[6] John xviii. 36 (Douay version).
[7] Luke ix. 54–6 (Douay version).

to kill him, to kill the greatest possible number, to do him injury in life and belongings, with means ever more powerful and murderous! What shall we say when the war is between brothers?"[8] The introduction of the myth of holy war in the present conflicts from which Europe suffers would be an irreparable calamity. By creating on one side, and associating with religion a deep sense of moral injury and an incurable resentment, by favouring, on the other side, an internal alteration and, as it were, an Islamization of the religious consciousness itself, it is at Christianity that such a myth would strike the hardest blow. And could its inevitable effect, given our human weakness, be less than to multiply sacrilege everywhere?

God forbid that I should pronounce a single word to wound a single soul in its sincere conviction. In Spain I have friends in both camps, I know that their hearts can be touched to the quick and that a word suffices to exacerbate their suffering. From men scandalized not to have their war deemed a holy war I have received insulting letters, which matter very little. But I have received other letters marked by a deep sense of injury, and these have distressed me. Yet I must call things by their names. Sacrilege in the strictest sense of the word, insulting God with respect to what is almost physically consecrated to Him, and by an act expressly intended against Him; or sacrilege in a more spiritual and not less serious sense, insulting God with respect to what His love has made His own, and by an act charged with contempt for Him; it is a horrible sacrilege to massacre priests – even if 'Fascists', they are ministers of Christ – out of hatred for religion; and it is another act of sacrilege, horrible also, to massacre his poor children – even if 'Marxists', they are Christ's own – in the name of religion. It is manifest sacrilege to burn the churches and the holy images, sometimes in blind rage, sometimes, as in Barcelona, methodically and systematically in all the cold fury of doctrinaire Anarchism; and it is another act of sacrilege – this time in religious form – to rig out Mohammedan soldiers with images of the Sacred Heart in order that they may slaughter in holy zeal the sons of Christians[9] and to claim to have enrolled God

---

[8] Pius XI, *Discourse to Spanish Pilgrims*, September 14, 1937.

[9] In a solemn assembly, at the *alcazar* of Seville, General Franco said recently to Moors whom he was receiving upon their return from their pilgrimage to Mecca:

n the passions of a struggle where the adversary is considered unworthy of all respect and of all pity. It is sacrilege to profane the holy places and the Holy Eucharist, to be zealous in persecution of everything that is consecrated to God, to dishonour and torture nuns, to exhume corpses that they may be made objects of derision, as we saw in the dark days immediately after the outbreak of the war; and it is sacrilege to shoot down, as at Badajoz, hundreds of men as part of the celebration of the Assumption, or to annihilate by bombing from the air, as in Durango – for a holy war hates even more than the infidel the faithful who do not serve it – churches and the children of the people who filled them, and the priests who were celebrating the mysteries; or by bombing, as at Guernica, an entire city with its churches and tabernacles, with poor creatures mowed down by machine-gun fire as they sought to escape.[10] The horrors perpetrated by the Reds in all their revelation of human savagery have several times been publicized; and the number of crimes and extortions due to the hysteria of crowds and the violence of individuals is doubtless even greater than we imagine. Eye-witness accounts of the White

---

'Spain and Islam have always been the peoples who have best understood each other.' *España y el Islam han sido siempre los pueblos que mejor se comprendieron.' (Diario Vasco de San Sebastian,* April 4, 1937.) This statement is doubtless even truer than the man who made it realizes.

[10] A letter from Saragossa speaks with legitimate indignation of the Red aviation several months ago dropping three bombs (which fortunately did not burst) on the church of Our Lady of the Pillar. It carried on heavier and more destructive bombardments, too. But those who rightly consider this an act of vandalism ought to be the first to condemn with all their hearts the destruction of Guernica.

For the sake of those who were scandalized by the protests of a certain number of French Catholics against this destruction, may I observe also: 1. that these Catholics condemn all bombardments of open cities, whatever may be their source (it will be recalled that the *Osservatore Romano* has called attention to the false allegation of some that it had 'called the former to task' on this subject). If some day the Red aviation, according to the principles of total war, destroys a city in the White zone just as German aviation destroyed Guernica, they will not fail to raise their protests; 2. that the assassinations, the acts of sacrilege, the massacres of priests committed in the Red zone have been denounced from the start and with the greatest vehemence by a French Catholic whose political positions are opposed to insurrection by the military. (Cf. Francisque Gay, *Dans les Flammes et dans le Sang.*) Elementary good faith requires us not to forget this fact. Moreover, the criminal acts in question have been the object of solemn condemnation by the Holy See; and since they were broadcast by the press, no special effort seemed called for to make them known to the Catholic conscience. It is an act of stupidity and calumny that only war psychosis can explain to imagine that Christians can find any excuse for such crimes.

terror are beginning to come in, and even the early accounts suggest that the level of cruelty and contempt of human life reaches a rare elevation. Worse still, in the name of holy war, all this is accomplished under the banners and standards of religion; the cross of Jesus Christ gleams like a symbol of war over the death-throes of men shot down in cold blood; and neither the heart of man nor human history will stand for that. A man who does not believe in God may conclude that, everything considered, it is only the price we must pay for a return to order and that one crime is as good as another. A man who believes in God knows that there is no worse disorder; it is as though the bones of Christ which even the executioners at Calvary could not touch were broken on the cross by Christians.

It may be that in Spain every war tends to become a holy war: in that sense the term 'holy war' no longer signifies something of a determinate objective nature, but refers to a well-marked trait in the historical temperament of a people. And since the myth of the Revolution, as it developed in the Socialistic and Anarchistic schools of the nineteenth century, can be regarded as the old idea of a Crusade transposed and laicized, we shall have to admit quite logically that the Red militia are waging their holy war. Who would dare ask to speak with less than respect of the heroic sacrifices Spain has exhibited on both sides? Who would deny the admirable courage, and the ardent devotion to an elevated cause animating so many men – White volunteer *requetes* or peoples' Militia, Basques or men of Navarre – men intent only on mutual slaughter? But the criterion for judging war is to be found elsewhere, in the consideration of the objective causes and conditions of the conflict, and in the question of justice. And the curse of civil war, especially when reinforced by the myth of holy war, consists precisely in the fact that it permits one side to see only the aberrations of the other and blinds the brothers in blood on both sides to the valour with which, in spite of so many nameless crimes, brave men in both camps bear witness to the common patrimony of virtue in their country.

Mr Christopher Dawson remarked recently that if a great European war breaks out in the near future, it will be less a Capitalist war for markets than a 'war between faiths for the possession of men's minds. The Fascist powers will believe that they defend

Christianity and European culture against Communistic atheism, while the Democratic and Socialist states will believe that they are defending peace and justice against militarist and Capitalist tyranny.' Hence that danger of *international civil war* that the *Osservatore Romano* pointed out a few months ago. In this phase of history the warmongers will be above all the 'idealists and propagandists', and 'principles will play a role as important as toxic gases'.[11] These observations corroborate our remarks on the danger for civilization of the myth of holy war; they show that anyone who really wants peace and the welfare of civilization must work to protect men's minds against this idea. Here, too, a maxim from the Gospel can be used to serve temporal politics and to save from the ruin of universal war what still subsists here below of historical Christianity, as well as the germs of a new Christianity. What peace in the world demands is not the opposition of ideology to ideology but a vigorous effort of concrete intelligence to permit existing states and existing historical forces to give each other mutual support along the road of history 'by agreeing with your adversary quickly while you are in the way with him'.[12]

The war being waged in Spain is a war of extermination; it tends not only to destroy the Spanish nation from top to bottom, but also to provoke a universal conflict; everywhere it exasperates passions that will never forgive; it is in process of dishonouring Europe. It is a grave menace to our France in certain essential conditions of external security.

A foreigner should be the last person to take sides in this civil war; he lacks sufficient information, direct experience of affairs, and competence.[13] The way in which the passions of party in all countries have exploited the tragedy in Spain is positively indecent, and the aim has been to bring the level of hatreds even higher.

Not that a Catholic can avoid feeling to the very depths what

[11] *The Colosseum*, March 1937.

[12] Matthew v. 25 (Douay version).

[13] We have presented for consideration, in two other studies, not this time with special reference to the war in Spain, but in a general fashion and with a view to consequences that may result elsewhere, the problem that the present crisis of civilization poses for the consciences of men as well as our personal position in relation to this problem. (Communication of January 23, 1937, to *L'Union pour la Vérité*, to appear in the *Bulletin* for June–July; and *Sept*, February 12, 1937; these two studies have appeared in Spanish in the magazine *Sur*, April 1937.)

concerns both his brothers in faith and the future of religion in Spain. We know that the Church has the promises of Jesus Christ, and that Spain has never been able to content itself with the purely terrestrial; we know also that Christianity, however cruelly it may feel certain historical wounds in its sides, can always count on the suffering of the saints that God can call forth, and upon that healing power. Yet when, in the face of the drama before our very eyes, one side represents any such things as a 'crushing' *dénouement* in favour of the Reds as the ruin, at least for a generation or two, of religious institutions in Spain, and as marking the advent of a militant anti-religious policy or of a religious 'anti-ecclesiasticism' much more dangerous than political anti-clericalism, so that a baptized people, the people of Saint Theresa and Saint John of the Cross, would then be deprived of its rights to be instructed in the divine truth, and the labour of propagation of the faith would have to start all over again, and from the catacombs up; and when the other side represents a *dénouement* of defeat as equally 'crushing' in turn since it would not only impose upon religion, considered a means of government or 'incorporated' in a political programme, the kind of protection that enslaves, but also would open up between it and the people an abyss of bitterness and resentment, and would dry up the inner springs of its own vitality, so that the underlying causes of the spiritual evils of our time would continue to poison history – we are not inclined to minimize the dangers of a contrary type thus indicated. What can we and must we hope but that the destiny of Spain may be spared both kinds of peril? If, even *after* the horrible constraint imposed upon consciences by recourse to the irreparable and the unchaining of violence, it were towards a *third solution* that Providence, after all, should incline events, that would be strong confirmation of the views of those who, belonging to countries hitherto preserved from civil war, think that this third solution, which will impose itself sooner or later, must be found and applied at all costs *before* a complete political catastrophe. And it is not only from the point of view of spiritual values, but also from that of temporal values, and of establishing a new order in harmony with the dignity of the human person that the world expects a third solution.

So far as Spain is concerned, whatever may be the sympathies, or an equal sense of reserve, that a foreigner, because of his philosophical view of the problems of our day and his general political tendencies, may feel towards one or the other side in this war, he has something better to do than to assert his preferences: if he is at all aware of the multiple perils that we have just outlined and is concerned for the general welfare of civilization, he will want to act in favour of peace in Spain. We believe that men of good will, in particular those whose religious faith requires a special interest in matters of peace and justice, have from this point of view an urgent talk to accomplish; not only may they bend every effort in aid of refugees and victims, to whatever side they may belong, and, wherever it is possible, save human lives; they can also organize themselves in order to set up beforehand, as fully as any outside contribution permits, the conditions for civil and religious pacification in Spain. Does this mean mixing water and fire, in accordance with the too-easy metaphor of men resigned to the worst? Or, in terms of another equally easy metaphor, to wash one's hands of good and evil equally? No, this means recognizing that all the good is not on one side and all the evil on the other; and hoping that one day there will emerge a new mode of existence, in which, after the terrible purification we are now undergoing, certain historical values will appear as complementary which today, mingled with so many errors, hurl unhappy men in exasperation against each other. In the event that one of the two sides – after how long, and at what cost in human lives? – should obtain the victory, a victory which might well render all these hatreds permanent; or in the event that a peace not due to the sole force of arms could be envisaged, thanks perhaps to some international initiative (which should aim first of all to provide conditions for the Spanish people freely to declare and realize their will and to vote for the political and social regime of its choice), it is of primary importance that a programme of pacification, very difficult, without doubt, but not impossible, be undertaken, which will have to be focused especially upon international public opinion, in order to bear witness *after all* to the spirit of Christ. This is not the place to examine in detail ways and means in such a programme, nor the obstacles of all kinds it will encounter, which we make no effort to conceal. We have only wished to point to its necessity.

(Translation by Angelo P. Bertocci)

The Witnesses

Although from various backgrounds and in Spain for different reasons, the witnesses saw events more clearly than almost all other writers. They particularly saw the tragedy of the war, the victims – military and political – and they focused their accounts on them. These writers, in a sense, bore witness to the Spanish Civil War.

Georges Bernanos and Simone Weil consciously place their writing in the religious tradition of bearing witness. Bernanos, a French Catholic and Rightist, cannot deny what 'I've seen with my own eyes': the Nationalist terror in Majorca. Repeatedly, he tells us what he 'saw', had 'to witness', and he concludes that 'It is a cruel thing when what you were born to love becomes degraded before your eyes.'

Simone Weil writes in response to Bernanos' book about Spain. She tells him what she saw in her visit to Catalonia. In this letter, as in all her writing, she tries to see the inner nature of mankind: '. . . one found immorality, cynicism, fanaticism and cruelty, but also love and fraternal spirit, and, above all, that concern for honour which is so beautiful in the humiliated.' What eluded the tourists on their short visits to Spain was somehow accessible to Simone Weil.

Antoine de Saint-Exupéry is a more secular kind of witness. His flying enables him to write from a great height. He does not care to spot political nuance, he only sees the broad outlines and he calls the war a plague in which both sides are 'struggling blindly against infection'.

Before the Spanish war, G. L. Steer had been a military correspondent for *The Times*. By chance, he was touring the Basque provinces at the time of the bombing of Guernica. His professional knowledge enabled him to reconstruct the awful event in detail. Steer's account, so different from the French writers' moral judgements, moves us because of its overwhelming specificity of detail. And, in the end, his detail forces us to become witnesses and, like Picasso's painting, to bear witness to the systematic murder from the sky.

T. C. Worsley was a British expatriate living in Malaga at the outbreak of the war. With the fall of the city (related by Koestler in The Reporters section), he joined up with a British ambulance corps. Beneath the surface horror of his account are layers of ironic perception about his travelling companions, Hesketh and Rathbone, and his own viewing of events: he had seen 'the procession [of refugees] as you view a film unrolling itself in front of you, the reality of which . . . you could somehow diminish . . . But the moment we stepped out from the security of the interior and mixed with the people, we found ourselves engulfed . . .' Thus, he must see the Spanish Civil War. (Ed. note: After many years of public silence on the subject, Worsley recently published a fine novel about the war, *Fellow Travelers*.)

Martha Gellhorn, an American writer, spent much of her time in Spain with Hemingway (she later became his third wife). She remained after he departed and she wrote some anecdotal but moving snapshots of Barcelona in the third and last winter of the war. Her strength is that she is unable to avert her eyes from the final human tragedy: "Would you like to see the medical ward?" the tall lanky boy said. "Well," I said. Well, no I thought. "I like the children" [he said]. So we went.'

Hugh (Humphrey) Slater wrote the finest work of fiction in English about the Spanish Civil War. Almost unknown and long out-of-print, *The Heretics* is based on the author's experiences in Spain, in the Communist Party, and his understanding of the political infighting on the Left during the war. Paralleling the adventures of three orphaned Albigensian children during the Children's Crusade (the Albigensians were a medieval heretic sect) with three British intellectuals during the Spanish Civil War, Slater achieves a unique synthesis in English fiction: a novel of political ideas. Slater is also one of the few English writers who portrayed the political victims of the war: those men and women crushed – not by Franco's bombs or bullets – but by the collision of their idealism with political expediency and cruelty.

In the writing of the witnesses, the victims of the war speak to us through the authors as mediums. What distinguishes the witnesses from all the other writers in the collection is the minimum of authorial intrusion, the lack of ego insistence. There is one partial exception: Gustav Regler, a political commissar in the International Brigade, was obsessed by the first person singular (his massive ego can barely fit between the covers of his autobiography, *The Owl of Minerva*). Yet when Regler witnesses the fall of the Republic, his description brushes his ego aside long enough for us to see the sad flight of the refugees.

Regler stands at the French border: 'That afternoon the Republican troops came. They were received as though they were tramps.' And when he quotes the dying Machado, we see the final paradox of the Spanish war: its brutality, its destruction, but also, its luminous hope:

> *Know how to hope –*
> *await the rising tide*
> *like a boat ashore*
> *and do not fear for the departure.*

George Orwell's *Homage to Catalonia* is probably the best single work in English about the war and it seems appropriate to end the anthology with his final pages: his summing-up and his journey back to England. This selection is set off as an epilogue entitled, 'The Journey Home'.

Georges Bernanos

From *Les grands cimetières sous la lune* (*A Diary of My Times*)

Over there, in Majorca, I saw lorry-loads of men pass over the Rambla. They rumbled like thunder on a level with the many-coloured terraces, freshly washed and running with water, gay with the murmur of country fairs. The lorries were grey with road-dust, the men too were grey, sitting four by four, grey caps slung crosswise, hands spread over their tent-cloth trousers, patiently. They were kidnapping them every day from lost villages, at the time when they came in from the fields. They set off for their last journey, shirts still clinging to their shoulders with perspiration, arms still full of the day's toil, leaving the soup untouched on the table, and a woman, breathless, a minute too late, at the garden wall, with the little bundle of belongings hastily twisted into a bright new napkin: *A Dios! Recuerdos!*

The sentimental appeal? God preserve me from it! I merely wish to say, and I shall never tire of saying, that those people had neither killed nor hurt anybody. They were country-folk like those you know, or rather like those your fathers knew, those your fathers shook hands with, for they made me think of the hard-chiselled faces in our French villages.

. . . We are always too sure of ourselves. Three week's innocent revelry at Montmartre can sometimes reawaken in a respectable gentleman over fifty, living quietly on his investments in the provinces, the vicious adolescent he had never given a thought to for years, and believed to be dead. The smell of blood, also, can suddenly go to the head of that type of person. I saw many strange things. I saw a woman of thirty-five, appertaining to the inoffensive category which over there we call *beata*, living peacefully in the bosom of her family after an interrupted novitiate, spending among the poor whatever time she did not spend in church, show sudden signs of incomprehensible nervous terror, speak of possible 'reprisals', and refuse to go out alone. A very dear friend whom I cannot name here, took pity on her, and in order to re-assure her, offered her shelter. A little later the devotee decided to return home. The day she was leaving, her charitable hostess questioned her affectionately:

'Come, child, what have you to fear? You're one of God's little lambs – who could possibly wish out of the way such a harmless creature as you?'

'Harmless? That's all you know! You don't think me capable of serving Religion. Everybody thinks as you do, and nobody's frightened of me. Well – you can find out for yourself. I had eight men shot, madame . . .'

Yes, I was privileged to witness many strange things. I know at Palma a young man of exquisite breeding, of most affable sim-plicity, most cordial, at one time a general favourite. His small aristocratic hand holds in its soft dimpled palm the secret of a hundred deaths, maybe . . . A lady called on him one day and saw a magnificent rose on his drawing-room table.

'Are you admiring that rose, my dear?'

'Why, yes . . . ?'

'You would admire it still more if you knew where it came from.'

'How do you expect me to know?'

'I took it from the cell of Madame M— whom we executed this morning.'

You may hate to read of this. Believe me, I hate to write of it. Above all, I hated the sound and sight of it. We stuck it out, my wife and I, not through bravado, not even hoping to be of much use – there was so little we could do, after all – but rather out of a deep sense of solidarity towards a group of decent people, of which there were more each day, who had known our hopes and illusions, stubbornly held their ground against overwhelming evidence, and now finally shared in our sorrow. They were not free, as we were. I remember those young Phalangistas, those old priests – one of them for having spoken his mind too freely was made to swallow, on pain of death, a litre of castor-oil. Had I lived there among the Left, it is possible that their methods of protest might have awakened in me certain partisan reflexes which one is not always able to control. But distillation, distress, pity, and shame, bind one far more closely than revolt or hate. You arise wearily from your bed, you are on your way, and there, in the street, at a café table, on the church steps, is one whom you thought was on the side of the killers, and he suddenly cries out to you, with eyes full of tears:

'I've had enough! I can't go on! Look – look what they've done now!'

The mayor of a small town was hidden by his wife in a tank. At each sign of danger the poor fellow crouched down in a sort of nook, a few inches from the still water. They dragged him out one December night, shaking with fever. They took him to the cemetery and put a bullet in his belly. Then as he was in no haste to die, his executioners who were drinking a few steps away, returned a little tight, with the empty bottle of brandy, thrust it in the mouth of the dying man, and smashed it on his head.

These facts, I insist, are known to all. I fear no contradiction. The atmosphere of Terrorism is not what you think. At first it is like some gigantic misunderstanding, mixing everything up, inextricably entangling good and evil, innocent and guilty, enthusiasm and cruelty. Can I believe my eyes? Can I have understood . . . ? They say it'll soon be over, that it *is* over. We breathe again. We breathe until the next killing, which cuts us short. Time passes, passes . . . And then? How can I explain it? Priests, soldiers, that banner of gold and black – 'neither gold could buy it, nor blood could sell it . . .'

It is a cruel thing when what you were born to love becomes degraded before your eyes.

I have seen – I've seen with my own eyes, I tell you – a small Christian people, with peaceable traditions, extremely, almost absurdly, friendly – I've seen them suddenly turned to stone, seen their faces hardening, even their children's faces. So it is no good to claim that we can keep a hold on certain emotions once they are let loose. Shall we make use of them whatever they are like? Shall we run this risk? Shall we drown in blood, as did the contemporaries of Philip the Second, these great heresies hardly above the surface as yet, but to be heard even now rumbling underground? For months, in Majorca, killer-gangs, swiftly transported from village to village in lorries requisitioned for the purpose, shot down in cold blood for everybody to see, thousands of persons who were held to be suspect, but against whom the military tribunal itself could not produce the faintest legal allegation. The Bishop of Palma was informed of this fact, like everybody else. Nevertheless he showed himself to be on the side of the executioners whenever he could – though it was notorious that some of them had the blood of a hundred men on their hands. Will this be the Church's attitude tomorrow? In the future the question will hold much less importance for the Spaniards than for us. It really seems likely that the Generals of the *Pronunciamento*, in order to save their skins, will allow the Monarchy they destroyed six years earlier to be re-established. The adventure will merely have cost a million men. Certainly this appears an enormous expense, but it will be worth it to Spain to be disqualified for a long time from taking part in any sort of Crusade at all. She dwells behind her mountains, as in the past, on the fringe of Europe. And for her the purge is over.

At Majorca I lived in a tiny seaside village, actually a suburb of Palma, about three miles away. I am bound to say that Porto Pi, even in the midst of civil war, was not a very 'lively' spot. The young men were fighting on one side or the other, or on neither side, according to where they found themselves in the world when the thing happened, for Majorcans are great travellers.

Those who stayed at home were not to be seen except on Sundays at church, followed of course by all.

I remember . . . I remember . . .

There was an old rag-picker who used to keep the streets clean. He rode in a queer wagon drawn by the ghost of a donkey covered over with a skin that looked as though it had been borrowed from another animal of the same kind, because it seemed far too large for his bones. Although the only son of this 'government official' had been slaughtered by the rebels, a charitable pub-keeper allowed him to sleep in the stable beside his curious beast. My little girl, Dominique, was most attached to them both. But on Easter day she found her old friend hanging – hanging between his dust-bin and his donkey – Easter day, a triumphant Easter day, with the morning full of white seagulls . . .

There was that fat wench, who used to stand next to me for Communion every Sunday. One day we spied beneath her jacket that had accidentally come unbuttoned – a police-badge: a bright new badge!

We had a cook, too, much loved by my children. A gendarme with the face of an evil priest called on her one day at dawn, bowing and scraping to me.

'Get ready,' he said. 'I'm coming back for you at four.'

She put on her black silk, which was now much too tight for her, and bursting at the seams. She tied up her bundle and wept great heaving sobs the whole of that interminable day. I met her in the road, plodding behind her master, and she gave me the Fascist salute. Horrible!

The dead must be atoned for. Reparation must be made for the dead, that they may deliver us when the time comes. The reconciliation of the living is only possible when the dead have been reconciled.

It is not so much the errors and sins of the dead that poison our national life as the malice and disgust which has survived them, exploited by a few party leaders whom we could count on the fingers of one hand. Let us look them in the eyes for the last time, those enemies of humankind, before turning from them to the pages of another book.

We shall not die at their hands.

Letter to Georges Bernanos (1938?)

Monsieur,

However silly it may be to write to an author, since his profession must always involve him in a flood of correspondence, I cannot refrain from doing so after having read *Les grands cimetières sous la lune.* Not that it is the first book of yours to touch me. The *Journal d'un curé de campagne* is in my opinion the best of them, at least of those I have read, and really a great book. But the fact that I have liked other books of yours gave me no reason for intruding upon you to say so. This last one, however, is a different matter. I have had an experience which corresponds to yours, although it was much shorter and was less profound; and although it was apparently – but only apparently – embraced in a different spirit.

I am not a Catholic, although – and this must no doubt appear presumptuous to any Catholic, coming from a non-Catholic – nothing that is Catholic, nothing that is Christian, has ever seemed alien to me. I have sometimes told myself that if only there were a notice on church doors forbidding entry to anyone with an income above a certain figure, and that a low one, I would be converted at once. From my childhood onwards I sympathized with those organizations which spring from the lowest and least regarded social strata, until the time when I realized that such organizations are of a kind to discourage all sympathy. The last one in which I felt some confidence was the Spanish CNT. I had travelled a little in Spain before the Civil War; only a little, but enough to feel the affection which it is hard not to feel for the Spanish people. I had seen the Anarchist movement as the natural expression of that people's greatness and of its flaws, of its worthiest aspirations and of its unworthiest. The CNT and FAI were an extraordinary mixture, to which anybody at all was admitted and in which, consequently, one found immorality, cynicism, fanaticism, and cruelty, but also love and fraternal spirit and, above all, that concern for honour which is so beautiful in the humiliated. It seemed to me that the idealists preponderated over the elements of violence and disorder. In July 1936, I was in Paris, I do not love war; but what has always seemed to me most horrible in war is the position of those in the rear. When I realized that, try as I would, I could not prevent myself from participating morally in that war – in other words, from hoping all day and every day for the victory of one side and the defeat of the other – I decided that, for me, Paris was the rear, and I took the train to Barcelona with the intention of enlisting. This was at the beginning of August 1936.

My stay in Spain was brought to a compulsory end by an accident. I was a few days in Barcelona, and then in the remote Aragonese countryside on the banks of the Ebro, about ten miles from Saragossa, at the very place where the river was recently crossed by Yague's troops; then I was at Sitges, in the palace converted into a hospital, and then again in Barcelona. A stay of about two months in all. I left Spain against my will and with the intention of returning; but I later decided voluntarily not to do so. I no longer felt any inner compulsion to participate in a war which, instead of being what it had appeared when it began – a war of famished peasants against landed proprietors and their clerical supporters – had become a war between Russia on the one hand and Germany and Italy on the other.

I recognize the smell of civil war, the smell of blood and terror, which exhales from your book; I have breathed it too. I must admit that I neither saw nor heard of anything which quite equalled the ignominy of certain facts you relate, such as the murders of elderly peasants or the *Ballillas* chasing old people and beating them with truncheons. But for all that, I heard quite enough. I was very nearly present at the execution of a priest. In the minutes of suspense I was asking myself whether I should simply look on or whether I should try to intervene and get myself shot as well. I still don't know which I would have done if a lucky chance had not prevented the execution.

So many incidents come crowding . . . but they would take too long to tell; and to what purpose? Let one suffice. I was at Sitges when the militiamen returned, defeated, from the expedition to

Majorca. They had been decimated. Out of forty young boys from Sitges nine were dead, as was learnt when the remaining thirty-one came back. The very next night there were nine revenge operations. In that little town, in which nothing at all had happened in July, they killed nine so-called Fascists. Among the nine was a baker, aged about thirty, whose crime, so I was told, was that he had not joined the 'Somaten' militia. His old father, whose only child and only support he was, went mad. One more incident: in a light engagement a small international party of militiamen from various countries captured a boy of fifteen who was a member of the Falange. As soon as he was captured, and still trembling from the sight of his comrades being killed along-side him, he said he had enrolled compulsorily. He was searched and a medal of the Virgin and a Falange card were found on him. Then he was sent to Durruti, the leader of the column, who lectured him for an hour on the beauties of the Anarchist ideal and gave him the choice between death and enrolling immediately in the ranks of his captors, against his comrades of yesterday. Durruti gave this child twenty-four hours to think it over, and when the time was up he said no and was shot. Yet Durruti was in some ways an admirable man. Although I only heard of it afterwards, the death of this little hero has never ceased to weigh on my conscience. Another incident: A village was finally cap-tured by the red militia after having been taken and retaken over and over again. In the cellars there was found a handful of hag-gard, terrified, famished creatures and among them three or four young men. The militiamen reasoned as follows: If these young men stayed behind and waited for the Fascists the last time we retired from here it means that they must be Fascists too. They therefore shot them immediately, but gave some food to the others and thought themselves very humane. Finally, here is an incident from the rear: Two Anarchists once told me how they and some comrades captured two priests. They killed one of them on the spot with a revolver, in front of the other, and then told the sur-vivor that he could go. When he was twenty yards away they shot him down. The man who told me this story was much surprised when I didn't laugh.

At Barcelona an average of fifty people were killed every night in punitive raids. This is proportionately much less than in

Majorca, because Barcelona is a town of nearly a million inhabitants; moreover, it had been the scene of a three-day battle of sanguinary street-fighting. But statistics are probably not to the point in such a matter. The point is the attitude towards murder. Never once, either among Spaniards or even among the French who were in Spain as combatants or as visitors – the latter being usually dim and harmless intellectuals – never once did I hear anyone express, even in private intimacy, any repulsion or disgust or even disapproval of useless bloodshed. You speak about fear. Yes, it is true that fear played some part in all this butchery; but where I was it did not appear to play the large part that you assign to it. Men who seemed to be brave – there was one at least whose courage I personally witnessed – would retail with cheery fraternal chuckles at convivial mealtimes how many priests they had murdered, or how many 'Fascists', the latter being a very elastic term. My own feeling was that once a certain class of people has been placed by the temporal and spiritual authorities outside the ranks of those whose life has value, then nothing comes more naturally to men than murder. As soon as men know that they can kill without fear of punishment or blame, they kill; or at least they encourage killers with approving smiles. If anyone happens to feel a slight distaste to begin with, he keeps quiet and he soon begins to suppress it for fear of seeming unmanly. People get carried away by a sort of intoxication which is irresistible without a fortitude of soul which I am bound to consider exceptional, since I have met with it nowhere. On the other hand, I met peaceable Frenchmen, for whom I had never before felt contempt and who would never have dreamed of doing any killing themselves, but who savoured that blood-polluted atmosphere with visible pleasure. For them I shall never again be able to feel any esteem.

The very purpose of the whole struggle is soon lost in an atmosphere of this sort. For the purpose can only be defined in terms of the public good, of the welfare of men – and men have become valueless. In a country where the great majority of the poor are peasants the essential aim of every extreme-Left party should be an improvement of the peasants' conditions; and perhaps the main issue of this war, at the beginning, was the redistribution of land. But those peasants of Aragon, so poor and so splendid in the pride they have cherished through all their umiliations – one cannot say that they were even so much as an object of curiosity to the militiamen. Although there was no insolence, no injury, no brutality – at least I saw none and I know that theft and rape were capital crimes in the Anarchist militias – nevertheless, between the armed forces and the civilian population there was an abyss, exactly like the abyss between the rich and the poor. One felt it in the attitude of the two groups, the one always rather humble, submissive, and timid, the other confident, off-hand, and condescending.

One sets out as a volunteer, with the idea of sacrifice, and finds oneself in a war which resembles a war of mercenaries, only with much more cruelty and with less human respect for the enemy.

I could say much more on the same lines, but I must limit myself. Having been in Spain, I now continually listen to and read all sorts of observations about Spain, but I could not point to a single person, except you alone, who has been exposed to the atmosphere of the Civil War and has resisted it. What do I care that you are a Royalist, a disciple of Drumont? You are incomparably nearer to me than my comrades of the Aragon militias – and yet I loved them.

What you say about nationalism, the war, and French foreign policy after the war is equally sympathetic to me. I was ten years old at the time of Versailles, and up to then I had been patriotically thrilled as children are in wartime. But the will to humiliate the defeated enemy which revealed itself so loathsomely everywhere at that time (and in the following years) was enough to cure me once for all of that naïve sort of patriotism. I suffer more from the humiliations inflicted by my country than from those inflicted on her.

I am afraid I have bothered you with a very long letter. I will only add an expression of my keen admiration.

Mlle Simone Weil, 3 rue Auguste-Comte, Paris (VIe)

P.S. I wrote my address automatically. I expect, for one thing, that you have better things to do than to answer letters. And in any case I am going to Italy for a month or two and if a letter from you should be forwarded it might be held up somewhere.

Antoine de Saint-Exupéry

From *Terre des Hommes* (*Wind, Sand, and Stars*)

My guides were Anarchists. They led me to the railway station where troops were being entrained. Far from the platforms built for tender farewells, we were walking in a desert of signal towers and switching points, stumbling in the rain through a labyrinthine yard filled with blackened goods wagons where tarpaulins the colour of lard were spread over carloads of stiffened forms. This world has lost its human quality, has become a world of iron, and therefore uninhabitable. A ship remains a living thing only so long as man with his brushes and oils swabs an artificial layer of light over it. Leave them to themselves a couple of weeks and the life dies out of your ship, your factory, your railway; death covers their faces. After six thousand years the stones of a temple still vibrate with the passage of man; but a little rust, a night of rain, and this railway yard is eaten away to its very skeleton.

Here are our men. Cannon and machine guns are being loaded on board with the straining muscles and the hoarse gaspings that are always drawn from men by these monstrous insects, these fleshless insects, these lumps of carapace and vertebra. What is startling here is the silence. Not a note of song, not a single shout. Only, now and then, when a gun-carriage lands, the hollow thump of a steel plate. Of human voices no sound.

No uniforms, either. These men are going off to be killed in their working garb. Wearing their dark clothes stiff with mud, the column heaving and sweating at their work look like the denizens of a night shelter. They fill me with the same uneasiness I felt when the yellow fever broke out among us at Dakar, ten years ago.

The chief of the detachment had been speaking to me in a whisper. I caught the end of his speech:

'. . . and we move up to Saragossa.'

Why the devil did he have to whisper! The atmosphere in this

ard made me think of a hospital. But of course! That was it. A
ivil war is not a war, it is a disease. These men were not going
ıp to the front in the exultation of certain victory; they were
truggling blindly against infection.

And the same thing was going on in the enemy camp. The pur-
oose of this struggle was not to rid the country of an invading
oreigner but to eradicate a plague. A new faith is like a plague. It
.ttacks from within. It propagates in the invisible. Walking in the
treets, whoever belongs to a Party feels himself surrounded by
ecretly infected men.

This must have been why these troops were going off in silence
vith their instruments of asphyxiation. There was not the slightest
esemblance between them and regiments that go into battle
ıgainst foreign armies and are set out on the chessboard of the
ields and moved about by strategists. These men had gathered
ogether haphazardly in a city filled with chaos.

There was not much to choose between Barcelona and its
:nemy, Saragossa: both were composed of the same swarm of
Communists, Anarchists, and Fascists. The very men who collec-
ed on the same side were perhaps more different from one another
han from their enemies. In civil war the enemy is inward; one as
;ood as fights against oneself.

What else can explain the particular horror of this war in which
firing squads count for more than soldiers of the line? Death in
:his war is a sort of quarantine. Purges take the place of germ-
carriers. The Anarchists go from house to house and load the
plague-stricken into their tumbrils, while on the other side of the
barricade Franco is able to utter that horrible boast: 'There are
no more Communists among us.'

The conscripts are weeded out by a kind of medical board; the
officer in charge is a sort of army doctor. Men present themselves
for service with pride shining in their eyes and the belief in their
hearts that they have a part to play in society.

'Exempt from service for life!' is the decision.

Fields have been turned into charnel-houses and the dead are
burned in lime or petroleum. Respect for the dignity of man has
been trampled under foot. Since on both sides the political parties
spy upon the stirrings of man's conscience as upon the workings
of a disease, why should the urn of his flesh be respected? This

body that clothes the spirit, that moves with grace and boldness that knows love, that is apt for self-sacrifice – no one now so much as thinks of giving it decent burial.

I thought of our respect for the dead. I thought of the white sanatorium where the light of a man's life goes quietly out in the presence of those who love him and who garner as if it were an inestimable treasure his last words, his ultimate smile. How right they are! Seeing that this same whole is never again to take shape in the world. Never again will be heard exactly that note of laughter, that intonation of voice, that quality of repartée. Each individual is a miracle. No wonder we go on speaking of the dead for twenty years.

Here, in Spain, a man is simply stood up against a wall and he gives up his entrails to the stones of the courtyard. You have been captured. You are shot. Reason: your ideas were not our ideas.

This entrainment in the rain is the only thing that rings true about their war. These men stand round and stare at me, and I read in their eyes a mournful sobriety. They know the fate that awaits them if they are captured. I begin to shiver with the cold and observe of a sudden that no woman has been allowed to see them off.

From *The Tree of Gernika*

Monday was the weekly market day of Gernika, when the town existed. At about 4.30 the market, in summer, was at its fullest. The civil war had not made great difference to the Gernika farmers who brought in their animals and produce for sale from the rich valley. Rather there was better business. In Gernika, where the population was usually seven thousand, there were now an additional three thousand refugees and two Basque battalions, who had plenty of pesetas to spend. A few of the facious rich had been jailed or run away, but only a few. Their fine stone houses with the floreate blazons engraved hugely over wide doors were shut; but they never had used the market much, and most of them visited peace-time Gernika little.

Gernika remained a modest Vizcayan country town. The population behaved itself, the priests walked about in the cloth, mass was held in the churches all day and every day. The two Basque Nationalist battalions quartered to the north of the town, where a water-green avenue of plane trees rippled out towards Bermeo, were popular with the people, and in Gernika itself there was the usual post of Basque motorized police. There were no troops retreating through the town. The armies were beyond Markina, miles to the east, and at Oitz, miles to the south. Gernika lay well behind the front, on part of its communications with Bilbao; to destroy it would cut off the retreating armies from the General Staff and their base.

After four there were farm carts coming into Gernika, rolling on solid wooden wheels and drawn by oxen whose heads were shaded under fleeces of sheep. Basque peasants in their long puckered market smocks walked backwards in front of them, mesmerizing the oxen to Gernika with their slim wands, with which they kept touching the horns and yoke gently. They talked to the oxen. Others were driving sheep to market. There was an assembly of animals near the parish church, a stately structure cavernous, tall and dark within, standing upon a flight of thin steps like leaves piled one upon the other.

It is improbable that anyone was thinking about the war when at 4.30 the church bell rang out loud. All over Spain a peal on a single bell is an air-raid warning. The population took cover and the sheep in the square were left to their own devices.

There were numerous air-raid shelters in Gernika, constructed after the terrible raid on Durango on March 31. Any cellar was covered with sandbags, and the entrance protected in the same way: a cardboard at the door painted ornamentally *refugio* showed where the people had to dive. Though there had been few raid warnings at Gernika since the war began, the whole Basque population by now took their church bells seriously.

In a few minutes a Heinkel 111 came over and dropped six medium bombs, probably fifty-pounders, near the station, with a shower of grenades. A director of the railway company who was in the office rang up Bilbao to inform them that an aeroplane was bombing Gernika.

A few minutes later another Heinkel 111 appeared, to bomb the same area, but nearer the centre. The telephone with Bilbao was now cut. The plane from its slant and speedy sides machine-gunned the town at random, then veered homeward.

The parish priest, Aronategui, left his church with the sacraments, for dying people were reported near the railway station. He went calmly through the deserted streets with the holy oil. No fires had yet started.

Fifteen minutes passed, and the people were coming out of their shelters. A heavy drumming of engines was heard to the east. It was what we called in lighter moments the *tranvias* – the trams – the Junker 52s, who were so clumsy that they seemed to clang rather than to fly. These were the heaviest bombers that Germany had sent to Spain.

Over the town, whose streets were once more empty trenches, they dispersed their load a ton at a time. They turned woodenly over Gernika, the bombs fell mechanically in line as they turned. Then came the crack of the explosions; smoke stood up over Gernika like wool on a Negro's head. Everywhere it sprouted, as more heavy bombers came.

Besides many fifty- and hundred-pound bombs, they dropped great torpedoes weighing a thousand. Gernika is a compact little town, and most of these hit buildings, tearing them to pieces vertically from top to bottom and below the bottom. They penetrated refuges. The spirit of the people had been good, but now they panicked.

An escort of Heinkel 51s, the same perhaps that had molested us that afternoon, were waiting for this moment. Till now they had been machine-gunning the roads round Gernika, scattering, killing, or wounding sheep and shepherds. As the terrified population streamed out of the town they dived low to drill them with their guns. Women were killed here whose bodies I afterwards saw. It was the same technique as that used at Durango on March 31, nearly a month back.

The little fighting planes came down in a line, like flashing dancing waves on shingle. They burst in spray on the countryside as they merrily dived. Twenty machine guns working together in line, and the roar of breakers behind them from ten engines. Always they flew nose towards Gernika. For the pilots it must have been like surfing. The terrified people lay face down in ditches, pressed their backs against tree trunks, coiled themselves in holes, shut their eyes and ran across sweet green open meadow. Many were foolish, and fled back before the aerial tide into the village. It was then that the heavy bombing of Gernika began.

It was then that Gernika was smudged out of that rich landscape, the province of Vizcaya, with a heavy fist.

It was about 5.15. For two hours and a half flights of between three and twelve aeroplanes, types Heinkel 111 and Junker 52, bombed Gernika without mercy and with system. They chose their sectors in the town in orderly fashion, with the opening points east of the Casa de Juntas and north of the arms factory. Early bombs fell like a circle of stars round the hospital on the road to Bermeo; all the windows were blown in by the divine efflatus, the wounded militiamen were thrown out of their beds, the inner fabric of the building shook and broke.

On the shattered houses, whose carpets and curtains, splintered beams and floors and furniture were knocked into angles and ready for the burning, the planes threw silver flakes. Tubes of two pounds, long as your forearm, glistening silver from their aluminium and elektron casing; inside them, as in the beginning of the world in Prometheus' reed, slept fire. Fire in a silver powder, sixty-five grammes in weight, ready to slip through six holes at the base of the glittering tube. So, as the houses were broken to pieces over the people, sheathed fire descended from heaven to burn them up.

Every twenty minutes fresh raiders came. And between the explosions and the spurts of flame as the burning metal seeped into curtains and beams, doors and carpets, while a grey pall stood over Gernika supported from below by white pillars where fires were starting, in the pauses of modern battle the population ran about the street to clear away the doors of smothered refuges, to pull children and other small worthless belongings from houses afire.

There was much groaning in Gernika, much breathless work to dig out wounded people before the next planes came. Twenty minutes was the interval between fire, and the priests spoke to the people to keep them calm. By now something like a spirit of passive resistance had been built up in them. Gernika's face was turning to ashes, everybody's face in Gernika was ash-grey, but terror had reached a condition of submissive stubbornness not seen before in Vizcaya.

In the interval people moved out of the town, but the fear of the fighting plane and separation from their families persuaded many to remain in Gernika. And then the planes returned with their tinsel tubes to shower over Gernika, and another part was destroyed, and more were buried in the *refugios*.

I do not know whether you have ever sat in a railway station having lost one train and waiting for another which will come in two and a half hours' time. A country railway station, where you can buy nothing to read or smoke or eat; and the hours take days to pass if you cannot go to sleep. Now in Gernika it was wellnigh impossible to go to sleep, except in an obligatory sleep which had no morrow in Gernika, or Vizcaya, or this world. And since there was nothing to eat or smoke, and fumes prevented one from reading, no other diversion remained but to allow terror to expand those hours past days into months and years. Years half-spent in dug-outs that might crash at any moment, and half-spent in streets of an unrecognizable town looking for people who may now be unrecognizable.

And so you see that to be in Gernika when it was destroyed, was in a limited sense, like waiting for a train in a country station. Time in both cases passed slowly.

Soon there was little of the town to move about in. The Church of San Juan was burning fiercely, with a huge bomb-hole through its roof and its altar and pulpit rippling fire. Even a few isolated buildings were touched; at the old parish church of Andra Mari, in the corner of the square where the sheep had been gathered, the chapel behind the altar was aflame.

As the people not trapped in the refuges moved northwards before the general fire the planes that raided Gernika came very low. It must have been difficult for them to sight their target in the smoke and grit which rose from the spreading campfire below them. They flew at six hundred feet, slowly and steadily shedding their tubes of silver, which settled upon those houses that still stood in pools of intolerable heat; then slipped and dribbled from floor to floor. Gernika was compact as peat to serve as fuel for the German planes. Nobody now bothered to save relatives or possessions; between bombardments they walked out of Gernika in front of the stifling smoke and sat in bewildered hundreds on the roads to Bermeo and Mugika. Mercifully, the fighters had gone. They no longer glanced down to mutilate the population in movement and chase them across the open fields. The people were worn out by noise, heat, and terror; they lay about like dirty bundles of washing, mindless, sprawling, and immobile. There was nothing to save in Gernika but the few old mattresses and pillows, kitchen tables and chairs which they had dragged out of the fire. By seven-thirty that evening fire was eating away the whole of crowded little Gernika but the Casa de Juntas and the houses of the Fascist families. These, being wealthier than the others, lived in stone mansions apart from the rest of the people; their properties did not catch the infection of the running fire even when under pressure of the wind it stretched its savage arms to stroke them.

At 7.45 the last plane went away. One could hear now, through ears half-numbed by the engines of the heavy bombers and explosions of the heavy bombs, the nervous crackle of arson all over the town and the totter and trembling collapse of roofs and walls. Gernika was finished, and as night fell and the motorized police stumbled along the road to ring up Bilbao to say that all was over, the total furnace that was Gernika began to play tricks of crimson colour with the night clouds. Very gently and softly they throbbed reflections of her death movement. They lay over her like a crimson-cushioned ceiling, like the hangings of a dying monarch, billowy and rich, stirring to the Gernika light.

Around the corpse of the Basques' oldest village *caserios* aflame in the hills made candles. The aviation had spent the residue of its fire upon them and had struck many.

Beginning to talk and to try to understand their experience, the Basques asked each other how many planes had attacked their town. Some said eighty, others one hundred, others two hundred, others more. They could not tell; but those who were outside Gernika the whole afternoon say that between forty and fifty German planes attacked her, including ten fighters. The bombers reappeared again and again with fresh loads.

To the people within Gernika it was not a question of figures, but of inquantitative and immeasurable terror. All they could hear was the drumbeat of the engines and the split of the explosions again and again until they sounded dull enough. They could see no more but the trembling doors of their refuges and their own helpless faces, and sometimes if they were in the streets the points of fire where the silver tubes struck; these fell many at a time, for they were dropped twenty-four together on a single spinning rod. Sometimes, too, before they bolted below they saw through the smoke the stiff, stubborn wings of the planes which molested them and heard the wingless flight of the metal that spurted blindly all over the town, crushing walls and roof tiles and stripping trees of their leaves and branches.

When they crept back to the town between the soft breeze of the flames now blowing on every house they saw what I saw later that night.

'Malaga Has Fallen'

From *New Writing*, Spring, 1939

The road out of Almeria turned and twisted, following the indented coast. It was cut out from the dark grey rock, which fell away steeply down to the sea on one hand, and rose steeply up on the other; pitched between the rising hills and the shore, it was very beautiful, but the going was slow, with its sharp blind turns and narrow bridges.

We had only gone about ten miles when we came on a few straggling parties of peasants, each grouped round a donkey or a mule, burdened not only with a mother or child, but with household possessions, pots, blankets, mattresses, piled high on the beasts' backs.

'Refugees,' Dr Rathbone said. 'I wonder where they're coming from?'

They looked very tired; the animals were walking with listless, shuffling steps, and the people the same. All big families, the father and mother carried a small child, while the eight- or nine-year-olds walked behind, clinging, many of them, to the tails of the animals, to help them along.

For the next three or four miles we met these parties regularly at intervals of a hundred yards. Rathbone was puzzled:

'Don't remember seeing so many refugees. I guess there's more than we ever saw outside Madrid, eh, Hesketh? Where have they come from? Malaga, I reckon ... and they must have started a long while back ... Say, look at this Bethlehem group; take a picture of 'em, Hesketh.'

There came by a girl-mother, with a baby at her breast, perched on a donkey, which a middle-aged peasant, tall, thin, brown, wearing a sombrero, was leading by a string. We stopped a moment for Hesketh to take a photograph.

Round every corner they came, seeming to get a little thicker, the distances between each group receding: the top-heavy donkeys and mules emitting an occasional pathetic bellow, the children plodding behind mostly barefooted, the women and men with typical peasant faces, creased and prematurely old; unsmiling and uncomplaining they seemed to be going through an unending routine with fixed automatic movements.

The intervals between them continued to decrease: until down one side of the road there was a continual thin line, a long colourless procession, like a grey rope threading the twisting road: until they became a part, simply, of the road itself, merging into the dust and the dark grey rock.

The road took a turn away from the sea and cut for twenty miles across a plain. As we breasted the hill which led on to it, we found the thin line almost perceptibly swelling, so that it was taking up now a quarter, now a half, now three-quarters of the road, the straggling line of donkeys, women, peasants, spread out over it, so that there was barely room for the lorry to squeeze slowly past. Inside we had fallen quite silent.

As we reached the top of the hill, and the plain spread out in front, the road was visible for some ten or fifteen miles. At least not the road, but the people on it; a long, winding procession, blacking out the road as far as one could see, winding away over the horizon; and beside the dark, broad main stream, rivulets, and tributaries, striking out individual paths across the heath and the foothills.

We stopped the lorry in sheer amazement. The long winding stream of people, struggling and shifting, black against the green heath, was like some vast Old Testament exodus, spread out before us: the illusion heightened by the donkeys and the grey-white single-piece cloak folded like a hood round the heads of many of the women and children; others in black, with long thick shawls draped over head and shoulders: all swarthy, dark-skinned: all with differentiations of dress and colour almost obliterated by the dirt and dust which enveloped them.

As the lorry stood there, the stream seethed round it, poured round and on, as if it were a tree stump, solid in the slow, ceaseless movement of a sluggish stream.

'Christ!' Rathbone said, 'Look at 'em, look at 'em. As far as you

an see. There's ten thousand of them; yeh, a good ten thousand.
hope they're expecting them in Almeria . . . there didn't seem
o be much for them there . . . Did you ever see anything like it?
od, they're like ants, like an army of ants! Come on, boys, we
ust get on. We must see what's in back of 'em.'

It was difficult going; we had to push our way through, nosing
y, and sounding the horn continuously. And then we began to
otice among the refugees some militiamen, with stubbled beards,
oking dead to the world.

'Bloody Anarchists, I reckon,' Hesketh muttered. 'What are
hey going this way for?'

'Deserters I guess,' Rathbone said.

Soon the proportion of militiamen increased: a troop of
avalry came by, with a helpless defeated air, covered with mud
nd sweat, the horses dragging; often they carried a double load,
child or a girl up beside the rider, while some men were leading
heir mounts, having given up their place to old women or children, who sat astride the cavalry horses slumped down on the
addles.

More cavalry and then more: and behind them the militia, in
uniforms none of which matched, all torn, ragged, dirty. Those
who were old enough had stubbled beards, but most were too
young; an army of boys, routed and leaderless, straggling desperately past with their rifles, many of them carrying their boots
tied round their necks. No single person ever seemed to speak to
any other; no smile, no touch of emotional colour, relieved the
dark despair of the procession.

'It's a rout,' Rathbone whispered. 'It's not a defeat, it's a bloody
rout: Christ, what are they doing? There's a whole army here.
Why aren't they covering the retreat? Christ, look, there are
thousands of them, thousands, and they haven't been fighting.
You can see they haven't been fighting.'

'They look pretty done,' I said.

'Yes, they're done all right, but not with fighting, with running
away; that's what's done 'em. We haven't seen a single officer;
the first one we see we'll stop and ask. Probably the buggers got
away a long time since in fast cars.'

As the soldiers began to thin, and the peasants to predominate
again – but the size of the unceasing stream never diminished – we

stopped and tried to find out what was happening. No one seeme
to know for certain. The Fascists were sweeping up the road; n
one knew where. They were coming somewhere behind; no on
knew how close. The militia? They had been ordered to fall bac
on Almeria; they were going to make a stand there.

Inside the lorry they had been completely externalized; we ha
viewed the processing as you view a film unrolling itself in fror
of you, the reality of which by focusing your consciousness on th
seat you occupy, on yourself, and your immediate surrounding;
you could somehow diminish; so that the stream of people ha
been outside, was performing with the unreal realism of actors
But the moment we stepped out from the security of the interio
and mixed with the people, we found ourselves engulfed in th
atmosphere of that road; an atmosphere through which panic an
rumour ran like a flame which burned out of the people ever
thought but one: 'The Fascists are behind, push on, push on.
There was little confusion or wildness, none of the stampeding
violence of other panics; everyone was too exhausted. But pani
was there in their refusal to explain, to talk, to smile, to stop, to d
anything but move on mechanically and ceaselessly until the
should reach the safety and protection of – whatever lay in front
'Scared' they were, as Rathbone said, desperate with fright, bu
their desperation expressed itself only in the urge to get on
without even a rest, until they were safe.

As we stood in the crowd, asking questions of the moving
mass, who wouldn't stop to answer them, we were caught in the
emotional tension of the atmosphere, its unreasoning ignorance
of the situation, its listening only to the rumours, which came
breathing up from behind, blowing over them like a dry gust of
wind; and serving only to lock their silence, and to carry their feet
doggedly on.

'I can't see any point in going on,' Hesketh said, 'until we find
out what's happening; let's think it out. I only wish we'd brought
that rifle; we haven't even got guns, and we might run into the
Fascists round the corner.'

'How can we find out? No one knows anything. There's only
one way to find out,' Rathbone replied, 'to go on.'

I was between the two; I was as frightened as Hesketh, and at
the same time, unnaturally excited as my imagination ran ahead

picture a situation where, round a corner, we saw the Fascists in the distance, and hastily backed, turned, and fled, with bullets whistling past; and I began estimating the size of the lorry, and the width of the road, and calculated that it was far too big and clumsy a vehicle for that kind of manoeuvring.

We stood wavering in a little group round the lorry, watching the set faces of the despairing procession. Ordinarily the lorry, with its brightly painted sides, aroused excited interest, but now no one troubled to look at it, or at us; eyes were straining blankly ahead, or fixed on the ground, as they trod out their set, mechanical rhythm; a few disjointed shouts or cries alone contesting with the noise of the shuffling feet and hooves.

Suddenly Rathbone made a decisive gesture; he pulled me round by the shoulders, and pointed up at the painting on the lorry with a dramatic finger, and read out the script with an emotional quiver in his voice, like a 'ham' actor doing his big moment.

'AMERICAN BLOOD TRANSFUSION UNIT – FOR SERVICE TO THE FRONTS. See that, boys. FOR SERVICE TO THE FRONT. To the front we go.' And with a swagger and a smile he climbed into the driving seat and jerking his head at us to follow, started up the engine. We climbed in beside him.

Now we were winding back by the sea again; the refugees still filled the road and the farther we got the worse was their condition. A few of them were wearing rubber shoes, but most feet were bound round with rags, many were bare, nearly all were bleeding. Donkeys became scarcer and scarcer.

We passed through a little village, which was cleaned out, as bare and stark as a picked skeleton. You could imagine the crowd descending on the village and sweeping up the inhabitants, who would catch the panic, and picking up everything they valued, tie it to their donkeys and make off. The walls of the empty houses still good, but nothing more; they were empty and deserted except for a few stragglers who sat resting on the doorsteps. The emptiness, and the streets strewn with rubbish, the squatters on the doorsteps, and the bedraggled group round the pump, heightened the sense of confusion and misery to a terrifying degree.

From the comparative comfort of the interior of the lorry, the

procession had ceased to be marvellous – a spectacle. It had be
come pitiful, tragic. There were seventy miles of people, desperat
with hunger and exhaustion, and still the stream showed no sig
of diminishing. 'Not ten thousand: thirty thousand, fort
thousand,' Rathbone muttered. 'Poor devils, our imaginatio
can't reach their suffering.'

A little way past the village coming round a corner we though
for a moment that we had reached the end. In front the roa
stood, for a few hundred yards, bare and white. To see a roa
bare and white was something so strange that we automaticall
slowed down.

'Stop, Rath,' Hesketh suddenly shouted. 'Quick, planes!' W
drew up and jumped out, and high in the far distance behind wer
two bombers, whose faint hum was only just audible. The side
of the road, the rocks, and the shore were dotted with the refugees
pressed down on their faces, burrowing into holes. Children la
flat, with one frightened eye turned up towards the sky, with
their hands pressed tight over their ears, or folded backwards t
protect their vulnerable necks. Huddled groups crouched every
where; mothers already on the brink of exhaustion, held dow
their children, pushing them down into every cranny and hollow
flattening themselves into the hard earth, while the planes drone
nearer, and then roared overhead and swept past.

And then, slowly, as the sound of the planes died away, fear
fully and distrustfully, as if this might be a trap, in solitary two
and threes, they emerged, rising from the ground as if from
grave, and straggled back on to the road.

'These poor bastards have been bombed before,' Rathbone said
as we got in again. 'They know only too well what to do.'

The sun was setting over the sea in a flaunting blaze of rich
deep rose, which suffused the whole scene. But no one noticed it
it added no comfort to the road. We were passing now betwee
fields of sugar-cane; the road was strewn with the trampled leaves
desperately, the people waved and shouted to us to go back
groups of militiamen, gathered round buses which had run out o
petrol, formed barriers across the road to intercept us. '*Al Frente
Al Frente*,' Rathbone shouted, and, as he drove at them, they
melted.

It was dark the moment after sunset; and now our lights,

iercing the darkness, blinded the stream flowing against us, and wild chant, 'Lights, lights, put out your lights' rose up; and the cries continued even when, turning out the headlights, we travelled with only the pin-points of side-lamps; even they might attract the bombers.

The milestones marked only twenty, and Hesketh, consulting the map, discovered that not Malaga, as we thought, but Motril was zero. 'We'll make Zero anyhow,' Rathbone said, gripping his lips together. But the darkness deepened and the confusion increased; the mass seemed to swell and gather, so that we were hardly moving at all. For an hour we struggled on reducing the mileage only to twelve. Rathbone pulled up.

'It's no good, boys. We can't get on in this. I guess we'll fill the truck with kids. I've been counting; there must be some twenty thousand kids under ten on this road. Kids only.'

With the greatest difficulty in the darkness, he turned the lorry on the narrow road and opened the back. Instantly we were the centre of a mob of raving, shouting people, entreating and begging, at this sudden miraculous apparition. The scene was fantastic, of the shouting faces of the women holding up naked babies above their heads, pleading, crying, and sobbing, with gratitude or disappointment, and Rathbone coolly in the middle of them, soothing, calming, rejecting, and selecting. But the reeling crowd, fighting like animals, and the darkness, were too much for him; the inside was crammed with the women and children nearest him and the back was shut up.

'Now, Hesketh, I want you to take this load back to Almeria. Take 'em to the hospital. We'll start walking back, Tom and I. If you can get back here, good. But I guess it won't be possible. I reckon Almeria's going to be the most confused town in the whole of the world, for the next few days. Don't worry about us; we'll make it somehow.'

Rathbone and I each took a mackintosh, and the loaded lorry slowly nosed off, pushing its way through the still shouting crowd.

We stood watching the lorry disappearing, while the crowd broke up and resumed its march. 'Got a cigarette, Tom?' Rathbone asked. I hadn't; neither had Rathbone.

'So what now? I'll tell you what I'd like. I'd like to push on to Motril. See what's happening down there. What do you say?'

I was tired of these dramatics. For the last ten miles I had thought that our behaviour, driving through the people, pushing them out of the way to this side and that, blinding them with our headlights and dramatically shouting 'To the front, to the front,' while it stimulated a certain vein of vanity – we alone dashing towards the enemy while sixty thousand people fled – was pointless, extravagant play-acting.

Besides, I was frightened; the Fascists must be certainly in Motril; I couldn't see the point of walking deliberately into them. But in the face of Rathbone's fearlessness I hardly liked to say so; instead I said, 'Well, I don't know if you're a good walker, Rath; we're more than eighty miles from Almeria, and it looks as if we shall have to walk the whole way. That's going to take us about three days; and it seems a pity to put ourselves any farther off.'

'I guess you're right,' Rathbone agreed, and turned back a little regretfully from the direction of Motril. 'Vamoos. But I wish we had a cigarette.'

We joined the procession; it was half past ten and too dark to see any of the others. There were sounds only, a ceaseless shuffling of feet, dragging along the road, feet softly shod; an occasional cry from a driver to his donkey; the plaintive whine of tired children; and from the women a continuous moan of sorrow, a bitter low sound, 'Pheu, Aiee,' which took me suddenly back to my school days. 'Aiee, Aiee.' Cutting across it were shouted names, 'Antonio, Madre, Antonio.' In the confusion of the darkness a lagging child would be lost; it might easily have slipped down in exhaustion, and not been missed for the moment. Now the mother came fearfully along, her frightened cry joins the other night sounds as she stumbled back.

The night was fine and clear, but sharply cold. By the side of the road fires of dried palms were being lighted, and family groups gathered round them, the children falling instantly into exhausted sleep, the elders mumbling quietly to each other and stretching out gnarled hands to the flames. They all kept one eye on the road behind them. The flames blazing up here and there along the road threw the bowed figures round them into silhouette.

After an hour's walking Rathbone suggested, 'Let's get some sleep, Tom. I'm done.' We went off the road and lay down behind a row of palms. Rathbone seemed to sleep, but I couldn't; the flickering pictures of the seemingly endless procession and the huddled groups at the roadside danced on one's strained nerves. And the cold crept in and round. I walked restlessly up and down to keep warm, and to avoid my thoughts. And soon the Doctor gave up too, and we set off again.

Within half an hour we came across the low houses of a village. 'We'll find something here,' Rathbone said hopefully. Personally I didn't want to stop. The fear, which two hours before had been vaguely distant, moved up and took hold of me. If the Fascists had been in Motril, three hours ago, they must be up to us soon; there was no time to lose. I wanted to put a good five hours' walking between myself and the enemy; but Rathbone was looking about.

'Swell: Here we are, Tom, just the thing.' At the back of one of the cottages he had found a donkey stable, low-roofed and empty; the floor was covered with straw and dung, soft and warm. So we lay down and Rathbone turned over to sleep.

I only dozed fitfully. Outside I could hear the shuffling feet, endlessly moving by, the cries, the whines, the low 'Aiee' and, every now and then, a confused shouting which made the fear leap up and claw at my chest and heart. And I would creep out and round the outbuilding and look into the road. But the sight was always the same, seemingly the same people with the same actions of exhaustion, the same cries of fear and sorrow, flickering in the lurid light of the flames from the glazing palm leaves.

It was easy to see why the stable had remained empty; no one dared to stay that long. I joined a group by one of the fires; listlessly they made room for me; but in a few minutes the children were woken from their sleep and pushed back on to the road. Another group would come up and take their place, add a few more sticks and leaves, and, in ten minutes, set off again, to be succeeded by yet another.

Eventually I crept back into the stable and lay down again, my nerves listening through a troubled sleep for any variation in the now familiar rhythm of sounds, any change which might indicate the end of the march or the coming of the enemy.

The Doctor, too, slept fitfully, and was repeatedly sick; it was the smell of the dung. But we stayed there inside, until, at about five, I urged the Doctor to start again. The procession seemed to be thinning a little; and we hadn't gone far, when the first grey light of dawn appeared. Then two dimmed headlights came round the corner; it was our lorry.

Almeria, Hesketh reported, was in complete confusion; the people were streaming in, and there was no provision for them, no shelter, no food, but he had managed to obtain enough petrol for one more trip.

'This time I want you to drive,' Rathbone said to me, 'and Hesketh's to go with you. Hesketh's to go to bed at Almeria as soon as you get there, and you come back and pick me up. I'll be on the road.'

A new load, women and babies, was piled in, the doors shut, and I drove off.

Hesketh procured from Almeria two guards who were placed on the running-board each side, carrying rifles.

'Christ, it was a terrible journey!' he told David a little melodramatically. 'The militiamen along the road are getting tough. They've got the jitters. Trying to jump a ride. They'll steal our petrol if they get half a chance. The great thing is to go as fast as you can. Don't on any account stop. Don't even slow down, or give 'em a chance of jumping the truck. And if people won't get out of the way, ride 'em down.'

By the time we got going it was light. I nosed my way gently through the crowd, blowing the horn, and presently, the guards, thinking that there was still room after all on the lorry, allowed two men to jump up and clamber on to it.

Almeria was almost unrecognizable when we reached it. The quiet little seaport we had left the day before was jammed to overflowing with refugees, still constantly flowing in. The streets were a black shifting mass of people, who pushed their way up and down, undirected and still unfed. Hesketh steered us to the hospital on the outskirts of the town, a high Moorish building still surprisingly empty.

In the centre of the town, where we came back to get the necessary documents for more petrol, we met an official of the Government, who had hurried down from Valencia to report on the situation. I suggested to him that I should take out a load of food to the refugees.

'Food?' said the official. 'We've got no food; there's none in the own. We've sent for some, and it ought to be coming soon. But this is all there is here. Have it; you must be hungry.' And he offered me two figs. Then he asked us to go along to the Civil Governor and tell him about the situation. 'You're the only people who've been down that road. The Governor wants to see you.'

The Governor seemed capable and efficient; he was pale and rather stout, with an intelligent face. Five people were talking to him at once. Messengers kept hurrying in and out with dispatches, and his three telephones were ringing incessantly: secretaries answered them. We told him that he must expect at least a hundred thousand refugees in all and showed him the place on the map where we had been; and finally asked him to send out lorries to bring in the refugees, 'Otherwise many must die of exposure, exhaustion, or hunger.'

'Couldn't you send food, and lorries for the sick and exhausted?'

'It isn't possible,' he said, striding up and down the room. 'How can I? I've got no food – we were short before – now we've got none. As for lorries, I've got to get troops together. Soldiers are the first thing. I must send some soldiers down. The enemy must be checked.'

We were interrupted by an important telephone call. He answered it and came back to us. 'Two more aeroplanes down near Motril; that makes four this morning. This is terrible . . . Thank you, gentlemen, I will do what I can, but soldiers first; the lorries shall take the soldiers and bring back the refugees. We must do it at once. Juan!' A secretary hurried up and was given orders, the telephone rang, dispatch riders came and went, the Governor turned away. But Hesketh still wanted something, a vale for petrol. Over his shoulder the governor gave the order to another secretary. 'And one thing more,' Hesketh insisted, in spite of the telephones, the secretaries, the dispatches.

'No, come on,' I said, 'he's far too busy.' Neither Hesketh nor Rathbone would ever realize their comparative unimportance.

'No, we've got to have 'em, better guards than those two, they were no bloody use,' Hesketh said, and he insisted on explaining, slowly and circumstantially to the harassed governor. The guards were granted, and I was asked to take an interpreter with them, to report on the situation.

The interpreter was a businessman, too carefully oiled and groomed; I mistrusted him from the first. Whether he was a Fascist or not he was certainly nervous. We hadn't been going fifteen miles before he began suggesting that they had gone far enough. There were plenty of people there, he said; why not pick *them* up? He frankly didn't believe me when I told him that we had to go right on to pick up the Doctor; he expected the Fascists round every corner, and was not reassured by my telling him that we could go another hundred and twenty kilometres in perfect safety.

At about the eighty mark, we met Rathbone riding on the running-board of a car.

'I've picked up three aviators here, badly wounded – rushing 'em back to hospital – got to operate. Came down over my head. You go on as far as you can. See you in Almeria.' And the Doctor was gone.

We went on until we came to the village where Rathbone and I had slept. There, sitting on the steps, was a crowd of despondent women, who looked as if they had given up the struggle. I stopped the car and turned it round.

It was the same procedure as before, but with myself in charge I realized it more vividly. I found myself, that is, the centre of a howling, crying mob, who clutched me and held up their children, imploring, beseeching, begging, and clung to the lorry, so that I couldn't even open it. The guards had remained sitting passively in the front seat with the interpreter between them. Without undoing the back I went round and asked the interpreter to come and help. Reluctantly he and the guards came out.

'Tell them to be quiet,' I told the interpreter. 'And that I'm taking only the children and the sick.'

This produced only another surging rush from the crowd, who were all sick and mostly had children. The guards and the interpreter edged away and left me to manage by myself.

There was no question of selection. This was the first time I had seen them plainly in the daylight. The eyes of the women were running with pus and gum, their faces blotched with tears, dust and suffering. The babies they held up wore, for the most part, one small garment, and their legs and bottoms, which were bare, were a mass of sores and rashes.

My only piece of selection was to put in a woman with a broken leg. I kept shouting, 'Women and children only,' and the few men there, responding, helped the women and children up. Like frightened animals they clambered in and herded at the entrance, refusing to move up. I swore and shouted and pushed while around me shouted and pushed the three hundred for whom there were no places.

Things on the road had got really desperate by now, for the tougher and fitter had got farther on; only the sick and the ailing were stranded up here, and those who had started late.

The lorry was packed full to suffocation, and still the people below pressed round it entreating and beseeching.

'Not for me, Compañero, it's not for me I'm asking. But take the child. Save my child.' 'Holy Mary, save the little one.' 'Mother of God, don't leave us.'

They put their arms round me; they fell to the ground and clutched my knees, holding their babies and imploring my compassion.

And then from out of a house came a man carrying in his arms a little boy unconscious with a high fever. 'He's dying,' the man said. 'You must take him to a hospital, you must. You can't leave him here to die.' Tears were running down his brown wrinkled face; the mother followed, weeping too; with a baby sucking at her breast, she looked at me, dumbly, imploring.

There didn't seem to be an inch of room; but running my eye over the load I noticed one woman who had no child; she looked strong and hefty, and healthier than the rest. She must come out, I explained to my helpers. 'Come on, Camarada, you must come out and make room for the child.' I jumped up and caught her wrist; she struggled and screamed, with heart-rending, tortured cries; she seized the side of the lorry and gripped it with all her strength. Getting angry, I wrenched her hand free and forced her to the back of the lorry, jumped down myself, and pulled her off.

Through her tortured screams the woman lifted up her skirt and exposed her body, pinching out her belly with her hand. She was great with child. In an agony of remorse I helped her in again; her screams turned to tears of gratitude; she put her arms round me, called me saviour, and began to climb up again. In her overwhelming relief she couldn't restrain her water which trickled down on to my head and shoulders as I helped her up.

Still there was the father weeping and holding out his dying son; but the commotion with the pregnant woman seemed to have cleared a little space. The mother and baby were hauled up and the woman with the broken leg was given the dying boy to hold. This was the last inch of room. And as I turned round from fastening up the back of the lorry, the women were kneeling in the road holding their children towards me.

I tried to tell them: 'I'll be back again soon; make on as best you can. There'll be other lorries coming.'

I had forgotten about the seats in front where the guards were sitting with the interpreter. If they were turned out that would give room for several more. And now standing looking reproachfully at me was the father of the dying boy, with eight other children round him, all under ten. Two were weeping copiously and uncontrollably; I asked the interpreter who they were.

'The rest of the children of the mothers inside.'

The weeping ones were the brothers of the boy who was dying. I explained to the father, 'I've no room for you but I'll take the children,' and he pushed them all into the cabin, where they squeezed in on the floor and on the seat. The brothers bubbled over into louder tears at being separated. 'Padre, Padre,' they called through the window. Three wounded militia boys had climbed on to the roof; I didn't disturb them. The guards and the interpreter sulked on the running-board. There was room for another two or three on the front wings, but I decided to reserve that in case we came across any more wounded on the road. Besides, I felt that the load was as much already as the lorry would stand.

When we were forty miles from home, I decided to fill up the spare spaces, and choosing a group of three wounded militiamen, fitted them in, one between each headlamp and wing, and one on the roof.

And shortly afterwards the trouble began.

For some time I had thought that the clutch on the lorry was wrong, but the last two days had been too exacting for us to pay much attention to it. Now suddenly it began to get worse; a small incline and the engine barely pulled up it; the motor raced, and our speed got slower and slower.

It couldn't be disregarded. We had to abandon the men we had just picked up, and the boys on the roof. They had been so delighted and pleased at their unexpected luck; now they looked puzzled and reproachful, as they joined the walking procession again.

But it didn't make the least difference. The engine went faster and faster, the lorry went slower and slower, until finally, half-way up a small hill, it stopped.

'Get them all out,' the interpreter suggested, 'then it may go.'

I knew it wouldn't, but I went round to the back to explain.

Directly I opened the doors, the hot rancid smell from the inside hit me in the face, the smell of rancid sweat, garlic, urine, and vomit, in thick hot waves. And I realized at once that it would be very difficult to move them. As soon as I suggested it, they clung a little tighter to the sides, and looked at me with the uncomprehending glance of animals, afraid they would be hurt. I went back to the interpreter.

'You must walk to the nearest telephone and get help. Ring the Sanidad and the Civil Governor,' I gave names and instructions, but all the time I knew that the interpreter would do nothing.

Then I remembered the dying boy, and remembered, too, that somewhere at the very inside of the lorry there was a small bottle of brandy. I must get the people out.

I went round to the back again. The boy was still unconscious, still had a high fever, and was shivering: he had been very sick. The atmosphere inside was unimaginable; they must be moved, for that if nothing else. I pleaded and argued and persuaded in my few words of Spanish. When I tried to force them they clung to the lorry and fought. But with the departure of the interpreter, the guards seemed to become more friendly.

The sun was shining and warm; the grass was soft; we pulled out some mackintoshes from inside and spread them on the grass. Frightened and suspicious, still suspecting a trick, they at last allowed themselves to be persuaded and climbed slowly out. Each one that came down seemed to be more bedraggled, dirty, wretched and ill than the last.

I took off my coat and wrapped the sick child in it, and, finding the brandy, forced some down its throat. It lay on the cushions in an unresponsive, huddled heap, and the two brothers came shyly back into the lorry and stroked it, and, sitting down beside it, let the tears pour slowly down their cheeks. I tried unavailingly to cheer them up, and then took the bottle of brandy to the people outside.

They were sitting pathetically miserable on the grass, and every single one, from the oldest mother to the youngest baby was crying, a continual loud wailing, rising up from them, as they rocked gently to and fro in grief. Beside us, the long string of stricken people ceaselessly and remorselessly padded past. In front the wretched bedraggled party, each woman clutching a tiny crying baby to her naked breast and crying in time to their cries.

I took round the cognac and gave a mouthful to each; I took off my sweater and put it on a twelve-year-old who was complaining of the cold; and the child looked so ridiculous that several of the children stopped crying and smiled – a little wanly.

Determined to follow this up, we moved among the group, encouraging the mothers and ragging the boys. And in an hour we were rewarded; they had all stopped crying. Some of them even began to laugh, the rest sat patient. Soon, we told them, there would be another lorry, any moment now. They needn't worry.

Now that they were calm some of the women began to talk; I could make out the gist of it. They were all from Malaga; some from beyond the town. They had been on the march three, four, five, and some even six days, and they had had no food. All of them were nursing mothers; and I noticed their feet blistered, torn, bleeding, scratched, shredded; many of them could hardly move.

They talked fast and bitterly and I only understood a little, but their gestures and the words I did grasp were enough. Only two had husbands alive, they had left them to come in the lorry; the rest were dead, shot in Malaga. Malaga and the road out had been an inferno. Shelled from the sea, bombed from the air, and then machine-gunned. The terror was alive and blistering in their eyes as they imitated the stutter of machine guns. Soft at first; then louder as their hands described planes swooping: sharp and powerful as their hands dived. Only one family there was left complete.

The tears started up again, and they leaned on me, touched me and kissed my hand, 'But what shall we do now, Compañero? No homes, no man, no future. Compañero, what shall become of us and our children?'

Unable any longer to keep up the pretence of keeping up their spirits, I walked away from them; but it was impossible to avoid it; the misery was inescapably there, on the road, too, crawling past, and fifty thousand still to come.

It was another wonderful sunset; the sky flushed crimson and gold and rose, as the sun disappeared. But its importance for the road was not in terms of beauty, but of heat. My party was beginning to cry again. One or two started; the mothers joined in, and soon they were all at it. I went over to them; they looked up at me, and cried, '*Frio, Frio*, cold, cold,' and begged to be allowed inside the lorry again. None of them thought of moving there without my permission. And when I agreed, they were pathetically grateful, as if I were conferring on them the greatest blessing in the world; they kissed my hands again, calling me their saviour. Once inside, they sat in their self-generated heat, the children mostly sleeping, the women whimpering.

The night dragged intolerably; I had to stay outside to try to stop a car and get a message back to Almeria. But no one would stop, any more than earlier, we had stopped. A night dew added to the misery of the cold and the darkness and 'Frio, Frio,' rose up from the endless dragging procession.

And all the time people would keep detaching themselves from the crowd, and coming up to me, murmur their sorrow as if I, because I stood outside it, must in some way be able to relieve them. I could do nothing but touch them with sympathy, old men, old women, and children, and they merged back into the dark mass of the crowd re-adding their individual sorrow to the collective agony.

Some I had to help. Once, I noticed a little boy who couldn't have been more than eight, standing swaying with his finger in his mouth, looking vacantly at the lorry. Thinking that he was lost, I went over to him and asked where his mother and father were. The child who could only speak in a hoarse whisper answered unemotionally and dully, 'Dead, all dead.' He had walked from Malaga by himself. Five days on the road, alone and without food. And now he was complaining of the cold. I picked him up and put him into the cabin on top of the others; it was at least warm there. He dropped instantly asleep.

Later, there came a woman with a son of about twelve. 'He's so cold.' She stood there, stating it as a mere fact. She was too tired to gesture or to plead. Her movements, as she walked up, were the movements of a woman of eighty, slow, shuffled, tiny, stiff steps with no trace of spring in them; the boy was sobbing. Four days they had been walking without food. They waited there, not asking, nor pleading, waiting as if it was their last hope that I should make some saving suggestion.

The cabin of the lorry was packed with children, lying on top of each other on the seats and the floor. But I determined to squeeze one more in, and took the child round. 'But not without my mother,' the boy protested, and in a last access of strength broke away and ran to her. She persuaded him to go in, and, as he went away, sank down where she stood on the road, drawing her cloak over her head.

And then a boy of about fifteen, long-legged, overgrown. Thin, pale and hoarse, he had been walking for five days, alone. He came up to me, too tired to speak. He pointed interrogatively at the lorry. Gently I shook my head. 'It's full, I'm sorry.' There was the faintest shrug of the shoulders in resignation, and then he spun, toppled, and fell: out: done: it had been his last effort.

They were a few out of the thousands. 'Feed my sheep.' The text kept running through my head with the derisive irony of a phrase of music. 'Feed my sheep.' And I suddenly found myself cursing and shouting at the top of my voice: 'Well, why don't you feed your bloody sheep? . . . Why don't you?'

Still the people shuffled by, and one would detach himself and come up to me and dumbly turn away from my ineffective sympathy. Still from inside the lorry the crying of the women and children rose and swelled and fell away again, and steam slowly ascended from the foetid atmosphere inside.

Once I lit a match to examine the unconscious child. And from the people on the road a frightened cry went up: 'Lights, put out the light,' and the women inside, with tears in their eyes, begged me to put it out. When I asked the guards what was the matter, they pointed down the coast to the lights of a battleship thirty miles away; there was a faint sound of firing. 'They are afraid she will see the light and bomb us.'

At half past three there was a roar in the distance, and the lights of powerful cars. Thirty fast lorries ploughed an opening through the crowd, by the power of their sirens and headlights, taking no notice of the cry of 'Lights, lights'. As they slowed down to pass them, I saw that they were a company of the International Brigade going down to Motril; no one cheered or cared.

An hour later after many useless attempts, I managed to stop a car going to Almeria. It was a staff car and one of the officers could speak French. He was most sympathetic and asked for written instructions, which I hastily scribbled. 'It probably won't be till morning,' the officer said, 'but I promise you something will be done.'

By this time I was very tired; it was my second night on the road, and it was very cold. I decided to make room for myself in the front of the lorry by taking one of the children on my knees.

I opened the door and shook the child nearest, half-ashamed of myself for waking it: only at last did it sit up, looking round sleepily. I tried to explain what I was doing, but the boy couldn't understand and I had to pick him up; there wasn't enough room to get in without first putting it outside. It cried out protesting, 'No, no, you can't turn me out,' and clutching the steering wheel, clung desperately. I pulled its hands free, set it for a moment in the road, and climbed in. But when I turned to pick it up again, after squeezing a place among the jumbled bodies of the other children, it had begun to stumble off uncomprehendingly down the road, crying and rubbing its eyes with the back of its hands.

I called to it and leaning out, drew it up, set it on my knees, and slammed the door. As it understood, it gave a tired smile, pushed up its face against my cheek and kissed me; and in almost im-mediately the same movement it fell back asleep against my shoulder.

The sun was just rising when a relief lorry rumbled up beside us. Soon they were all packed into the new lorry. They had brought a rope to tow us back with, but it looked too thin. The broken lorry was filled up with more people; there was no limit now to the load; they sat on the headlights, the wings, the running-board and the roofs.

My mistrust of the rope proved well founded: every time the towing lorry changed gear, it broke. It must have broken twenty times in the thirty miles; and by the time we reached Almeria it was half-past ten: and the rope was so short that the lorries almost touched.

From *The Heretics*

Cordova read the letter carefully and told Elizabeth he thought it meant Paul was not dead, and she said she hardly dared to think that was what it meant. She said Paul had always signed his letters from school in that way. Luap was Paul spelt backwards and anyway they had no Auntie Ethel: it certainly was Paul's writing and it said definitely he was alive and that the report was wrong. The letter's facetious tone was too characteristic to have been written by anyone else. Then she read it again and noticed Paul had been careful to give no address but to put in an obvious clue to where he was and through whom he might be found.

Because of the maid, they talked in English all the morning. By lunchtime they had agreed the most likely explanation was that through having gone to the front with the POUM[1] militia column Paul was on the SIM's list for liquidation. They had both been anxious about this ever since the May events in Barcelona, which were followed by the declaration of the POUM's illegality. Now they were both certain Paul had had himself reported killed in order to evade the SIM, and Elizabeth insisted that he would not have risked saying how he could be traced if he had not had a very definite, perhaps urgent, reason for doing so. She was convinced, she said, that Paul needed her help badly but did not dare to say so in a letter. It must be really serious, she thought, because to mention the mayor of Avallo was obviously very dangerous to both of them.

Cordova tried hard to dissuade Elizabeth from starting off to Avallo. He said there was the possibility she might be followed and anyway there was nothing she could do without making Paul conspicuous. For an ordinary militiaman to be seen talking intimately to a foreign female journalist was itself suspicious. As soon as she began to make inquiries her name might be remem-

[1] *Partido Overo Union Marxista* – United Marxist Workers' Party [Author's note].

bered as being the same as that of a listed political criminal. Some guilty connection between them would be assumed and she would be constantly watched: all she would do would be to lead the authorities straight to Paul.

Elizabeth said she knew it was a risk to take but she understood Paul better than Cordova did: she was positive he would not have written so indiscreetly without some imperative reason. She had lived with Paul all her life and considered he had one of the clearest heads of anyone she knew; the schoolboyish style of the letter was affected deliberately to divert any suspicions the censor might have had.

As Cordova's arguments against Elizabeth's intention became less reasonable he stated them more aggressively and in the end he announced that he forbade her absolutely to go off to Avallo.

Elizabeth went out of the room and walked to the Press Censorship office and arranged there for a car to take her to the Aragon front. She said she had been commissioned to write a series of articles with a British historical slant and she had decided to begin with Catherine of Aragon. The chief censor was an educated Castilian woman who was accustomed to the foreign journalists' efforts to carry out their persistent instructions to write up their material from the American or British or French or Mexican angles. She was an eager feminist and was always glad to favour people like Elizabeth.

She telephoned from her desk and arranged for a car to be ready in an hour's time.

Elizabeth did not want to go on arguing with Cordova so she went out to wait in a café. She bought two dozen ham rolls and enough cigarettes to last for four days. She then telephoned Cordova to say she would be away for a day or two and rang off before he could begin shouting again. She looked round the café and saw a reporter she knew and sat down at his table: they talked for a few minutes before her acquaintance got up to go to the lavatory, leaving his jacket hanging over his chair.

Elizabeth could see his wallet in the inside pocket. The table was in a corner and there were few other customers. Elizabeth saw her chance to solve a difficult problem and she took the wallet and slipped out the journalist's identity card, and his authorization to circulate on all fronts. Then she put the wallet back.

The diagonal scarlet and black flag of the FAI hung over the door of the Town Hall in Avallo. Elizabeth climbed out of her government car and looked at the scowls of the dozen or so young bandits with rifles who stood about on the wide stone steps. They did not make way for her and she had to talk up to them from the pavement level. She asked if she could see the comrade mayor, and none of them answered, but one, an older man, shouted the name 'Manolo' into the building. Nobody answered and then one of the young men smiled suddenly and lifted his shoulders at Elizabeth and said:

'Out.'

She asked when he would be in and smiled back effectively. The young man did not know and Elizabeth said she would wait: she stood there and took out a pack of cigarettes and then offered one to the youth. He took the cigarette and thanked her and broke it in half and gave away the rather larger piece to a friend standing next to him. They smoked for a few minutes and Elizabeth asked how things were at the front.

'Nothing,' one of them said, 'nothing new.'

She had only seen Anarchist badges and flags in the villages for the last fifty miles of her journey and she had noticed the FAI armbands of all the men in the streets of Avallo. She had known before she left Barcelona that the Anarchists had controlled this front since the beginning of the war but she had not expected to be received with such very blatant hostility. She supposed most of the visitors in grand motor-cars who came to Avallo had been interfering government officials whose business it was to demand the disbanding of the collective farms or to raise legalistic difficulties about the banknotes which the municipality preferred to print for themselves locally.

Elizabeth offered more cigarettes but they all refused with dignity. She said they did not have to be so unamiable, she had nothing to do with the government.

'Are you a Communist?' one of them asked.

'Certainly not,' she said.

Then in a more amicable way they began to talk curiously about her business in Avallo. Elizabeth said she was on a personal visit to discuss family affairs with the comrade mayor who was a friend of a friend of hers.

The young man to whom she had given the cigarette offered to take her to see Manolo and the others laughed and as he and Elizabeth walked down the street together they shouted improprieties after them, implying they had fallen for one another. When they were out of sight of the Town Hall, Pepe, Elizabeth's companion, suggested she should give him a packet of cigarettes.

They went into a large café and the young man led Elizabeth over to a table where the mayor, Manolo, was sitting drinking coffee with six armed guards.

The mayor was a small man with a very dark complexion and unshaven cheeks and chin. He wore a black cloth cap and a dirty black suit and his ragged blue shirt had no collar: a large revolver stuck out of his red waistband. His six companions wore old civilian shirts and trousers and each of them had a new polished Mauser pistol fitted to its heavy wooden stock. They all looked at Elizabeth without moving and Manolo did not answer when she asked if she could talk to him. He told Pepe to tell him who she was.

Pepe said he did not know and the mayor, still ignoring her, asked him what she wanted. Pepe said she wanted to talk to him. Manolo looked round at the others and then told Elizabeth and Pepe to sit down.

Elizabeth said her business was private business to do only with the comrade mayor personally, but Manolo said they were all friends there. Elizabeth did not know how discreet these people would be and she was more than ever uncertain when two waiters and the occupants of the next table all crowded round inquisitively to hear what was going on. She could not decide how to begin and she started round the café hoping she would think of something to say. She read a notice on the wall which said:

'Comrades are respectfully requested not to use firearms in the café and to pay for what they drink.'

She realized she would have to risk making a mistake and said she wanted to take a photograph of the grave of a friend of Manolo's who was dead, and she hoped he might be able to show her where it was. It was a matter of sentiment; the picture was for the parents of the man: his name was Paul Berridge and he was English.

The mayor laughed very loudly and slapped his thighs with his

ɔig peasant's hands. His gay, deep voice encouraged the others to
ɹaugh too, though only some of them knew what the joke was.

With his thumb Manolo gestured to his guards and they stood
ɪp and two of them, on each side of her, helped Elizabeth up and
ǥuided her by the arms into the back room behind the counter.
ꓥll of them, including the waiters and Pepe and the customers,
ꓛollowed in and then the door was shut and locked. The mayor
ꓥsked for Elizabeth's papers.

One of the others spelt out the words of her safe conduct and
ꓥer press identity card. Manolo could not read but he was in-
ꓛerested in the fact that Elizabeth selected the papers she showed
ꓛrom among some others he could see she had. He asked for them
ꓥll, but Elizabeth said they were of no importance and she began
ꓛo buckle them in to the leather bag she carried.

One of the *pistoleros* twisted her wrist behind her back and
ꓥnother cocked his Mauser and pressed its muzzle into her stom-
ꓥch. They took the bag and found the papers she had stolen from
ꓛhe journalist in Barcelona and also a special priority pass, stamped
ꓥnd signed by the Minister of War, which Cordova had got for
ꓥer in case it might be useful if she were ever in any real difficulty.
When it was read out to him this document made Manolo so sure
ʃhe was an enemy that he only laughed again rudely when
Elizabeth in despair said Paul was her brother and if he had been
ꓥ friend of the mayor they should not treat her in such an un-
ꓛomradely way.

Manolo told three of them to search her. She knew if she
ʃstruggled one of the pistols might go off and she was too interested
ɪn getting them to change their opinion of her to make any
ꓛrouble, which anyhow would have been useless. She helped them
ꓛo undress her completely and she only protested verbally when
ʃhe was levered fairly gently on to her back on the floor and a not
very thorough search was made for anything she might have had
between her legs.

While she was dressing again she insisted she was Paul's sister
ꓥnd he would be very angry when he heard how they had behaved.

Manolo said he thought she had told him Paulo was dead.
Elizabeth was annoyed and also she began to see that nothing
but the most direct approach would be any use with these people,

so she answered that Manolo knew very well Paul was alive and
that she had good reasons for not saying so before she had found
out what sort of people she was talking to. She felt she was being
unwise when she said this but at the same time she realized that
their manifest disapproval of anyone they thought was a government agent proved, if she had been right about Paul's letter, that
she could trust them to be on his side. She said it was no good
going on arguing and they ought to get Paul to come and identify
her.

They shut her up in one of the penitentiary cells of the convent
of the Virgin of Pilar. On the way through the devastated chapel
Elizabeth thought with what malevolence the peasants must hate
the Church and how completely the ecclesiastical authorities must
have become identified with the persecutions and exploitations
of the centuries. Otherwise it was impossible to believe that these
illiterate, superstitious, and simple countrymen could have developed the vindictive loathing suggested by the thoroughness of
their destruction of the churches and the churchmen.

When Elizabeth was being interrogated in Avallo, Paul was playing cards with Manolo's son, Angelito, in a front-line trench near
Belchite.

Elizabeth had understood the letter very well: soon after the
POUM had been declared an illegal organization a truck-load of
SIM executives had arrived at Avallo with warrants for the arrest,
on capital charges, of Paul and three other foreigners who were
known to be serving on that sector. Angelito had been one of
those Paul had originally met in Barcelona and because he was
brave and intelligent he had become the leader of their band of
twenty-three mixed Anarchists and members of the Trotskyistic
POUM. The procedure of the SIM had been scrupulously correct:
they had applied to Angelito, as Paul's commanding officer, for
permission to take the wanted men from their firing position in
the front line. Angelito had naturally agreed, in view of the sub-
machine guns of the SIM contingent, and had directed them to a
part of the line six miles from where he knew Paul and the others
were. He then sent a motor-cyclist to his cousin who was in
charge there to say that when the SIM arrived they were to be

reated well and told that all the foreigners had been killed by a
shell which landed right on top of the dugout they shared.

The position had been at the far end of a mule-track and Angelito's cousin had had time, before the truck arrived, to stick a
notice on the soil of a recently filled-in latrine saying that there
lay the remains of four foreign volunteers who died gloriously in
the cause of democracy.

Because Angelito could not produce any proofs, like papers or
personal effects, the agents were not fully satisfied, but as these
were only four of the hundreds of names on the list of the SIM
men could not spend a disproportionate amount of time checking
them. And having failed to collect these four it had seemed to
them to be better to report their deaths as a fact than to indicate
any doubts in their report, which might involve the executives
themselves in the suspicion, at headquarters, of lack of efficiency
or zeal.

After this incident Paul and the others had thought it wise to
become members of the FAI and to get themselves transferred
away from the unit where they were known to have been in a
POUM group. Angelito remained a friend of theirs and they used
to meet him in Avallo whenever they moved back into reserve.
Their Spanish nicknames were used on all official lists.

For a year the front had been quiet and the troops on both sides
lived dull lives in their dirty trenches. Paul's column had established the routine of alternating between a fortnight in the line
and a fortnight resting in Avallo. They exchanged with the same
unit each time and only these holidays and their occasional
guerrilla raids deep into Fascist territory relieved the dreary
months of the static war.

But suddenly, a week before, Manolo had told them the
sensational news that as mayor he had been directed to find billets
for the International Brigades and the Army of Manoeuvre which
was moving over from the Central Front.

This decision had been taken by the government for both a
military and a political reason. The previous tranquillity in Aragon
made possible a secret concentration and a surprise attack; and
also there were political advantages in saturating these anarchist
provinces with disciplined Communist troops whose allegiance
to the government was absolute, and whose presence in the in-

transigent country would provide a means of forcing the FAI into greater conformity, and would also ensure a more thorough purge of Trotskyists than it had been possible until then to carry out.

Paul and his friends had discussed the news at a table in Manolo's café. They had agreed that they were likely to become more of a nuisance to their friends than they were a danger to the Fascists. There was no point in their hanging furtively about concentrating their energies on the problem of evading being killed by their own side. Their original purpose had been to fight Fascism but now they felt they had too little military value to justify the liability they would be to everyone they knew. The sensible thing was to leave Spain.

So far they had not dared to move out of the forward area, and it was certain they had no hope of applying for exit visas without bringing the SIM down on them. The frontier was tightly guarded and to board a ship without permits or friends would be too hazardous to be worth trying. They did not think they would be very welcome at the British Consulate in Barcelona and anyhow they felt it would be unwise to be seen walking up to the front door and ringing the bell. All the consulates were certain to be watched.

In the end Paul had decided to write to Elizabeth so as to have some respectably documented person through whom to work. He had not doubted that she would come flying up to Avallo as soon as she got his letter and he had thought it best to present Manolo with an accomplished fact rather than to risk his disagreement by telling him beforehand that she would probably be arriving.

As soon as he had taken the decision to try to get out of Spain they had stopped talking and had sprawled round the table, each of them suddenly enervated by a flaccid sense of the most desolate depression. They had looked at their glasses and their fingers and had avoided one another's eyes. After their earnest talk about what to do the abrupt silence and their disinterested preoccupation with their own thoughts became embarrassing and soon Paul had said how wretched he felt about it. The others had agreed and by sharing their dejection they had begun to be able to plan again.

By three in the morning when the café was beginning to be less crowded, Paul said he had thought of a way to improve their morale and qualify the regrets they might have for the rest of their lives if they became deserters from the front: he suggested that on their own they should do one more raid into Fascist territory and really smash something up. Then at least they would be able to comfort themselves that they had made one definite concrete contribution to the winning of the war.

The next day they had borrowed a truck from Manolo and had driven up to a sector where they knew there was a Fascist train which regularly chugged across the front from Saragossa; it was about ten miles behind the enemy's most forward line but was visible through binoculars from Angelito's observation post. For months the troops there had indented for a gun big enough to carry that far, but it had never arrived. Every piece of artillery had been needed for the Madrid offensive.

Paul and the other three decided to destroy the train as it passed through a tunnel in a ridge of hills about twelve miles away.

The morning Elizabeth was arrested they were playing cards with Angelito waiting for it to be time to start. It would have been best to take three or four days over the patrol; to travel only after dark and to hide up during daylight but they had guessed they had little time left before the troops from Madrid arrived and they had therefore decided to make the journey that night, to blow the tunnel the next morning, and get back to the front by five the same day so as to be able to slip home into their own trenches under cover of the regular 'exchange of newspapers' which happened each week at that time.

Since the beginning of the war there had been an arrangement with the enemy troops to have a truce for ten minutes once a week during which they exchanged bundles of newspapers and were able to enjoy the news from the two opposite propaganda angles. Paul's patrol would go out in Fascist uniforms borrowed from prisoners and be able on the return journey to mix in the small crowd of arguing men which always formed in the middle of no-man's-land; they would be back in the Republican trenches before the ten minutes was up.

The four of them played cards with Angelito all day and watched the distance of the sun from the tops of the far mountains. Paul found he became less frightened as the sun dropped but when it was dark he noticed his hands were still shaking slightly and he had to repress a superstitious presentiment that in every sense it would be their last patrol.

Angelito kissed them when they were ready to go. He helped to strap up their huge packs of gelignite and he watched them climb out from the trench and begin crawling into the blackness. He listened for what seemed to him to be two or three hours and then suddenly at least six enemy machine guns banged and clattered opposite him. The Republicans replied and within a minute the whole front for miles in each direction was blazing and howling with rifle and machine gun and mortar fire. The uproar went on all night and petered out when the sun came up.

Three days after Elizabeth had been arrested two guards came for her and led her out with their pistols pointed at her back. She asked what they were going to do and one of them gestured with his finger across his neck and made a gargling noise in his throat.

She was walked through the streets to the town hall.

Manolo and Angelito were there with a group on the steps and Paul grinned from behind them. He waited for her to come up to him and then he put his arms round her shoulders and said in English that she was a good girl. He introduced her to the mayor and Angelito and she shook hands as if she had not met Manolo before. They all laughed and slapped Paul on the back, and Elizabeth was so relieved to see him she laughed too and made bantering remarks to Manolo whom she accused of not being a gentleman. Manolo enjoyed being teased and his heavy booming laughter echoed in the narrow street. The rest chuckled and repeated Elizabeth's joke to one another and laughed loudly again in company with Manolo.

As soon as he had got in from the patrol Paul had been given Manolo's message to come back immediately in connection with an affair of importance. Paul was in good spirits because everything was working out well. Their raid had been successful, except for the death of one of them, and Elizabeth's prompt appearance had reduced his anxiety about the difficulty of arranging their escape from Spain.

Paul and Elizabeth went off with Manolo for a meal at the café. They sat round the table all the afternoon drinking white wine

ind arguing happily about politics. Manolo attacked Paul for his
support of the POUM and its Marxist approval of the dictatorship
of the proletariat which, Manolo said, was bound to develop into a
tyrannous regimentation of the proletariat. Paul answered that a
dictatorship of the proletariat in alliance with the peasantry was
exactly what Manolo himself was operating in Avallo.

The mayor laughed and denied it with violent blasphemous
words.

Paul said he thought the POUM was right to consider that a
revolution had happened in Spain in 1936. In the early days power
was certainly in the hands of the working class, but it had gradually been lost through the FAI and the CNT[1] not having organized
that power politically. The Spanish proletariat, concentrated
mainly in Barcelona, was traditionally anarchist and against all
politics and politicians, and this unpractical though understand-
able attitude meant they would never be able to compete with
either the Capitalists or the orthodox Communists, and must
certainly fail against the present combination of both.

Elizabeth said Paul was wrong to suggest there was a united
front of capitalists and Stalinists. She thought his trouble was that
he was too pre-occupied with old-fashioned Bolshevism: as she
understood it he was thinking in terms of repeating in Spain the
Leninist revolution in St Petersburg. In fact history could not
repeat itself and nowadays the whole question of the Socialist
world revolution had been transformed by the existence of the
Soviet Union. Now the proletarian revolutionism of the POUM
was out of date. In the old days it was necessary for Socialist
working men to proclaim and expect violent revolutions. The
thing was that if they succeeded in achieving political power by
peaceful parliamentary means the reactionaries were bound to
start the violence and the rebellion themselves. This had been
proved, for example, in Spain, where the progressive government
had not even been mildly Socialist or working-class. But, Elizabeth said, a really new factor was now developing: increasingly
as time went on reactionary counter-revolutionaries would find
themselves having to fight the whole power of the Soviet Red
Army. In fact any new Socialist government would now have as
much more military power behind it than its opponents could

[1] The Anarcho-Syndicalist Union [Author's note].

possibly muster. This meant, she said, that the proletarians of the world could now afford to approve the methods of gradualism, reform, and alliance with the timid middle classes. It was now possible to be more moderate, more patient, and less sectarian because they were sure to win anyway.

Paul said it did not sound much like the world revolution to him.

Elizabeth said her view was in fact more effectively revolutionary than Paul's. The world revolution would expand inexorably from a centre – the Soviet Union. The first loyalty of revolutionary Socialists throughout the world must be to the USSR and the Red Army and not to their own patriotic little parish pumps. The interests of the Soviet Union as a nation must now be not only associated, but identified, with the cause of humanity.

Paul said he thought she had a serious case, but for him it seemed unpleasantly sophisticated, almost cynical. He supposed she had picked it up among her big-time Soviet friends at the Lord Gaythorne. He did not think such a degree of self-abnegation, such an arid repudiation of all national traditions and aspirations could be really healthy. To substitute a feeling of awe for a powerful nation for the old enthusiasm for a great cause seemed to him a wretched backward move. The idea of Russia, as the expanding Nucleus-Nation was to him just as stupidly philistine as Hitler's Master Race. All the same, he added, from the point of view of the historian two hundred years hence Elizabeth might be right: that was why he did not approve of the bitterness of the orthodox Trotskyist's criticisms of Stalin's policies. They were inclined, he thought, to give ammunition to the enemy.

Manolo said he was an older man than Paul and he could tell him he was talking a formidable nonsense. Any criticism of anything always may be used by the opponents of that thing: if for fear of pleasing the reactionaries there were never to be any criticism of policies within the progressive movement, then that would be the end of all improvement, all vitality, all mental life; it would be an intellectual suicide which would delight all established authorities far more than any disagreements among their opponents could. Manolo said if the Russians could not take criticism, then that proved there was something 'obscenity' wrong with them.

Paul and Elizabeth laughed because they liked Manolo's rude
sagacity. Elizabeth felt she understood why Manolo was so respected in the town, and so powerful. She smiled when she
wondered how much serious criticism he himself had been prepared to swallow since he had been in charge.

They stopped talking for a time and filled up their glasses; then
Paul said the tendency for anyone who is sure he is right to impute
disreputable motives in those who do not agree was not a characteristic peculiar to the Communists; the medieval church also had
always regarded heretics as ill-willed and evil; that was why it was
considered legitimate to imprison, torture, and kill them.

Elizabeth thought of the intricate position Paul was in and admired his ability to talk so dispassionately; and she said that although there certainly was such a universal tendency to suspect
sinister motives in critics, it was in the contemporary world only
really violently manifested among Fascists and Communists.

Manolo said it should be opposed equally in both and it was
time they got down to arranging what to do about Paul and the
other two foreign heretics. Also, he said, they had to decide
whether it would be wise to let Elizabeth's chauffeur out of jail,
or whether to have him reported killed by an enemy sniper at the
front.

The next day Elizabeth and Paul and two other Englishmen
motored back to Barcelona. Paul used the journalist's safe conduct
which Elizabeth had brought with her and the other two showed
the British passports, now invalid, with which they had originally
entered Spain. It would probably have been impossible for them
to get through government controls on the outskirts of Barcelona,
without everyone showing a proper authorization, if Elizabeth
had not been able to overawe the sentries with her Special Priority
Pass and their official car and chauffeur.

They left the car at the censorship and walked back to Elizabeth's flat. Cordova was there trying to mitigate his dreadful
anxiety by drinking whisky and listening to a concert from Paris.
When Elizabeth came in he knocked over his glass and embraced
her and murmured incoherent and clumsy words of relief and
affection. Because Elizabeth was also hysterically pleased to see

him, they stood close together and mumbled and stroked one another. The three Englishmen stood about just inside the door waiting unhappily to be introduced. When Elizabeth remembered them, they shuffled forward and shook hands and, because General Cordova controlled his embarrassment by behaving with inappropriate formality, they all felt as if they ought to have saluted and clicked their heels.

Cordova had a case of whisky he had been given by the captain of one of the French gun-running freighters from Marseilles, and when they had finished their second tumblers, they had become more accustomed to one another. They talked and joked and Paul began to tell Cordova about Elizabeth being searched at Avallo, but she was able to shut him up without Cordova, who she knew would not have laughed, having noticed that she did so. The Brandenburg Concerto, dimmed down, made them shout at one another, and with the whisky it increased their exhilarated mood.

Elizabeth had always been sure Cordova would do his best to help her brother, but she was surprised at the generous, almost enthusiastic way in which he was assuming the whole responsibility for looking after them and for organizing their escape. After they had eaten a meal of cold rabbit, Paul and Elizabeth began to speak more seriously of the alternative possibilities before them but Cordova suggested they should forget practical affairs for the time being. He would make a certain reconnaissance in the morning, he said, and let them know what the plan of campaign was at lunchtime. He asked them to stay in the flat for the night and not to go out until he got back in the morning; they had better be careful to speak English while they were there because of the maids.

They were talking about Bach when the telephone rang. Elizabeth answered it and shouted with pleasure when she found it was Simon: she told him to come straight round, she had a surprise for him.

Simon came in soberly in sombre navy blue corduroys. He had a revolver and looked as he had done in Madrid after they had smartened him up for dinner at the Lord Gaythorne. He smiled and shook hands and spoke to Paul self-consciously. He said he congratulated him on not having died a martyr to the cause of Trotskyism after all. Paul was feeling too excited to notice the lack of warmth in his friend's voice and Elizabeth interrupted them with a drink for Simon before they had time to start one of their theoretical wrangles.

Because Simon was sober and the others had been drinking for some hours his presence in the room disturbed the spontaneity of their conversation. It was difficult to know what to talk about because it would have been rude to leave Paul's Aragon friends out by speaking for too long about family topics, and Elizabeth was careful to steer them away from the political quarrel she could see beginning when Simon mentioned that he was in the International Brigade.

Cordova turned the radio on for the news from London and they were able to sit silently for twenty minutes without feeling embarrassed by the uneasy atmosphere. Then they talked for a time about Professor Harrington and his adventures while evacuating his monkeys and apes by American gunboat from Malaga to Gibraltar.

Soon Simon said he had to be back in barracks by eleven, and Elizabeth went with him as far as the street door. She told him to be especially careful not to let anyone know he had seen Paul or that he knew he was alive; she said the SIM was after him and Cordova was going to fix his escape within the next day or two.

Simon said he would come round again at six the next day and walked off after he had kissed Elizabeth good night.

After Simon had gone they all felt suddenly exhausted and went to bed. Elizabeth and Cordova talked in their room until very late. Cordova told her why he had behaved so badly about her going to Avallo. The thing was, he said, he particularly did not want to attract any attention to the flat because he needed to use it as a meeting-place for a group of officers and politicians who were urging the acceptance of the 'French Plan'. They had definite information, Cordova said, that the Soviet Union had decided to pull out of Spain. The Russians' entanglement with the Spanish Government was leading, the Kremlin considered, to a too dangerous diplomatic isolation of Russia from the Western Democracies. Moscow had decided, therefore, to withdraw all Russian personnel and to stop the supply of arms to Spain. Without the Russian materials, Cordova said, there was not the slightest hope of winning the war against the increasing number of German and Italian divisions on Franco's side. Therefore the only practical thing to do was to make peace on the basis of the 'French Plan' which was a scheme to allow Franco to control all of Spain except Catalonia, which should be an independent and democratic Republic under French protection. The opposition to Franco would have to go underground and a guerrilla warfare could be conducted from the safe Catalonian base.

Cordova said they had reason to believe this compromise solution to the war would be approved by the non-intervention committee and by the British and French Governments – who would be willing to press its acceptance by Franco by threatening to supply arms to the Republicans if he refused.

Elizabeth protested that this was the most horribly treacherous idea she had ever heard in her life, practically a capitulation. But Cordova insisted it did at least have some chance of stopping the Fascists getting complete control of absolutely everything, which was bound to happen when the Russian arms dried up. Cordova said that for reasons of Communist politics, as distinct from Russian diplomacy, Moscow was in favour of the war in Spain being fought on for as long as it was possible to keep it going, because every week of the fighting was increasing the power of the Spanish Communist Party in relation to all other organizations. For this reason, he said, Moscow was opposing all discussion of the 'French Plan' or any thought of its acceptance. In fact, Cordova said, if the SIM found out we were having meetings about it here we should all be shot for treason. The method of the Soviet Union, Cordova said, was the subtly dialectical one of combining Russian state diplomacy with Comintern politics – both pulling out themselves and saying 'Fight on, comrades' to the Spanish people.

Elizabeth told Cordova how sorry she was she had had to complicate things for him by bringing in Paul and his friends and she stroked his hair and said how wonderfully kind he was being. She said it was impossible for her to decide whether he was right to advocate the 'French Plan' because she loved him so dearly she would probably support him whatever he did. It was a humiliating thought, she said.

Then they kissed and talked less seriously, and played until it was nearly light.

Without difficulty Cordova arranged the next morning for Paul
and the others to leave Spain that night on the gun-runner whose
captain he knew. They would sail soon after dark for Marseilles.
Captain Carboni had been a professional smuggler all his life and
Cordova had found it easy to broach the subject and to buy, at a
high price, three sets of French seamen's papers, with which Paul
and his friends would be able to pass the sentries at the dock gates.

But all the afternoon they fidgeted about in the flat feeling
dejected and apprehensive. They tried to play poker but were
unable to care whether they won or lost. After the wild romance
of the first revolutionary months in Barcelona and at the front it
seemed despicable to be sneaking away again to the safety of the
old Philistine world. They were glad when Simon came in at six,
and interrupted their dreary game, and they were all disappointed
when he said he had only looked in for a few minutes but would
see them some time the next day. Elizabeth tried to persuade him
to stay with them until it was time for Paul and the others to go
down to the ship, but Simon said definitely it was a pity he had
not known they were leaving so soon because he had an appoint-
ment he could not break.

When he had gone they felt even more deflated than before.
Paul envied Simon's established position as a member of the
admired and applauded International Brigade and felt slighted by
Simon's self-composure and his lack of sympathy for, or even
interest in, the difficulties of his less respectable friends. Paul felt
there was something almost snobbish in Simon's casual manner
and his polite, uninterested questions about the name of the ship
and the time they would be leaving.

By the time it was dark and they began to say good-bye,
Elizabeth and Cordova were ashamed of their relief and their impatience for Paul and the others to go. Elizabeth went out into
the street first to make sure there was no one watching the front
door. She came back and said it would be all right; it was far too
dark in the blacked-out streets for anyone to be able to follow
them. They slipped out self-consciously and walked quickly without their rope-soled shoes making any sound on the pavement.
They said nothing until they began to speak French as they
approached the control post guarding the way to the docks. They
showed their papers and were able to avoid conversation with the

sentries by pretending not to understand Spanish. They mumble
their way through on to the quay.

They could see their freighter against the sky a few hundred
yards away: the three red lanterns by the gang-plank were the
signal Cordova had arranged with the captain, so as to be sure
they would not mistake the ship. When they were within ten
yards of the lights a figure came out of the darkness in front of
them and asked for their papers in French; they showed their
seamen's passes and the man fumbled with his torch until six
other armed men had converged in to surround them. They could
feel the revolvers in their backs.

Paul and the two others were taken away to SIM headquarters
in a dark blue, forty-horsepower limousine. Simon was not one
of the group that made the arrest; he had agreed with his superior
that his past connection with the accused made it unsuitable for
him to be personally involved in the actual apprehension.

Simon had said he met Paul by chance in a café, because he had
his own reasons for wanting to be able to go on seeing Elizabeth.
He excused himself for pretending this by thinking it would be
uneconomical to get too many people unnecessarily into trouble.

The Third Winter'

from *The Face of War*

November 1938

In Barcelona, it was perfect bombing weather. The cafés along the Ramblas were crowded. There was nothing much to drink: a sweet fizzy poison called orangeade and a horrible liquid supposed to be sherry. There was, of course, nothing to eat. Everyone was out enjoying the cold afternoon sunlight. No bombers had come over for at least two hours.

The flower stalls looked bright and pretty along the promenade. The flowers are all sold, señora. For the funerals of those who were killed in the eleven o'clock bombing, poor souls.'

It had been clear and cold all day and all day yesterday and probably would be fair from now on. 'What beautiful weather,' a woman said, and she stood, holding her shawl around her, staring at the sky. 'And the nights are as fine as the days. A catastrophe,' she said, and she walked with her husband towards a café.

It was cold but really too lovely and everyone listened for the sirens all the time, and when we saw the bombers they were like tiny silver bullets moving for ever up, across the sky.

It gets dark suddenly and no street-lights are allowed in Barcelona, and at night the old town is rough going. It would be a silly end, I thought, to fall into a bomb hole, like the one I saw yesterday, that opens right down to the sewers. Everything you do in war is odd, I thought; why should I be ploughing around after dark, looking for a carpenter in order to call for a picture frame for a friend? I found Hernandez' house in a back street and I held my cigarette lighter above my head to see my way down the hall and up the stairs and then I was knocking on a door and old Mrs Hernandez opened the door and asked me to come in, to be welcome, her house was mine.

'How are you?' I said.

'As you see,' old Hernandez said, and he pushed his cap back on his forehead and smiled, 'alive'.

It wasn't much of a home but they looked very handsome in it. A wick floating in a cup of oil lighted the place. There were four chairs and a big table and some shelves tacked on the wall. The ten-year-old grandson was reading close to the burning wick. The daughter-in-law, the wife of their youngest son, played quietly with her baby in a corner. Old Mrs Hernandez had been working over the stove, and the room was smoky. What they would have to eat would be greens, a mound of cabbage leaves the size of your fist, and some dry bread. The women start cooking greens long in advance because they want to get them soft at least. Boiled flavourless greens go down better if they are soft.

The picture frame was not ready, Hernandez could not get the wood. Wood is for dugouts and trenches, bridges, railroad ties, to prop up bombed houses, to make artificial arms and legs, for coffins. He used to collect the fragments from destroyed houses, he said, not to work with, but for firewood, but now that is all saved for the hospitals. It was hard to be a carpenter, there wasn't much wood or much work any more.

'Not that it matters about me,' Hernandez said, 'I am very old.'

The little boy had been listening. His grandmother kept looking at him, ready to silence him if he interrupted while his elders spoke.

'What do you do all day?' I said.

'I stand in the food line.'

'Miguel is a good boy,' Mrs Hernandez said. 'He does what he can to help his old grandmother.'

'Do you like doing that?' I said.

'When they fight,' he said, laughing to himself, 'it is fun.'

His grandmother looked shocked. 'He does not understand,' she said. 'He is only ten. The poor people – they are so hungry, sometimes they quarrel among themselves, not knowing what they do.'

(They put up a sign on the shop door, and word flies through the neighbourhood that you can get food today. Then the lines form. Sometimes they are five blocks long. Sometimes you wait all that time but just before your turn comes the shop closes. There is no

ore food. The women wait in line and talk or knit, the children
vent games that they can play standing in one place. Everyone
s very thin. They know perfectly, by the sound of the first
xplosion, where the bombs are falling. If the first bomb sounds
ollow and muffled, they do not move from their places, because
hey know there is no immediate danger. If they can hear the drone
f the planes too clearly or the first explosion is jagged and harsh,
hey scatter for doorways or refuges. They do this professionally,
ke soldiers.

The pinched women file into the shop and hand their food cards
ver the high bare counter. The girls behind the counter look
ealthy because they are wearing rouge. Then the food is doled
ut in little grey paper sacks. A sack the size of a cigarette package,
ull of rice: that will have to do two people for two weeks. A sack
alf that big, full of dried peas: for one person for two weeks.
Wait, there's some codfish too. The girl behind the counter pulls
ut a slab of the grey-white flat fish and cuts off a little piece with
pair of scissors. She cuts it with scissors, not a knife, because
cissors are more accurate. A piece as long as your finger and
wice as thick is the ration for one person for two weeks. The
woman with grey hair and a grey frozen face and exhausted eyes
eaches out to get her piece of fish. She holds it a minute in her
and, looking at it. They all look at it, and say nothing. Then
he turns and pushes her way through the crowd and out the
oor.

Now she will wait every day to hear whether the store in her
eighbourhood is open again, whether you can trade anything,
whether a farmer she knows is coming to town with a dozen eggs
nd four cabbages and some potatoes. Whether somewhere, some-
ow, she can get food for her family. Sometimes when the shop
uns out of food before everyone is served, the women are wild
with grief, afraid to go home with nothing. Then there's trouble.
The little boys don't understand the trouble, all they know is that
quarrel brightens the long hours of waiting.)

You don't go to school?' I said.
  'Not now.'
  'He did very well at school,' his grandmother said.

'I want to be a mechanic,' the child said, in a voice that was almost weeping. 'I want to be a mechanic.'

'We do not let him go to school,' Mrs Hernandez said, stroking the child's black head. 'Because of the bombs. We cannot have him walking about alone.'

'The bombs,' I said, and smiled at the boy. 'What do you do about the bombs?'

'I hide,' he said, and he was shy about it, telling me a secret. 'I hide so they won't kill me.'

'Where do you hide?'

'Under the bed,' he said.

The daughter-in-law, who is very young, laughed at this, but the old people treated the child seriously. They know that you must have safety in something; if the child believes he is safe under the bed it is better for him.

'When will the war end?' the daughter-in-law asked suddenly.

'Now, now,' said the old man. 'It will end when we have won it. You know that, Lola. Have patience and do not be silly.'

'I have not seen my husband for five months,' the girl explained, as if this were the very worst thing that could ever happen to anyone. Old Mrs Hernandez nodded her head, which was like a fine worn wood carving, and made a little sympathetic noise.

'You understand, señora,' Mr Hernandez said to me, 'I am so old that perhaps I shall not live to see the end of the war. Things do not make any difference to me any longer. But it will be better for the children afterwards. That is what I tell Lola. Spain will be better for her and Federico afterwards. Besides,' he said, 'Federico is learning a great deal in the Army.'

(The Internationals had left the lines and were waiting to go home, or were already gone. There was a parade for them, down the Diagonal, and women threw flowers and wept, and all the Spanish people thanked them somehow, sometimes only by the way they watched the parade passing. The Internationals looked very dirty and weary, and young, and many of them had no country to go back to. The German and Italian anti-Fascists were already refugees; the Hungarians had no home either. Leaving Spain, for

ost of the European volunteers, was to go into exile. I wonder
hat happened to the German who was the best man for night
atrols in the 11th International Brigade. He was a sombre man,
hose teeth were irregularly broken, whose fingertips were nail-
ss pulp; the first graduate of Gestapo torture I had known.

The Spanish Republican Army, which had been growing and
aping itself through two winters, now dug in for the third
inter of war. They were proud and self-confident soldiers. They
ad started out as militia companies, citizens carrying any sort of
fle, and had become an army and looked like an army and acted
ke one.

They were always a pleasure to see and often a surprise. On a
ear night, coming back very tired from the Segre Front, we
opped at divisional headquarters to look at maps and get some
inner too, if lucky. We were received by the Lieutenant-Colonel,
ho commanded ten thousand men. He was twenty-six years old
nd had been an electrician at Lerida. He was blond and looked
merican and he had grown up with the war. The chief of
perations was twenty-three and a former medical student from
alicia. The chief of staff was twenty-seven, a lawyer, a Madrid
ristocrat who spoke good French and English. Modesto, com-
anding the Army of the Ebro and a great soldier, was thirty-
ve. All the new corps commanders were in their late twenties
nd early thirties. Everybody you saw knew what he was doing
nd why; it was a cheerful army. The winter is the worst time of
ll in war and the third winter is long, cold, and desperate; but
ou couldn't feel sorry for that army.)

Both my boys are soldiers,' Mrs Hernandez said. 'Miguel's father
s the oldest, Tomas, he is at Tortosa; and Federico is up towards
érida somewhere. Tomas was here only last week.'

'What did he say of the war?' I asked.

'We do not speak of the war,' she said. 'He says to me, "You
re like all the other mothers in Spain. You must be brave like all
he others." And sometimes he speaks of the dead.'

'Yes?'

'He said, "I have seen many dead." He says that so I will under-
tand, but we do not speak of the war. My sons are always close

to the bombs,' she said in her blurred old voice. 'If my childre
are in danger, it is not well that I should be safe.'

The girl Lola had started to sing to her child, to keep it quie
and now she brought the baby over near the lighted wick, for m
to see. She turned down a greyish blanket showing the child
head and sang, 'Pretty little child, my pretty little girl.'

The face seemed shrunken and faded, and bluish eyelids reste
lightly shot on the eyes. The child was too weak to cry. It frette
softly, with closed eyes, and we all watched it, and suddenly Lo
pulled the cover back over the bundle in her arms and said, cold
and proudly, 'She does not have the right food to eat and there
fore she is not well. But she is a fine child.'

(The hospital was huge and ornate, the way all modern building
are in Catalonia. This one was built of orange bricks and was a re
horror to look at. It was new and well equipped and had a garde
The buildings, called pavilions, were placed around this garde
The children's pavilion was off to the right and we followed
lanky, quiet boy who was showing us the way. I did not want t
come, really. I knew the statistics, the statistics were enough fo
me. In Catalonia alone, there were approximately 870,000 childre
up to school age. Of these, the statistics announced, more tha
100,000 suffered from bad nutrition, more than 200,000 suffere
from undernourishment, more than 100,000 were in a state of pre
famine. I thought the statistics were no doubt mild, and I did no
want to think at all about Madrid, about the swift dark laughin
children in Madrid. I did not want to imagine how hunger ha
deformed them.

There were two great wards, the surgical ward and the medica
ward, and it was almost suppertime and the surgical ward wa
brightly lit. Small beds lined the walls. It was very cold, betwee
the stone floors and the plaster walls; there is no heat anywhere
The children looked like toys until you came closer – tiny whit
figures propped up with pillows, swathed in bandages, the littl
pale faces showing, the great black eyes staring at you, the smal
hands playing over the sheets. There was not one child in th
hospital for any peacetime reason, tonsils or adenoids or mastoi
or appendicitis. These children were all wounded.

A little boy named Paco sat up in his bed with great dignity. He was four and beautiful and had a bad head wound. He had been crossing a square to meet a little girl on the other side – he played with her in the afternoons. Then a bomb fell. Many people were killed and he was wounded in the head. He had gone through his pain quietly, the nurse said. The wound was five months old. He had always been patient with it, and as the months wore on he grew solemner and more elderly every day. Sometimes he cried to himself, but without making a sound, and if anyone noticed he tried to stop. We stood by his bed and he watched us gravely but he did not want to talk.

I asked if they had anything to play with and the nurse said, Well, little things, not much. No, not really, she said. Just once in a while someone brings a present for one of them. A jolly little girl, with pigtails and only one leg, was having a nice time making paper balls out of an old newspaper.

There were three little boys with shaved heads and various splints on them; one of them had his leg held up on a rope from the ceiling. They lived in a corner by themselves; they were not only wounded, but they had tuberculosis. The nurse said they had fever and that made them gay, particularly at this hour. They would not live, she didn't think they would live even if there was food to give them, or a sanatorium to send them to. The sanatoriums were all full. Anyhow, they were too far gone. It works very fast on them, the nurse said. The little boys had a sort of Meccano toy, it was on the bed of the boy who had a broken arm. A bomb fragment broke his arm, the nurse said; he did not suffer as much as some but he used to scream at night. The other two were now shouting instructions to their friend, how to play with the toy. They were building a bridge. When we stopped beside them, they grew shy and gave up their game. All the children were the colour of their pillows except the little ones with t.b., who looked quite rosy. They were unbelievably thin.

'No,' the nurse said, almost impatiently, as if it hurt and angered her to talk about it. 'Of course we haven't enough food to give them. What do you think? If only they didn't bomb all the time,' she said, 'it would help. When the children hear the siren they go crazy, they try to get out of their beds and run. We are only four nurses in these two rooms and we have a hard time with them. At night it is worse. They all remember what happened to them and they go crazy.'

We went into the second room. A little boy was crying noisily and the other children were listening to him, frightened by his grief. The nurse explained that he had been wounded today, in one of the morning raids, and of course he was in pain but mainly he was homesick. He wanted his mother. He was also hungry. We stood by his bed helplessly and promised to bring him some food tomorrow if only he would stop crying and we promised that his mother would come right away, only please stop crying. He twisted on the bed and sobbed for his mother. Then she came. She was a dark witch of a woman, outdone by life. Her hair straggled from a knot on top of her head, and her bedroom slippers were worn through and her coat was pinned together with two safety pins. She looked gaunt and a little mad and her voice was as harsh as stone scraping on stone. She sat on the bed (we had been careful not to touch the bed, not to move or shake the small aching wounded child) and talked to him in her shrill voice, telling him of the family's catastrophes.

Their house had been destroyed by the bomb that wounded him, though he was the only one hurt. But now they had no home, no furniture, nothing to cook with, no blankets, no place to go. She told the round-eyed child the story of woe and he listened with interest and sympathy and wasn't homesick any more. Then she took a pot from some pocket, it materialized like a rabbit from a hat, and gave it to the child, and said, 'Here, eat.' He began to scoop up cold rice from the pot, just cold rice boiled in water. He ate it, his face close to the pot, spilling a little on the bedclothes and stopping to collect the greyish rice grains with his fingers. He seemed happy then and at home. His mother was now talking with another woman, in her hard tormented voice, and presently the little boy went to sleep.

'Would you like to see the medical ward?' the tall lanky boy said.

'Well,' I said. Well, no, I thought.

'I like the children.'

So we went.

Three blue lights were burning and the ward was in shadow. The children sat up in bed, silent and waiting. We stepped aside to let the dinner wagon pass. It made a metal clanking sound on he floor, and I watched their eyes follow the wagon down the yard. There was the seven-months-old baby with tuberculosis who did not notice and there was another child, like an old-faced doll against the pillows, who turned away her head. On the wagon were four lumps of something green and cooked, four shrunken lettuces, I think, and a great cauldron of soup. The nurse went over to the cauldron and lifted a ladleful and let it spill back into the pot. It was clear pale-beige water. That was supper. 'The children cry for food most of the time,' she said, looking at the thin soup with hate.

'What is the matter with them?' I asked. She evidently thought I was not very sound in the head.

'There are only two things the matter with them. Tuberculosis and rickets.'

The old-faced doll reached out a tiny white hand. I walked over to her and her hand curled around my fingers and she smiled. She was, the nurse said, seventeen months old and her name was Manuela.

Manuela let go of my fingers and began to cry. Had I done something bad? 'Only hungry,' the nurse said. She picked the child up, lightly and gently, and tossed it in her arms. The child laughed aloud with pleasure at this lovely game. As the nurse held her you saw the rope-thin legs and the swollen stomach of rickets.

'Will she be all right?' I said.

'Certainly,' the nurse said and she was lying, you could see that in her face. 'Certainly she'll get well. She has to. Somehow.'

'Yes, she's a fine child,' I said to Lola Hernandez, but I thought, maybe we can stop looking at the child, when we all know she's sick with hunger and probably will not live until summer. Let's talk about something else, now, just for a change.

'Have you been to the opera?' I said to Lola.

'I went once,' she said, 'but I do not like to go. All the time I was there, I kept thinking, What if this minute my husband is wounded, or what if he is coming home on leave. I almost thought he had come home and then I would have missed an hour with him. So now I stay home.'

'We all stay home,' the old man said, 'I like the house. We have
been here for twenty-five years.'

'Do you go often?' Lola asked.

'I've been,' I said. 'It's wonderful.'

(The opera is not as funny as the movies, though the people of
Barcelona don't think the movies are funny. But you can't help
laughing when you go to see Jane Eyre, and it is all about a life
none of the audience ever knew or imagined, and then in the middle the film flickers off and you hear the bombs falling somewhere,
while the audience groans with irritation, knowing it will take
half an hour before the current comes on again, and they are dying
to see what happens to Jane and her handsome gentleman friend,
and they are fascinated by the madwoman and the burning house.
I particularly liked the Westerns, and seeing the horse stopped in
mid-leap for an air alarm, knowing that the dangerous activities
of the hero and his horse were much more thrilling to the
audience than a mere covey of bombers flying at a great safe
height and sending down indiscriminate, expensive steel-encased
death and destruction.

It costs about two pesetas for the best seats at any show, and
nobody earns less than ten pesetas a day. The only thing you want
to spend money on is food, and there is no food, so you might as
well go to the opera or to the movies. It would be very stupid to
save up to buy furniture, the way the city gets bombed. Besides,
it's warm inside the big overdecorated theatre, because there are
so many people, and it's friendly, and sitting there with something
to look at on the stage you forget for a while that you aren't really
safe, you aren't really safe at all. And also you might even forget
how hungry you are.

But the opera was a wonder. Some afternoons there was opera
and some afternoons there was the symphony orchestra. The
people of Barcelona crowded to both. The opera house was far
too near the port for comfort, and bombs had ruined much of the
neighbourhood. It was surprising that the singers had energy to
sing, considering how little they eat. It was surprising to see such
thin singers. The women were any age at all, wearing the pre-war
costumes, a little mussed now but still brilliant and romantic. All

the men were old. The young men were at the war. The opera
house was full every day and everyone enjoyed the music immensely, and roared with laughter at the stale formal opera jokes,
and sighed audibly at the amorous moments and shouted 'Ole!'
at each curtain. We used to sit and scratch, because everyone had
fleas this winter, there was no soap any more and everyone was
very dirty and malodorous indeed. But we loved the music and
loved not thinking about the war.)

The Hernandez' only daughter now came home from her job, and
there was much loud gay talk as if they had not seen each other for
weeks, with everyone reporting on the day's air raids. She wore
her dark hair in braids around her head and was glowing with
rouge, and quite well dressed. She earned plenty of money because she worked in a munitions factory.

'I must leave,' I said. 'Please forgive me for staying so long.
Good-bye, Miguel, after the war you'll be a mechanic.'

'After we have won the war,' old Mrs Hernandez corrected me.
'We will invite you to come here and eat a big supper with us.'

They were all delighted, delighted with winning the war and
delighted with eating a big supper.

'You will see Federico too,' Lola said.

'Yes,' I said, 'that will be a great pleasure. Good-bye, good-bye,'
I said, shaking hands all around, 'and many thanks.'

We were standing up now, and looking at them I suddenly said,
'The third winter is the hardest.'

Then I felt ashamed. They were strong brave people and didn't
need me to say cheering words for them.

'We are all right, señora,' Mrs Hernandez said, making it clear
at once, saying the last word in her home about her family, 'We
are Spaniards and we have faith in our Republic.'

Gustav Regler

From *The Owl of Minerva*

A year later, in March 1939, the war in Spain ended with the defeat of the Republicans. The Fascist superiority in numbers and equipment, which had been unavailing at Guadalajara in 1937, triumphed after a winter of starvation. For a year the members of an international commission had been paid salaries to supervise the withdrawal of foreign troops on both sides. The remains of our brigades were shifted aimlessly from one base to another. Sometimes they rebelled and were allowed to take part in a battle. But Franco's Condor Legion kept its artillery always ready for action, while the German generals sat in famous castles making their plans and the Junkers and Messerschmitts made daily sorties. Now they could fly over Barcelona without encountering any opposition. The Spanish sky was theirs, and presently an officer of the Falange appeared in Port Bou, where two and a half years earlier I had smuggled in the printing press and the film projector in my van, and raised the hated flag of dictatorship.

I heard in Paris of the fall of Barcelona, and was filled with rage and despair. Where were the remains of the brigade? The Commission would not worry about them any more. Events had done their job for them, and they would now depart and apply to the League of Nations for their expense money. But the men of the brigade would fall into Franco's hands and be summarily executed. This had happened throughout the war. We were held to be worse than the Spanish Communists, since we had interfered in Spain's 'domestic affairs'. No mercy was shown us. I felt that I must search for the brigade and render it my last service as commissar. I did not know how grotesque and grave were the circumstances in which I was to find it.

In the Grand Hotel in Perpignan I ran into the Correspondent of the *New York Times*, whose name was Matthews. On the table lay a telegram from his editor warning him not to send in any sentimental stuff about the (impossible) refugee camps.

A gramophone was playing in a corner of the room – '. . . for we have lost our home, our home today is before Madrid.' It was the record which the singer Ernst Busch had made with the German volunteers in 1937.

'Come with me,' said Matthews, switching it off. 'Come and see for yourself. Perhaps you'll find out something about your own lot.'

We drove to the frontier. It was as though we had arrived too late at a vast public meeting which was just breaking up. We threaded our way through the crowd hurrying homewards. The landscape was a tragic one. Beneath a flowering shrub lay a man dying, his face yellow, his eyes staring up at the blossoms. Men lay huddled together, drinking at a stream. A shaggy-haired man with a donkey, which had apparently refused to go any farther, was seated on the ground, waiting.

The frontier, when we reached it, was like a medieval picture of the Crucifixion. Groups of men in civilian clothes were streaming down from the hills. They bore themselves with dignity, advancing with evident trust towards the fate that awaited them on the guarded plain teeming with soldiers.

Some still had earth clutched in their hands which they had snatched up as they left their villages. When I saw one of the *gardes mobiles* forcibly open one of these clenched hands and scatter the soil in disdain I knew that the soldiers of France did not understand the meaning of the word 'home', and I wished that one day they might pay for it. It was an impermissible wish, a meaningless one, but at that moment rage at defeat, not reason, filled my heart.

Others came singing. Just as the dying are sometimes seized with a lightness of heart, so did these fugitives display a boisterousness which caused us who watched them to marvel and which added to our grief. Had they already an inkling that before long the people of a dozen European nations would tread the same road? That is not an afterthought. Standing in the stink of the chloride of lime that had been strewn on the road, I seemed to catch, with the heightened sensibility of the defeated, the stench of tomorrow's corpses. I said so to Matthews.

'Smells like it,' he said dryly.

At that moment I saw the Frenchman, Aragon, coming down the road towards us with another group of journalists. It was a tragi-comical interlude, and to me it was as though a diabolical Puck sought jeeringly to remind me of the ass's head I had worn for two years. Nothing had changed in the attitude of the writer, who during that time had become the doyen of the French Communist array of half-talents. Here too he seemed unable to control his own arrogance. Like a peacock he walked a few paces back and forth, recoiled from the chloride of lime, glanced with theatrical contempt at the *gardes mobiles* and then went back to his car. I did not see him again in the town; he had left. Two days later I saw his picture in *Ce Soir*. He had been photographed surrounded by Parisian women who, so the caption said, had come to thank him for all he had done for the fugitives in Perpignan. The hundred eyes of the peacock! Even in the presence of despair they remained wide open in vanity. Like a circle – truly a vicious circle – the course of this lamentable man between September 1936 and that March of 1939 was rounded off. To me it was as painful as the snapping of handcuffs, but the steel springs closed on my heart.

Women came with children in their arms, others carrying small dogs, and one was carrying a hen in her apron. The Quakers had sent cars with milk and cocoa up into the hills, and some had picked up women they found on the way. One woman discovered, just as she was passing us, that the child she was carrying was dead. She covered it with her apron and pressed it the more tightly against her. A policeman thought it necessary to ask her name and age, and what brought her here. She did not answer, but after a pause another woman said, 'Anything is better than Fascism.'

That afternoon the Republican troops came. They were received as though they were tramps. We saw them in the distance marching towards us, with their rifles over their shoulders, still with a mile or more of Spanish soil between them and the frontier which represented the death of all their hopes – rifles of Madrid and Guadalajara, of Belchite and the Ebro – rifles of so many despairing victories ... There were five of us helpless onlookers, two Englishmen, Matthews, and an elderly Frenchwoman from the League of Human Rights.

The international bridge, the no-man's-land between the two

publics, lay in a gulley. We had been given permission to go
far as this. The Prefect of Perpignan was standing on the other
de of the road with some French generals and a young Spanish
fficer who recognized me and came over delightedly to greet me.
warned him that I was in danger of being put in a camp myself.
erhaps for the first time he realized what the position was. He
ld me with tears in his eyes that he had been appointed to act as
aison officer between his army and France.

The soldiers were now approaching the bridge. They knew what
he contingent of the *garde mobile* signified. As the first of them laid
own his rifle I saw Matthews turn away his head. 'I can't bear to
atch it,' he said. But I watched steadily, and I hope to be under-
ood when I say that I have never felt such close feelings of
omradeship for any army as I felt for those defeated soldiers of
pain. There was something of tenderness in the man's attitude
s he bent down over the rifle which he was relinquishing to the
riendly hands' of France. Before moving on he picked it up
gain, and for the last time ran his hand caressingly over stock and
olt, and barrel. And this was too much for the *garde mobile* who
tood facing him. He snatched the rifle from him, and it looked
o us as though he was afraid that he was going to shoot.

Then came the search. The Spaniards were asked what was in
he haversacks and ditty-bags they carried and they answered
hat in surrendering their rifles they had given up all the arms
hey possessed. But the French tapped disdainfully on the haver-
acks and demanded that they should be opened.

The Spaniards did not understand. Until the last moment they
ersisted in the tragic error of believing in international solidarity.
Madrid, capital of anti-Fascism, stronghold of courage high as
nountains, and of faith deep as an abyss!' But here there was
nother kind of abyss. The dirty road on which the disarmed men
tood was not merely the frontier between two countries, it was
n abyss between two worlds. Under the eyes of the Prefect and
he generals, the men of the *garde mobile* took away the bags and
undles containing the Spaniards' personal belongings and emp-
ied their contents into a ditch filled with chloride of lime.

I have never seen eyes of such anger and helplessness as those of
he Spaniards. They stood as though turned to stone, and they
did not understand.

Matthews lost all self-control and shouted, 'Don't you know
that Spaniards never lie?'

Underclothes and fragments of food were scattered in the
ditch. The first of the Spaniards was still standing there, his face
pale with shock. The *garde mobile* turned to the next, while the
Prefect and the generals chatted together, puffing cigarettes. And
then Herbert Matthews, with a gesture that I shall never forget,
bent down and began to pick the things up.

The Prefect frowned and sent a lieutenant to tell the guards to
show a little more courtesy. Then he lit another cigarette. Matthews straightened himself and tapped the Spaniard on the
shoulder. '*Lo siento*,' he said, as though he knew that his action had
changed nothing. '*No hay de que*,' said the Spaniard and smiled again.

'I need a drink.' said Matthews to me.

'So do I,' I said, and we took leave of the Spaniards and went
to our car.

'I have to find my boys,' I said.

'You will,' said Matthews.

We drove slowly back into the valley, past the silent procession
of a people going into exile. Laughing faces were often turned
towards us. It was as though the Spaniards wanted to comfort us.

After half an hour we came to a cross-roads of which one side
was barred by the police. 'I know how to deal with this,' said
Matthews, and leaning out of the car he signalled to the officer in
charge of the guard.

'Where can we get something to eat around here, Monsieur le
Capitaine?'

The scene changed as though by magic. The captain came to the
car and told us in the friendliest fashion that there was an excellent
restaurant half a mile away. The fish, *rouget à la provençale*, was
especially to be recommended. He waved his men aside and we
drove through the barrier, while the Spaniards were being herded
in the opposite direction, towards a concentration camp consisting
of primitive trenches in the sand of Argeles.

Matthews trod furiously on the accelerator.

'*Voilà le cœur français – l'estomac!*' he said.

At the restaurant of the widow X, I met a member of the

ternational Commission which had been charged with looking
ter the Brigade. He told me that nothing special had been done.
stormed at him and his whole League of Nations, and he soon
parted. Fortunately Matthews had kept calm, and found out
om him, before he left, where the remains of the Brigade had
st been seen. Shortly afterwards I met a member of the Society
Friends who took me with him.

Near a village in the mountains, of which I have forgotten the
me, I came upon the last handful of the Brigade. There were
out seventy-five of them, seated in a circle on the ground,
cing outwards. They had formed themselves into a phalanx
d with weary eyes and rifles in their hands were confronting a
oup of ten men who faced them from across the road, also with
les ready to shoot.

I thought at first, as we approached, that the smaller group was
mposed of Fascists who had captured our men at the last
oment but did not feel strong enough to disarm them. With my
uaker friend I withdrew behind the cover of an olive-tree and
ied to recognize faces. Suddenly a man in the larger group waved
me. It was Klaus Becker, an artillery officer who had worked
ith André Marty in Albacete. Scarcely had he raised his arm
ithout leaving his place in the circle, when a tall figure arose
om among the smaller group and looked towards us. I saw that
was Marty himself. Throughout the war he had never visited
our headquarters. I had only met him once, in the autumn of
936, and now he did not recognize me but merely took me for a
oreigner, presumably a press correspondent. He gave orders in a
w voice to the soldiers crouched on the ground around him.
hey returned their revolvers to their holsters, let fall their rifles
nd followed Marty, who, without looking at us, led the way
own a side-path to the lower valley. I looked at Marty's dark-
aced followers. They were all Communists, reliable Party men,
ho until yesterday had probably been his prison superintendents
nd worse. I had interrupted them in their last act of blood.

Klaus Becker sprang to his feet, ran to me and embraced me.
The others got up, some staggering with exhaustion. They had
een sitting there for hours.

Marty had been well aware that they all knew about his corrupt
dministration and summary executions in Albacete. He must

have thought that now they would weaken and make disclosur
in France. The bourgeois Press would pay them. Such things ha
happened before – the world was full of treachery!

I am convinced that his thinking was as naïve as this, for an
thing more subtle, or even human, was not in his nature. He ha
probably meant to machine gun them without warning, but Kla
Becker had suspected his intention and had passed the word in
whisper from man to man as they marched. Finally, they had con
to this small plateau. The condemned majority of the troop ha
by arrangement, suddenly broken away from the rest and forme
their defensive circles on the grass, with their rifles ready.

'At first I wouldn't believe it,' said a young Jewish boy wh
had once been in my signal detachment. 'But then Marty starte
cursing like mad, all about Trotskyites and counter-revolutio
aries. So then we knew for certain that he wanted to liquidate u
He nearly got away with it!'

'I should have shot him at once,' said an older man.

'Why didn't he shoot?' asked the Jewish boy.

'Because he is a coward. Because he knew he'd cop it himsel
Executioners are always cowards. It's a cowardly calling. Adolf
a coward, and so is Stalin.'

The Quaker broke into the conversation.

'Are you all Germans?' he asked. Apparently he needed t
know this for the purpose of his report.

'International,' I said. It was the last time I could identif
myself with the Brigade, and I knew that we should have to leav
the pine-woods around us, the meadows and the mountains, an
that tomorrow the Spanish countryside would be under Nationa
ist rule.

The Quaker went to the car and came back with a parcel o
slabs of chocolate. At once they all lined up.

'I can see you're Germans!' said the Quaker, laughing.

'This is the last pay we shall get,' said the young signaller wit
a choke in his voice. He put the slab of chocolate in his pocke
but then, when he saw the others eating, his hunger overcame hin
and he got it out again.

I learned that evening that the Spanish poet, Antonio Machada

s among those lying in the sand of Cerbère. One of his verses
ne to my mind:

> *Sabe esperar –*
> *aguarda que la marea fluya*
> *asi en la costa un barco*
> *sin que el partir te inquieta.*

> *Know how to hope –*
> *await the rising tide*
> *like a boat ashore*
> *and do not fear for the departure.*

Then the messenger went on to say that Machado had fallen
avely ill, and he added in a matter-of-fact voice that his heart
s broken.

I asked Matthews to drive me there; but at Argelès we were held
by Senegalese soldiers who told us in bad French that we should
arrested if we went any farther. I saw only their faces, which
oked very self-assured. The white of their eyes and teeth gleam-
in the light of the searchlight by which they were stand-
g.

I thought of the dead of Badajoz, whom Jay Allen had seen, of
ans Beimler, killed by a Moor, and of the wounded at Chinchon,
aughtered by Moors as they lay on stretchers. I thought of the
byssinian of the Garibaldi Battalion who had mastered his own
apulse, and I thought of Franco, who would now ride in
iumph through the streets of Madrid, accompanied by mounted
oors in white cloaks and red caps. And somewhere in the night,
ck and tired, ill-used by the murderers of his Republic, lay the
epublic's greatest poet, watched over by the Senegalese, ill-used
fricans.

'It doesn't make sense,' said Matthews, and started his engine
ain.

'No, it doesn't make sense,' I repeated.

e sat on the terrace of the hotel waiting for news. Matthews had
lephoned the Préfecture. We were drinking whisky. 'I'd like to

recite a verse,' I said to Matthews, and he knew at once who t
author would be.

'It's stoical,' I said. 'Perhaps it will help him:

> *Y si la vida es corta*
> *y no llega la mar a tu galira –*
> *aguarda sin partir y siempre espera*
> *que el arte es largo y, además, no importa.*
>
> *And if life is short*
> *and the sea does not reach your boat*
> *wait still without departing and be patient*
> *for art is large and that is all that matters.'*

A donkey cart rattled past. The lines sounded like the ebbi
of the tide. We had no more news that night.

It seemed the next day as though someone in Paris had inte
vened, but we learned that no doctor had yet been allowed in t
camp. Matthews drove out there and came back very depresse

'Nobody knows anything. How can all those thousands
expected to take any notice of a sick poet? They dug trenches f
latrines, and the wind blew the whole contents over them as th
lay asleep. It's shameful!'

The next morning he brought me a newspaper, pointed to
marked passage and went out again. I read that a lady had call
at the editorial offices to complain that 'the Red bandits' h
brought a dying man to her empty house on the beach. She d
manded that the body be removed at once.

I did not ask Matthews who it was that had died. I knew
had found out before showing me the paper.

Thus ended our war for freedom. Six months later the Seco
World War began.

'The Journey Home'

from Homage to Catalonia

In the end we crossed the frontier without incident. The train had first class and a dining-car, the first I had seen in Spain. Until recently there had been only one class on the trains in Catalonia. Two detectives came round the train taking the names of foreigners, but when they saw us in the dining-car they seemed satisfied that we were respectable. It was queer how everything had changed. Only six months ago, when the Anarchists still reigned, it was looking like a proletarian that made you respectable. On the way down from Perpignan to Cerbères a French commercial traveller in my carriage had said to me in all solemnity: 'You mustn't go into Spain looking like that. Take off that collar and tie. They'll tear them off you in Barcelona.' He was exaggerating, but it showed how Catalonia was regarded. And at the frontier the Anarchist guards had turned back a smartly dressed Frenchman and his wife, solely – I think – because they looked too bourgeois. Now it was the other way about; to look bourgeois was the one salvation. At the passport office they looked us up in the card-index of suspects, but thanks to the inefficiency of the police our names were not listed, not even McNair's. We were searched from head to foot, but we possessed nothing incriminating, except my discharge papers, and the *carabiñeros* who searched me did not know that the 29th Division was the POUM. So we slipped through the barrier, and after just six months I was on French soil again. My only souvenirs of Spain were a goatskin water-bottle and one of those tiny iron lamps in which the Aragon peasants burn olive oil – lamps almost exactly the shape of the terra-cotta lamps that the Romans used two thousand years ago – which I had picked up in some ruined hut, and which had somehow got stuck in my luggage.

After all, it turned out that we had come away none too soon. The very first newspaper we saw announced McNair's arrest for espionage. The Spanish authorities had been a little premature in announcing this. Fortunately, 'Trotskyism' is not extraditable.

I wonder what is the appropriate first action when you come from a country at war and set foot on peaceful soil. Mine was to rush to the tobacco-kiosk and buy as many cigars and cigarettes as I could stuff into my pockets. Then we all went to the buffet and had a cup of tea, the first tea with fresh milk in it that we had had for many months. It was several days before I could get used to the idea that you could buy cigarettes whenever you wanted them. I always half expected to see the tobacconists' doors barred and the forbidding notice 'No hay tobaco' in the window.

McNair and Cottman were going on to Paris. My wife and I got off the train at Banyuls, the first station up the line, feeling that we would like a rest. We were not too well received in Banyuls when they discovered that we had come from Barcelona. Quite a number of times I was involved in the same conversation: 'You come from Spain? Which side were you fighting on? The Government? Oh!' – and then a marked coolness. The little town seemed solidly pro-Franco, no doubt because of the various Spanish Fascist refugees who had arrived there from time to time. The waiter at the café I frequented was a pro-Franco Spaniard and used to give me lowering glances as he served me with an aperitif. It was otherwise in Perpignan, which was stiff with Government partisans and where all the different factions were caballing against one another almost as in Barcelona. There was one café where the word 'POUM' immediately procured you French friends and smiles from the waiter.

I think we stayed three days in Banyuls. It was a strangely restless time. In this quiet fishing-town, remote from bombs, machine-guns, food queues, propaganda, and intrigue, we ought to have felt profoundly relieved and thankful. We felt nothing of the kind. The things we had seen in Spain did not recede and fall into proportion now that we were away from them; instead they rushed back upon us and were far more vivid than before. We thought, talked, dreamed incessantly of Spain. For months past we had been telling ourselves that 'when we get out of Spain' we would go somewhere beside the Mediterranean and be quiet for a little hile and perhaps do a little fishing; but now that we were here was merely a bore and a disappointment. It was chilly weather, persistent wind blew off the sea, the water was dull and choppy, ound the harbour's edge a scum of ashes, corks, and fish-guts obbed against the stones. It sounds like lunacy, but the thing at both of us wanted was to be back in Spain. Though it could ave done no good to anybody, might indeed have done serious arm, both of us wished that we had stayed to be imprisoned long with the others. I suppose I have failed to convey more han a little of what those months in Spain mean to me. I have ecorded some of the outward events, but I cannot record the eeling they have left me with. It is all mixed up with sights, smells, nd sounds that cannot be conveyed in writing: the smell of the renches, the mountain dawns stretching away into inconceivable istances, the frosty crackle of bullets, the roar and glare of ombs; the clear cold light of the Barcelona mornings, and the tamp of boots in the barrack yard, back in December when eople still believed in the revolution; and the food queues and he red and black flags and the faces of Spanish militiamen; above ll the faces of militiamen – men whom I knew in the line and who re now scattered Lord knows where, some killed in battle, some naimed, some in prison – most of them, I hope, still safe and ound. Good luck to them all; I hope they win their war and drive ll the foreigners out of Spain, Germans, Russians, and Italians like. This war, in which I played so ineffectual a part, has left me vith memories that are mostly evil, and yet I do not wish that I ad missed it. When you have had a glimpse of such a disaster as his – and however it ends the Spanish war will turn out to have een an appalling disaster, quite apart from the slaughter and hysical suffering – the result is not necessarily disillusionment nd cynicism. Curiously enough the whole experience has left me vith not less but more belief in the decency of human beings. And hope the account I have given is not too misleading. I believe hat on such an issue as this no one is or can be completely truth-ul. It is difficult to be certain about anything except what you ave seen with your own eyes, and consciously or unconsciously veryone writes as a partisan. In case I have not said this some-vhere earlier in the book I will say it now: beware of my parti-anship, my mistakes of fact, and the distortion inevitably caused

by my having seen only one corner of events. And beware o
exactly the same things when you read any other book on thi
period of the Spanish war.

Because of the feeling that we ought to be doing something
though actually there was nothing we could do, we left Banyul
earlier than we had intended. With every mile that you wen
northward France grew greener and softer. Away from th
mountain and the vine, back to the meadow and the elm. When
had passed through Paris on my way to Spain it had seemed t
me decayed and gloomy, very different from the Paris I had know
eight years earlier, when living was cheap and Hitler was not hear
of. Half the cafés I used to know were shut for lack of custom, an
everyone was obsessed with the high cost of living and the fear o
war. Now, after poor Spain, even Paris seemed gay and prosper
ous. And the Exhibition was in full swing, though we manage
to avoid visiting it.

And then England – southern England, probably the sleekes
landscape in the world. It is difficult when you pass that way
especially when you are peacefully recovering from sea-sicknes
with the plush cushions of a boat-train carriage under your bum
to believe that anything is really happening anywhere. Earth-
quakes in Japan, famines in China, revolutions in Mexico? Don'
worry, the milk will be on the doorstep tomorrow morning, the
New Statesman will come out on Friday. The industrial towns were
far away, a smudge of smoke and misery hidden by the curve of
the earth's surface. Down here it was still the England I had
known in my childhood: the railway-cuttings smothered in wild
flowers, the deep meadows where the great shining horses browse
and meditate, the slow-moving streams bordered by willows, the
green bosoms of the elms, the larkspurs in the cottage gardens;
and then the huge peaceful wilderness of outer London, the
barges on the miry river, the familiar streets, the posters telling of
cricket matches and Royal weddings, the men in bowler hats, the
pigeons in Trafalgar Square, the red buses, the blue policemen –
all sleeping the deep, deep sleep of England, from which I sometimes fear that we shall never wake till we are jerked out of it by
the roar of bombs.

ibliography

l. Note: The following is a list of books cited or quoted from the text itself. It is neither a complete listing nor a guide to orks on the Spanish Civil War. For that, the reader is referred to ugh Thomas' bibliography in *The Spanish Civil War* and Hugh ord's in *A Poet's War*.

arcel Acier, ed., *From Spanish Trenches*, Modern Age Books, New York, 1937.

ıy Allen, 'City of Horrors', *The Chicago Tribune*, August 30, 1936.

ım Atyeo, *Up and Down Under: Being the Author's Adventures in Art and Diplomacy*, unpublished.

ʹ. H. Auden, 'Impressions of Valencia', *The New Statesman and Nation*, January 30, 1937.

ʹ. H. Auden, 'Spain', Faber and Faber, London, 1938.

·eorge Bernanos, *Les grands cimetières sous la lune*, Libraire Plon, Paris, 1938; translated by Pamela Morris as *A Diary of My Times*, Boriswood, London, 1938.

, Leslie Brewer, 'Too Late?', *Time and Tide*, October 24, 1936.

oy Campbell, *Flowering Rifle*, Longmans, Green and Co., London, 1939.

hristopher Caudwell, 'Last Letters', *News Chronicle*, June 28, 1937.

Jorman Cohn, *The Pursuit of the Millennium*, Harper and Row, New York, 1961.

ohn Cornford, *John Cornford: A Memoir*, ed. Pat Sloan, Jonathan Cape, London, 1938.

Jancy Cunard, ed., 'Authors Take Sides', *Left Review*, London, 1937.

ohn Dos Passos, *Journeys Between Wars*, Harcourt, Brace and Co., New York, 1938.

Theodore Dreiser, 'Barcelona in August', *Direction I*, New York, November–December, 1938.

Pierre Drieu la Rochelle, *Gilles*, Gallimard, Paris, 1939.

Hugh Ford, *A Poet's War*, Univ. of Pennsylvania Press, Philadelphia, 1965.

Martha Gellhorn, *The Face of War*, Rupert Hart-Davis, London 1959.

Cecil Gerahty, *The Road to Madrid*, Hutchinson and Co., London 1937.

Ernest Hemingway, *The Spanish Earth*, J. B. Savage Co., Cleveland, 1938.

Douglas Jerrold, *Georgian Adventure*, Wm Collins Sons and Co. London, 1937.

Arthur Koestler, 'Koestler's Own Story', *News Chronicle*, May 23–28, 1937.

Laurie Lee, *The Sun My Monument*, The Hogarth Press, London 1944.

Louis MacNeice, *Autumn Journal*, Faber and Faber, London, 1939

Louis MacNeice, 'Today in Barcelona', *The Spectator*, January 20 1939.

André Malraux, *L'Espoir*, Gallimard, Paris, 1938; translated by Stuart Gilbert and Alastair Macdonald as *Man's Hope* Random House, New York, 1938.

André Malraux, 'This is War', *Collier's Magazine*, May 29, 1937.

Jacques Maritain, 'The Idea of Holy War', *From the N.R.F* (*Nouvelle Revue Française*) ed. Justin O'Brien, Meridian Books New York, 1959.

Eoin O'Duffy, *Crusade in Spain*, Browne and Nolan, Dublin, 1938

George Orwell, *Homage to Catalonia*, Secker and Warburg, London, 1937.

Herbert Read, *Collected Poems*, Faber and Faber, London, 1946.

Gustav Regler, *The Owl of Minerva*, Rupert Hart-Davis, London 1959.

Antoine de Saint-Exupéry, *Terre des hommes*, Gallimard, Paris 1939; translated by Lewis Galantière as *Wind, Sand, and Stars* Wm Heinemann, London, 1939.

George Santayana, *The Letters of George Santayana*, ed. Daniel Cory Constable and Co., London, 1955.

George Bernard Shaw, *Geneva*, Constable and Co., London, 1946 ugh Slater, *The Heretics*, Secker and Warburg, London, 1946.

hn Sommerfield, *Volunteer in Spain*, Lawrence and Wishart, London, 1937.

ephen Spender, 'Guernica', *The New Statesman and Nation*, London, October 15, 1938.

ephen Spender, 'Heroes in Spain', *The New Statesman and Nation*, London, May 1, 1937.

ephen Spender, 'Pictures in Spain', *The Spectator*, July 30, 1937.

ephen Spender, *Poems for Spain*, ed. with John Lehmann, The Hogarth Press, London, 1939.

eorge Steer, *The Tree of Gernika*, Hodder and Stoughton, London, 1938.

onald Ogden Stewart, ed., *Writers Take Sides*, The League of American Writers, New York, 1938.

ugh Thomas, *The Spanish Civil War*, Harper and Row, New York, 1961.

velyn Waugh, *Scoop*, Longmans, Green and Co., London, 1938.

mone Weil, *Selected Essays*, chosen and translated by Richard Rees, Oxford University Press, London, 1962.

lexander Werth ['Dispatches from Spain'], *The Manchester Guardian*, December–January, 1937–8.

. C. Worsley, 'Malaga Has Fallen', *New Writing*, Spring, 1939.

. B. Yeats, *Collected Poems*, Macmillan and Co., London, 1956.